Intercultural Communication

1853592854

Multilingual Matters

The Age Factor in Second Language Acquistion
    D. SINGLETON and Z. LENGYEL (eds)
Asian Teachers in British Schools
    PAUL A.S. GHUMAN
Becoming Bilingual
    JEAN LYON
Competing and Consensual Voices
    PATRICK J.M. COSTELLO and SALLY MITCHELL (eds)
Coping with Two Cultures
    PAUL A.S. GHUMAN
Culture and Language Learning in Higher Education
    MICHAEL BYRAM (ed.)
The Guided Construction of Knowledge
    NEIL MERCER
Language Attitudes in Sub-Saharan Africa
    E. ADEGBIJA
Language Diversity Surveys as Agents of Change
    JOE NICHOLAS
Language, Education and Society in a Changing World
    TINA HICKEY and JENNY WILLIAMS (eds)
Language, Minority Education and Gender
    DAVID CORSON
Languages in Contact and Conflict
    SUE WRIGHT (ed.)
Language Reclamation
    HUBISI NWENMELY
Making Multicultural Education Work
    STEPHEN MAY
Mission Incomprehensible: The Linguistic Barrier to Effective Police Co-operation in Europe
    ROY D. INGLETON
Multilingual Japan
    JOHN C. MAHER and KYOKO YASHIRO (eds)
The Step-Tongue: Children's English in Singapore
    ANTHEA FRASER GUPTA
Three Generations – Two Languages – One Family
    LI WEI

Please contact us for the latest book information:
Multilingual Matters Ltd, Frankfurt Lodge, Clevedon Hall,
Victoria Road, Clevedon, Avon, England, BS21 7SJ.

Intercultural Communication

Pragmatics, Genealogy, Deconstruction

Robert Young

The University of Sydney

MULTILINGUAL MATTERS LTD
Clevedon • Philadelphia • Adelaide

Library of Congress Cataloging in Publication Data

Young, R.E. (Robert E.), 1940-
Intercultural Communication: Pragmatics, Genealogy, Deconstruction
Robert Young
Includes bibliographical references and index.
1. Intercultural comunication. 2 Communication and culture. 3. International
cooperation. 4. Ethnic relations. I. Title.
GN345.6.Y68   1996
303.48'2–dc20   95-25383

British Library Cataloguing in Publication Data

A CIP catalogue record for this book is available from the British Library.

ISBN 1-85359-286-2 (hbk)
ISBN 1-85359-285-4 (pbk)

Multilingual Matters Ltd

UK: Frankfurt Lodge, Clevedon Hall, Victoria Road, Clevedon, Avon BS21 7SJ.
USA: 1900 Frost Road, Suite 101, Bristol, PA 19007, USA.
Australia: P.O. Box 6025, 83 Gilles Street, Adelaide, SA 5000, Australia.

Printed and bound in Great Britain by WBC Book Manufacturers Ltd.

Dedicated to my Mother
Marcia Frances Young
for always being on my side

Contents

1 A Wager on Hope

There is, perhaps, no more important topic in the social sciences than the study of intercultural communication. Understanding between members of different cultures was always important, but it has never been as important as it is now. Formerly, it was necessary for empire, or trade. Now it is a matter of the survival of our species.

We stand at the beginning of the global age in human affairs, and the development of our human powers to affect each other and the planet we share has been so rapid and so great that we threaten our own survival. Whatever the solutions to the problems created by our inventiveness and fecundity, they cannot be found or implemented unless we are able to create intercultural understanding and cooperation on a scale never before achieved. Only effective intercultural communication can enable us to achieve cooperation and understanding on a global scale.

The key to an adequate understanding of intercultural communication is a simple one. We have no choice. We *must* succeed in doing it, we *have* succeeded in doing it in the past (here and there), and we must adopt ways of theorising it which recognise the imperative of extending our capacity to do it to a global level.

But we already know this. One glance is all it takes. Whether it was the glance of Melanesian people, gathered around a satellite television set in the Highlands of Papua New Guinea, or that of a group of African executives gathered around the same pictures in a boardroom in Nairobi, or the gaze of an American family in their living room — one glance was enough. The picture was the picture of the planet Earth, viewed from space.

It did not show the boundary line of nations, the net of political alliances among them — the coloured patchwork of the maps of power and control. It showed one, fragile but beautiful blue-green world — spaceship Earth it has been called. Once this image became part of the common heritage of humankind we knew, at a deeper level than language, or difference, what we needed to do and be.

Events have conspired to point to the same destiny. We have witnessed the end of the cold war, the growth of global rather than merely local

1

problems of pollution, increased trade and economic interdependence, greater levels of travel and migration, accelerating population growth, and increased electronic means for communication across planetary distances.

At the same time, we see everyday evidence of a terrible paradox. While we are clearly more involved in each other's lives than ever before, we appear no less deeply involved in brutal rejection of each other. While more people from more cultures are communicating and cooperating across differences, as many, it seems, are killing and maiming each other in the name of cultural and religious identity. At the same time, still virulent remnants of the forces of 19th and 20th century imperialism are at work among nations. The dilemma of the global age is that, while we have finally discovered that we are one people who must share one precarious world, we are profoundly divided by race, culture and belief and we have yet to find a tongue in which we can speak our humanity to each other.

To find that tongue must be our first and last endeavour, for the pursuit of peace, and freedom from pollution and poverty, are merely means to an end and that end is the celebration of our human possibilities. To peace, freedom from poverty and pollution we may add a more fundamental need — finding a voice in which to speak, first, in reaching the understanding on which we will assure peace, share wealth and live cleanly, and then, in the speech whereby we will freely utter our own becoming.

It is right, at the closing of the age of imperialism and colonisation, to busy ourselves with rooting out and destroying these things. It is right, to concern ourselves with the celebration of difference, the expression of the repressed, the assertion of the oppressed and the deconstruction of the theoretical and intellectual manifestations of imperial overstretch. However, if the price of this necessary radicalism is the renunciation of our common humanity and all possibilities of celebrating it, it is a price that is too great to pay, because, under present historical conditions, its payment threatens our very survival. It may be necessary to destroy the Eurocentric kind of humanism that prematurely celebrated the achievement of 'civilisation', but it is also necessary to save the humanistic hope that led to that celebration.

The central proposition on which all of the argument of this book is based is that we must make a wager — we will be able to find common ground while preserving genuine difference and diversity. If we do not succeed in this we will fail as a species. We *must* assume we will succeed. If we still fail, we will have lost nothing in the attempt. If we assume that we will fail, and we *could* have succeeded, we will have lost everything. This must be the touchstone of all our theorising. We will wager that success in finding a common tongue but preserving difference is possible.

The alternatives are not pleasant to contemplate. Basically there are two possibilities: The first is that we, or our descendants, will all be members of a single, world culture, perhaps clinging lovingly to minor regional differences in cuisine or folk music and this single culture will either be a genuinely new global culture, no doubt influenced by many prior cultures, but not a mere amalgam of them, or it will be a heavily American (or Chinese) imperial culture. Either way, we will have lost something precious — our diversity — and life will be less interesting for this loss.

The second possibility is that we remain roughly where we are or have been, with intercultural misunderstanding as common as it is at present, or, spurred on by population growth, pollution, scarcity of resources and war, more common and more deadly.

Neither of the two possibilities is worth contemplating. The notion of a new culture which is influenced by all cultures is attractive in some ways, but history tells us that we do not have enough time for this to come about. It is also highly improbable. Most cultural blending has come about by conquest and has only achieved the kind of mellowness which partially hides ancient imperialisms by the passage of a great deal of time — as is the case in the United Kingdom, for instance.

The imperial solution is even less attractive although entirely possible. The problem with this solution is that the structural and other violence necessary to bring it about appear unlikely to permit us to solve our planetary problems. An imperial culture is a culture blind to the conditions necessary for its own survival.

The second possibility — do nothing, or continue recent trends towards accentuation of difference — provides the most probable scenario, but it holds out very little promise of yielding the harvest of understanding and cooperation we must reap if we are to survive the winter of scarcity and bitterness that may be just ahead of our present world wide Indian summer.

The wager this book makes is that it is possible and desirable for all cultures to change, but not to change by blending with one another or being submerged by a single culture. Each culture must change to the extent necessary for it to recognise differences, to acknowledge the prima facie validity of other cultures, to incorporate some degree of tolerance of cultural diversity, and to discover some common ground in the new intercultural space thus created, ground upon which a conversation about intercultural understanding and cooperation can be built. The apparent paradox of this change is that there must be room in it not only for tolerance but also for critique, including critique of other cultures.

This approach to theorising is a pragmatic one, but it is also pragmatist, since it is not based on a narrow, ethnocentric practicality, in which the test of good theory is whether it is developed in the interests of the group of which the theorist is a member, but upon an ethnically decentred understanding of our global problems, as configurational problems which are a result of the human condition or situation, taken as a whole. Our propensity to be blind to moderation, to multiply, and to transform our environment, and in the process to use more and more natural resources, coupled with our ethnic and political fragmentation, means that the problems of peace, poverty and pollution can never be solved by either imperialism or separation.

Many of the goods for which we compete under conditions of an ever growing army of consumers are *positional* goods. Some goods are such that an individual or a nation can only have more if someone else has less, at whatever level of absolute abundance is achieved. You can only have prestige if someone else lacks it, power if someone else obeys you, wealth if someone is poor, even if their poverty is riches relative to someone in another context. Short of a global cultural revolution, this is a component of the human condition for the foreseeable future. We are blind to moderation. Two refrigerators are not enough, we want four — with built-in ice-making machines. Desire knows no bounds.

Under conditions of limitless desire and unlimited population, scarcity is perennial and the technological race not withstanding, growing. Imperialist solutions are by definition solutions based on elevation of positional goods, through power, over other desires and the desires of others. Imperialism, which is entirely lacking in moderation when it comes to power, is incompatible with moderation when it comes to consumption, except for a localised, enforced moderation achieved by the repression of the colonised. At a global level this is likely to be as temporary and unstable a process as it has proven at the level of past empires. But the alternative, cultural separatism, merely institutionalised competition for position. Imperialism leads to big conflicts, and the violence of repressive wars at the periphery of empire; separatism leads to small conflicts and pervasive, regional and local insecurity. Neither condition holds any promise for effective global management.

The necessary moderation is theoretical as well as substantive. Our theorising must steer a middle path between imperial universalism and separatist cultural relativism. So another touchstone of good theory in intercultural communication is moderation, not radicalism. The theory which is constructed in this book is a theory which seeks to steer a middle path between universalism and separation through a decentred understanding of culture, and through critical moderation. It seeks to recognise difference but not to absolutise it. As such, it will be a theory characterised as much by hope as accomplishment. At times, the promise of a reconciliation of opposites will have to stand in for the achievement. Among the many logical, conceptual and practical dilemmas that mark many if not most present discussions of cultural difference, a hopeful theory must sometimes assume resolution will be forthcoming where none yet exists. If that is to risk error, it is also the risk which makes this theory a wager rather than a certainty. But, then, how does this differ from life itself?

Dilemmas of Theorising Difference

Theory of cultural difference, like theory of communication, is beset by dichotomy and absolutism. It is easy enough to refute vulgar epistemology and to show that concepts of truth based on relatively unproblematic relationships between word and object, proposition and reality, are not coherent. It is similarly easy to refute vulgar cultural universalism and to show that concepts of difference that see it as a surface phenomenon, overlying a deeper level where we are 'all the same deep down' are without foundation. It is also easy to show that ideas of transparent mutual understanding among interlocutors who begin a conversation from the starting point of different life experiences are unduly idealistic.

But those, who like the French philosopher Derrida,[1] see themselves as destroying theory of truth-making and as banishing epistemology often fail to note that the view of truth they contest is one held by hardly any analytical philosophers today, and even fewer continental philosophers. Before Derrida was born, most analytical philosophers came to the view that 'truth' could only intelligibly be spoken of in a sense in which it was *relative to a language*. However, the real problem is with those who read Derrida in an absolutist way, as Derrida himself complains. It was not Derrida's intention to banish all truth seeking, just to de-absolutise it. Talk of truth could still make sense, as long as we recognised that hope and truth always met in it. How ironical that some followers of Derrida should espouse a new kind of absolutism by claiming that no truth talk could ever be meaningful.[2]

Cultural universalism has not been the majority viewpoint in cultural anthropology since before 1920. Certainly, some have continued to pursue such a view. It was, perhaps surprisingly, a corollary of Chomsky's search for deep linguistic structure. It was at least implicit in much comparative anthropology. But it would be reasonable to argue that the main message of American cultural anthropology since Margaret Mead's 1930s studies in Samoa, and in British social anthropology since Radcliffe-Brown's analyses of roughly the same era, is that all cultural traits are to be judged functional and acceptable relative to the cultures to which they belong and that talk of the *general* superiority of one culture over another is nonsense.

Nor has communication been considered a relatively unproblematic process of meaning transmission and reproduction, except by a small minority of communication theorists. George Steiner's[3] now classic review of cultural and linguistic difference concludes that all communication displays the problems of intercultural communication and translation, even communication among culturally very similar people. But before that, Benjamin and members of the Frankfurt School were probing the problems of the non-identity of sign and concept, thought and object, the constructive rather than transmissive or reproductive nature of communication and more, as we will see when we come back to these themes in a later chapter.[4]

Nevertheless, difference was incompletely theorised by mainstream theorists during the period in question. Many theoretical and practical inconsistencies remained. While stridently asserting the cultural relativity of values and practices most anthropologists nonetheless continued to claim culturally independent *methodological* capacity to explore, describe and explain cultures other than their own. Communication theorists continued to treat communication problems as problems of transmission, and social scientists of all stripes continued to behave as if the truths produced by their studies were not relative to the conceptual and methodological language in which they were embedded or to the hope of a future completion of understanding. Post-colonial, post-structuralist and post-analytical critique found that there was still work to do, even if it would be as reasonable to call that work a completion of the modern project as it would be to call it the beginning of the postmodern one.

Critique of Earlier Approaches to Culture

Postmodern

So much of recent discussions of culture and cultural difference has been characterised by what is loosely called 'postmodernism'.

But what is at issue when we speak of 'postmodern', 'postmodernity' and 'postmodernism'? Sometimes what is at issue is the notion of a succession of artistic or architectural styles, the postmodern having succeeded the modern. That is artistic postmodern*ism*. For other commentators, such as Lyotard,[5] the reference is to a broader social and cultural change, from modern *societies* to postmodern ones — postmodern*ity*. Others appear to focus on the kind of self-understanding that intellectuals have at a given time: faith in science, social progress and the rational management of human affairs (modernity) having given way to doubt, despair and cognitive pluralism. That is another form of postmodern*ism*. Some would weave all this together in a dizzying complexity that only a latter day polymath could unravel or challenge: fragments of reference, names of artists and architects, philosophers and mountebanks vie with disembodied statistics as an avalanche of examples and name dropping threaten to overwhelm all sensibility. The particular shards of a shattered modern optimism that are important for us to gather up here are those which have to do with the possibility of universal elements of culture and common ground in our common humanity.

In their attack on modernity, 'postmodern' thinkers have criticised the overextension of universalising tendencies in modern thought, and they have celebrated the marginal, peripheral and local. Against the decontextualised and abstract understanding of modern knowledge, they have restored the primacy of context and the concrete. In place of the theoretical and cognitive, they have put the practical, sensuous and embodied. In rejecting these features of modernity they have also seen themselves as rejecting the core of European culture, because Europe has been the centre of the development of the modernity which is being rejected. They are also rejecting what they see as the cultural imperialism of universal ideas which they believe are, in fact, universalisations of European culture, rather than genuine universals. They have been asserting the marginalised, local and sensuous, European or otherwise, against the centres of power, the metropolis, and the tyranny of theory.

But what they have been attacking may have been only one strand in modern thought and culture, which we can call High Modernity. If so, they are certainly not the first to do this. Since the 1930s, the critical theorists of the Frankfurt School, such as Adorno,[6] have been trenchant critics of just these tendencies in modern thought. The present critics seem at times to have short memories. They may also overdo it. Universal concepts are necessary to language and thought. You must see both individual trees *and* the woods to have a balanced view of an ecosystem. Surely what is at stake is to have a balanced view of the losses and *gains* of abstracting and generalising, constructing hypothetical universals and so on. Perhaps we might be permitted the heretical thought that European culture, being itself a product of the interaction of many cultures and influences, enriched by contributions from the Islamic world and the east, and the scene of extraordinary developments in human knowledge, may itself have something of value to offer to all humanity — that is, something universally valuable — whatever the uncertainty over just what is of universal merit and what is falsely thought to be so.

Toulmin[7] argues that modernity had two distinct phases and that it is the second imperialist phase, High Modernity, which is now being rejected. Callinicos[8] takes up the theme that the modernity that the postmoderns attack has itself already dissolved into a more pluralistic, ambiguous and complex state of affairs, of which postmodernism is, itself, merely a symptom.

Toulmin has made a case that High Modernity arose to meet a crisis of European self-confidence and spilled over into intercultural arrogance more or less accidentally, due to the imperial expansion and colonisation processes which were a by-product of the new level of inter-nation competition and rivalry that emerged in Europe with the formation of nation-states. In Toulmin's view, postmodern critique is mistaken in the object of its criticism. It has stepped forward bravely to administer the coup de grace to a mortally wounded modernity only to find it has been dead for some time. I will discuss this view here and in Chapter 4 I will add an argument to the effect that the would-be executioners of modernity are themselves an inverted expression of the very High Modernity they seek to slay. I will argue that, paradoxically, at least in the case of Foucault[9] and Derrida ('post-structuralists'), the position from which they attempt to speak is itself a kind of universal extra-cultural one.

Marxist and Liberal Critique of Postmodernism

Toulmin, a Liberal philosopher of science, calls High Modernity 'Cosmopolis' because he traces its origins to the political role of science and intellectuals in the early part of the modern era. The overemphasis on universals and abstraction from the local, culturally and religiously specific context was a prophylactic for a Europe that had endured thirty years of sectarian warfare (the Thirty Years War). The later extension of this political-cognitive system to colonial domination was a natural extension of what was already essentially a system of domination within Europe.

With Habermas, Toulmin accuses Descartes of the decisive break with an earlier much more balanced and humane modernity. The usual starting date for the modern era is 1630 or thereabouts — Galileo's decentring of humanity's place in the universe. Undoubtedly this was a significant event, but it ignores the 'modernity of the renaissance', the urbane scepticism of Montaigne (b.1533), Erasmus (b. 1467) or Shakespeare (b.1564):

> ...from Erasmus to Montaigne, the writings of the renaissance human-ists displayed an urbane open-mindedness and sceptical tolerance that were novel features of [a] new lay culture. Their ways of thinking were not subject to the demands of pastoral or ecclesiastical duty: they regarded human affairs in a clear-eyed, non-judgemental light that led to honest doubt about the value of 'theory' for human experience — whether in theology, natural philosophy, metaphysics or ethics. (*Cosmopolis*, p. 25)

The common picture of the era which followed, beginning with Galileo, is one of a break away from religious superstition, and the rise of autonomous reason, but this picture is anachronistic. It is a French-revolu-tionary reading of the triumph of reason, a Brechtian political retrojection, which is dispelled by elementary historical inquiry. Even for thinkers like Newton, the motivation was as much or more religious and political as it was that of disinterested inquiry. The world of knowledge and the world of human affairs was seen as one — as a cosmos joined to a polis, an ordered world, seen whole, with the same order in the cosmos at large as there should be in human affairs — cosmopolis.

A profound suspicion of scepticism and humanism marked this second wave of modernity, led by Descartes, consolidated by Leibniz and perfected by Newton. When Donne complained about individualism and antinomialism he was directing his remarks against the first wave of modernity, but not in order to re-establish the medieval understanding:

> Tis all in pieces, all Coherence gone,
> All just supply, and all Relation...
> For every man alone thinkes he hath got
> to be a Phoenix, and that there can bee
> None of that kinde, of which he is, but hee.
>
> (quoted in *Cosmopolis*, p. vi)

For Toulmin, what we need to do is to abandon the attempt to 'start with a clean slate' by producing a culturally and historically abstracted understanding of the world. We need to recognise the historically available resources of European culture as well as other cultures. The 'clean slate' was a myth of High Modernity, a celebration of the abandonment of all tradition, but a recognition of continuity and context is not necessarily a 'conservative' value — it is realistic. High Modernity's apparently final spasm of self assertion occurred in the inter-war period. The decontextual-ised view of scientific knowledge, characteristic of the Vienna positivists, and Popper, which was a product of the need for certainty in the economic and political turmoil of Europe in the 1920s and 30s has, since the 60s, perhaps finally, given way to a more historically contextualised understanding of science:

> Philosophical critics and defenders of Modernity are, thus, directly at cross-purposes. Many of the reasons that contemporary French writers give for *denying* the continued validity of 'modernity' refer to the same features of the 20th century scene that Habermas points to in *asserting* it. They take opposite sides on issues about modernity, but not for reasons of substance, but because as seen from their respective points of view — the word 'modern' means different things. French writers take 'modern' in a Cartesian sense. For them formal rationality has no alternative but absurdity... *Cosmopolis* (p. 173.)

But for the critical theorist Jurgen Habermas,[10] the recent developments of social movements, the effects of increased intercultural contact, the pluralism and cosmopolitanism, of the last few decades, is evidence of a resurgence of the critical process that has been an internal characteristic of the modern era since the beginning. As we will see in Chapter 6, the politics of social movements is an appropriate politics for minority cultural recognition. The burden of Habermas' criticism of the postmodernists is that they have failed to recognise how borrowed their clothes are and that they have indulged themselves in a rhetorical stance which is at odds with the narrative content of their utterances. We will explore Habermas' analysis in greater detail throughout the remaining chapters of the book.

Callinicos, a Marxist, makes a similar point (while apparently misunderstanding Habermas' views on a number of issues). Callinicos' juxtaposition of modernist statements from the late nineteenth century and the *fin de siècle* with 1960s and 70s statements by the so-called postmodernists is something of a tour de force refutation of the second, clearly locating them as a last gasp of modernity. One example will have to stand in for many:

> Compare these two passages:
> In the multidimensional and slippery space of Postmodernism anything goes with anything...disassociated and decontextualised [images] ...slide past one another...unable to fix meaning.

> The nature of our epoch is multiplicity and indeterminacy. It can only rest on *das Gleitende* [the moving, the slipping, the sliding] and is — aware that what other generations believed to be firm is in fact *das Gleitende*. (Callinicos, p. 12)

The first passage comes from a talk given by the postmodern art critic Suzy Gablik in Los Angeles in 1987, the second was written by the poet Hugo von Hofmannsthal in 1905.

The object of critique set up by those who follow the postmodern analyses is a curious one. It bears a striking resemblance to what others before have called scientism, positivism or objectivism. The construct of modernism undoubtedly identifies 'real' features of aspects of 'modern' society, and it is a concept which is more broadly based in the whole social institutional process than 'scientism', which focused largely on scientific and technological institutions. But modernism is a complex construct in ways other than its descriptive combination of social practice and professional ideology. It is implied that it is the dominant ideology of our time, at least in the technological advanced, post-industrial societies. Little attention is paid to the continuing critique of scientism, to surviving romanticism and conservatism and all the other complex currents in contemporary life.

However, I still want to agree that much of the main impetus of postmodern criticism is well directed. Many, but not all previous 'modern' critics of major tendencies of modern society had failed to extend their critique of truth, cultural universalism or reproductive theories of communication to their own practices. That is, they were not reflexive. Their critique had been insufficiently thorough. The major thrust of the second wave of critique (some of which is called postmodern) has been the reflexive application of this critique and the pursuit of the paradoxical implications of this *for the very idea of critique itself.*

Pessimism, Optimism and Critique

This state of affairs brings us to the starting point of this book. It would no doubt be a blessed relief to many if we could just get on and explore a few useful ways to communicate with members of other cultures — a compendium of handy hints on how low to bow in Japan or when to smile in Russia. The matter is not so simple. The current state of the art is such that once you get beyond the preliminaries, existing 'How to' manuals leave you without much guidance. Worse, different 'practical' guides tell you different things. For a serious student of intercultural understanding, there is no substitute for starting where the theoretical debate is now — in the debate (stimulated by postmodern critique) about the nature of good theory and the nature of critique.

Contemporary theorists who are pursuing the reflexive task of redefining critique at the same time as continuing to criticise society fall into several groups, whose work will be discussed in later chapters. Two important clusters of these differ in their attitudes to the modern project and to key ideas from its tradition. Critical theorists seek to establish a basis for critique which is not merely negative, and which preserves some continuity with the European philosophical tradition. This group is ready to admit that reason has limits, that philosophy has been ethno-and-Euro-centric, but it seeks to recognise something of value within the tradition and to transform it. The second group, postmodern theorists, as the various prefixes suggest (post-colonial, post-structuralist, post-analytical) see themselves as making a decisive break with the tradition. Habermas exemplifies the critical group, Foucault the post-group. Derrida could be located in either, depending on how seriously you take his protestations that he seeks to continue rather than destroy the tradition, or depending on whether you take up Gasché's or Rorty's readings of him. Much of this book will be attempting to steer a path between these groups, with leanings toward the critical side. However, what the rarefied air such theorists breathe desperately needs is a little of the oxygen of common sense and a touch of the perfume of hope. That is where pragmatism comes in. Our pragmatic wager is that it *must* be possible to preserve difference (but not absolute difference) while finding enough common ground to communi-cate and cooperate (without absolutising communication).

We should, perhaps, remind ourselves of what we already know. Communication in everyday life is an experience of both success and failure, of both oneness and difference. The separatists and communica-tion purists make a theoretical law of what for most of us is a merely passing fear that we can never be at one with others, that we can never understand or be understood.

The pessimists are wrong but, as I hope to show, they are not wrong simply because we can't afford that they be right. They are wrong because their pessimism, which arguably comes first, drives them to bad theory — or, perhaps, more accurately lousier theory. It was the historian of science, Imre Lakatos, who remarked that all theory was lousy theory — you could find arguments against anything, at least, as long as we don't know everything already — but our job, when presented with theoretical choice, is to choose the least lousy alternative. This inevitably means to make judgments about which faults in a theory are worse than others. Unless we are prepared to come to grips with judgements, and criteria of judgement in theory, we cannot choose between theories on any basis other than our mood on the day.

The pessimists are wrong because they apply criteria to their theory choice which would be limiting when applied to theorising *within a single culture*, let alone to communication between different cultures. They are also wrong because the criteria they apply cannot be applied to themselves without contradiction.

The pessimists fall into five kinds of error. They set standards for theory that theory cannot meet, then dismiss all theory as logocentric. They set up a straw figure, a scarecrow, of perfect communicative reproduction of understanding, and then make much of the fact that it is not achievable. They define 'meaning' as mysterious essence and complain that all we can actually achieve is ambiguity and they put forward a model of interpretation as reproduction of original meaning and use the absurdity of this model to prove that interpretation so defined, is not possible. Finally, they completely lose sight of our common experience of these things, which is an experience of success as well as failure.

In a certain strict and utopian sense, no two individuals ever fully understand each other. In a more practical, indeed pragmatist, sense, understanding is a matter of degree and is demonstrable. Even within our culture, and within one family, we might want to say, for instance, that identical twins understand each other *better* than other siblings in the same family. The existence of 'better' doesn't imply that at some level misunderstandings do not always exist but that some sort of *scale* of different degrees of misunderstanding and understanding is implied by our daily experience. Where on such a scale would we want to locate the kind of understanding between members of different cultures that will be necessary if we are to solve the problems of our common life on this planet? If our unstated standard is the kind of almost unspoken understanding that observers report characterises the communication of identical twins, we would clearly be asking too much. We would be asking for more than we ask for in most of our lives. Perhaps, realistically, we should aspire to the kind of understanding two well-disposed strangers might have or develop were they to be thrown together on a long train journey.

Derrida, who you will meet in Chapter 4, while problematising philosophical communication, acknowledges that everyday practical, face to face communication is exempt from his criticisms. Since the kind of communication between cultures that is necessary for the promotion of peace and the preservation of the environment will often be of a practical kind, a window of opportunity would seem to appear, even for Derrideans. Nevertheless, we might want to take issue with aspects of Derrida's critique of philosophical writing as well. In the meantime, let us look more closely at standards for theorising, and criteria for making sense of communication, meaning and interpretation.

And lest this talk of criteria, standards and making sense be seen to be yet another logocentric[11] attempt at the suppression of difference let us make an important distinction. There is a crucial difference between cultural plurality and theoretical plurality. It is true that our planet is characterised by the existence of many different cultures with different ways of life and different ways of viewing the world. It is also true that the multicultural, multilingual community of social theorists is characterised by a plurality of different ways of theorising culture, difference, and communication, with associated differences in political practices. But it is also true that these two areas of difference are *different*! They do not map onto each other. Sometimes, even often, members of different cultures espouse the same theories. Members of the 'same' culture, espouse different theories. No doubt there are some connections between the two domains of difference, but these have yet to be decisively demonstrated. The most powerful denunciations of, say, Eurocentrism, have come from, writers, such as Saïd, who have worked primarily within 'European' institutions and discourses. The critique of European thought is largely internal to it, although some of the important protagonists also draw on experience of other cultures.

It follows that an attempt to work through theoretical differences and develop or apply standards of some kind in our theorising is not *necessarily* an attempt to suppress cultural difference. Again, Derrida may be taken as an exemplary figure. He is not a theorist who is soft on attempts to employ logocentric standards to theorising. Yet he is also not a theorist without standards and his theorising is not without methodology. This is demonstrated clearly enough by Derrida's own protestations on this point. It is also demonstrated by the many commentators and critics, who, while disagreeing with Derrida about many things, have felt compelled to acknowledge Derrida's 'rigour'.[12] In what sense can Derrida's way of writing about writing in general and about other's writings be said to be 'rigorous', except in some sense which permits us to compare writings for their rigour? In this way, a standard is set up, but not an absolute, logocentric standard, extrinsic to the theorising being judged. The standard is intrinsic to a *discourse* and is fallibly relative to its development at any time — but it is a standard nevertheless.

Standards of Theorising

It might seem strange that it is necessary to begin a book about intercultural communication with a somewhat dry discussion about methodological standards, whether we can meaningfully use the word 'truth' and so on. The reason for this is quite straightforward. The present location of debate about both culture and communication is entirely a product of the attack on previous views of culture, language and communication by postmodern thinkers such as Derrida and Foucault and by those influenced by their views such as Bhabha, Spivak, Saïd and Niranjana. But the key postmodern ideas have been ideas about the nature and role of 'truth' in modern cultures and the nature of social theory and the validity of its claims. These very general philosophical insights have underlain all recent analyses of more specific cultural questions. The approach of this book is to take a pragmatic critical view of questions of truth, method and theory. It is argued that this approach can deal with postmodern objections to modern culture while allowing more useful things to be said than postmodernism can. Pragmatism, too, rests on the idea of non-absolute or intrinsic standards.

We can make a reasonable case for a number of such intrinsic or immanent standards. They are not absolute standards, nor are they standards which while relative, are somehow culturally imposed. They are intrinsic in two ways. First, any judgements we make about them will be relative to a discourse and to its boundaries and development. They will be fallible judgements which are related to arguments and comparisons couched within the terms of the discourse itself. Second, they are matters of choice. But the choices concerned are intrinsic to the moral life of people who do theoretical work. They are choices about how to see the world and its possibilities. In a way, everyone does theoretical work and makes such choices, but only some do it mindfully and self-consciously.

Being a matter of choice may seem to be a somewhat idiosyncratic characteristic for something we would want to call a 'standard'. After all, a standard *ought* to be necessary and unavoidable. If standards are optional they are hardly standards. Just so.

And intrinsic standards are both a matter of choice and a practical necessity. For instance, you can decide that you will not apply standards of mutuality and continuity to the voices in a discourse. That is, you can decide that it doesn't matter whether or not the voices in a discourse, say, discourse about cultural difference, address each other, or not. Or you can decide that any voice which ignores all others and does not position itself in respect of other voices, including prior voices, is, in some sense, denying the seriousness of the *problem* of difference. As Derrida tells us, this would also amount to disrespect for others. At a conceptual level, the choice is possible; at a practical level the choice has consequences for the mutuality, coherence and continuity of the debate. Derrida, for instance, is at considerable pains to show that his voice(s) are in some sort of dialogue with the voices of his predecessors (Kant, Husserl, Heidegger) and contemporaries (Habermas, Searle, Foucault).[13] It then becomes a matter of fallible judgement, for which we must call on argument and analysis of Derrida's writings, if we want to come to a judgement of how adequately Derrida has joined the discourse, how much he has changed it and how much he has failed to do so.

In the case of intercultural communication we already have a touch-stone, a wager, a pragmatic imperative. Choices which have consequences deleterious to our goal are already under judgement. In this sense, one of the standards we may legitimately apply to theories of intercultural understanding is the standard of completeness. Any adequate theory must provide a sufficiently complete account of culture, cultural membership, language, communication, meaning and interpretation, and relationships between cultures to provide working guidance for more effective communication between cultures. Or it should be open to further development in ways that promote this.

Translated to the level of theorising, completeness is a goal rather than a characteristic of completed theory. We will never know everything. In theory building, it is openness to further development that is crucial. However, this openness is not the same thing as a tolerance for unlimited theoretical pluralism. The present state of intercultural theorising *is* one of pluralism, but while this is not entirely desirable it is not without temporary value. In a practical sense, it is not always possible to specify in advance what elements might be necessary for a theory or be required to render a theory complete. Pluralism provides options — candidate part-theories and theoretical emphases — which challenge existing theory to grow and develop. Our standards for theorising should press us to find sufficient theoretical common ground to make our theorising practically useful, but should also permit us to be open to new theory, particularly through the recognition that the pluralism of current thought provides opportunities for theory development, only provided we can get the theories concerned to *engage* with each other rather than speak in grand soliloquy. It is possible to read theories as more or less in sympathy with each other. If we read for common ground we may make more sense. That is what this book tries to do.

We can also apply pragmatic standards of 'truth' to our theory. While we may not want to speak of our theory being true in any old-fashioned sense, we may speak of its usefulness and its adequacy to our experience. We may legitimately look at empirical experience in judging a theory.

The Reflexivity of Theorising

Since the turn away from positivist social thought towards a more 'linguistic' model for social theorising — the 'linguistic turn'[14] — social reality is not depicted as an external 'non-linguistic' or non-symbolic reality that we can objectively test theories against but rather is seen as the reality of symbols and meanings. These are constructed meanings but they take on 'facticity' — a fact like character. Thus, theorising can also be reality making. Meanings are fact like because once people possess these meanings they take on a certain inertia. It has often been said that social change is possible only because beings live for 70 years not 700. Ideas have a great deal of 'weight' — often they cannot be moved, only buried with their 'owners'. Theorising *can* create reality, but it would be a bold theorist who thought this was automatic.

This 'double-structure' of social theorising, the way the self-conscious act of theorising distances our everyday theories or beliefs from us, making them 'theoretic' rather than 'taken-for-granted', must be recognised in our theorising. But it doesn't excuse us from empirical work in connection with theorising. Otherwise we could fail to recognise that our theorising doesn't instantly change social reality (even though that reality consists only of other people's 'theories'), or fail to recognise that within a language, such as English, we can identify separate sub-languages, or logical languages and that through these cultures comment on (theorise) themselves. The last rather technical logical point is crucial for good theorising.

As the logician Tarski[15] pointed out, to say a sentence is true is to make a statement in one logical sub-language about a statement (the sentence) in another. Via sub-languages, language comments on itself. For Tarski, an object language is a language in which we talk about the world as directly as we can. Talk about the properties of our talk about the world takes place in a meta-language. In turn, we can talk about the grammar etc. of the meta-language in a meta-meta-language. There is no end to languages, but this need not lead to promiscuous mixing of them, because that, in turn, leads to all sorts of confusion. There is, of course, a circularity in this, which has been duly noted by Tarski among others. Just the same, there is a difference between talk about social reality and talk that *is* (everyday) social reality, even if, in its turn, talk about social reality, via education, newspapers, films etc. seeps out into the social reality it comments upon and becomes part of it. In this process we see at work nothing more than a wider circuit of a general characteristic of everyday talk — it comments on itself in such a way as to constitute itself as the kind of talk it is as it goes. Further, as ethnomethodology shows us, everyday talk would not be possible without this constant constitutive or rather self-constitutive dimension. The fact that social theorising is in the long run creative or constitutive of social reality does not mean that empirical experience of the way people act now is irrelevant to it, quite the contrary. The reflexivity of theory is not an excuse for equating theorising with mere invention, but it is a reason for responsibility, since theorising is, in a sense, a form of invention, to the extent that it does not rest content with describing the present facticity but opens itself to alternatives, what-might-bes, and as-ifs which may, eventually, be chosen by people as their identity.

All theory is elaborated as a kind of wager with the future, not just the theory in this book. To appropriate a grand word, we could say that theory is prophetic, providing we see that word written with a small, modest and open-ended 'p'. In parlance more in tune with the times we could say that theorising is like issuing a promissory note or writing a check on the basis of what we might someday have in our account if only we can draw it from the immense range of our human possibilities. Because theorising has a constitutive role, because even at a minimal level it is an act with ethical implications, the *describing* of social facticity to those who were oblivious of it is an ethical political act, and an act from which a further political strategy might issue. When we look back to the current incompleteness and pluralism of theory, and to questions of the relationship of voices in a discourse, it is reasonable to recognise a distinction between the political significance of particular theories and the internal politics of theorising, just as we recognised a distinction between levels of language. In the internal politics of theorising, when we decide to prefer one theory over another, we are not dealing directly with the repression of cultures and difference.

Theoretical differences at this level may be a resource for better theorising but in general there is a press for overcoming them in the name of the need to have or create sufficient common ground for a useful theory to emerge. And at the level of the external politics of theory, where there is direct interaction with the world situation, a theory is useful if it provides some common ground upon which culturally different interlocutors may touch. Ideally, that would in some sense be culturally neutral common ground created by some degree of theoretical agreement across cultural difference (as we will see in Chapter 4). At both levels, some of the ethical questions that arise are questions intrinsic to the ethics of communicative interaction, whether in theory building discourse or in practical discourse about managing our planet. It will be argued in a later chapter that the ethical requirements of effective communication (in the limited pragmatist sense in which the concept of communication is used in the present discussion) are characterised by a kind of communicative democracy.

Summary

The standards of theorising identified so far are that theorising should be pragmatic, realistic (rather than idealistic or absolutist), open to development (completeness), through harnessing pluralism of theory, via democratic but engaged dialogue among theorists, and through systematic relating of theorising to our empirical experience (while recognising the reflexivity of theorising). At the same time, theory should be optimistic and politically responsible. It is also important that we do not collapse all distinctions in the name of relationships. That one level of theorising is related to another does not destroy the distinction between levels of theorising. It is logically necessary to postulate levels of theorising in order to speak of relationships at all, even those characterised by deep and significant reflexivity and relatedness. Only a perfect one to one mapping of the levels on each other would justify abandoning such distinctions. In the final analysis there is a difference between theoretical work on the nature of intercultural communication and the work of communication between members of different cultures about wealth, power, pollution and peace, even if the two kinds of work are interrelated.

Problems for Theories of Communication, Meaning and Interpretation

The standards we have just discussed at a general level can be applied to more specific questions, permitting us to identify problem areas in theories of intercultural communication — areas where the standards are in trouble.

As we have already noted, a pragmatic and realistic theory of communication does not theorise communication as perfect reproduction of meaning. The paradox of (perfect) communication is that the conditions necessary for its perfection would render it unnecessary. Identical twins often know so much about each other (because they have shared so much experience since birth) that they do not need to speak. They already know how their twin is thinking and feeling.

This shared knowledge and experience, indeed, shared life, could be said to be the 'culture' of the twins concerned. But we might want to use the same analogy when we speak of genetically more distantly related members of the same family. Siblings, in general, might be said to share a way of life — a way of family life — and thus be said to share a kind of 'culture'. Clearly, this sharing, and the character of people's membership of a family, a social class, or a nation is a matter of degrees and levels, rather than absolutes. But we often speak of members of cultures as if their membership of a culture was a complete and total immersion in culture. In this way, we have the member *stand for* the culture, as a kind of existential point at which the giant abstract *system* of the culture expresses itself. Theorists speak this way even when their very speaking reflexively gives the lie to itself, at least as far as their own membership of (French?) culture is concerned. In later chapters this problem will be called the problem of *membership*.

It is also necessary to distinguish between the simple fact of communication of 'information' and the effect of communicating certain information under the conditions which prevail on a given occasion. Communicating information, cognition, semantic meaning etc. is rather like the activity of theorising — it does not change social reality, or rather, minimally changes it by changing the minds of theorists or other interlocutors. Rather, it is the further consequences of the information communicated that brings about change when the forces of social life are able to be channelled in different directions due to the information in question. The reflexivity of social theorising is partly a product of this double structure of social action. While there are distinct moments or levels of communication just as there are distinct moments or levels of social theorising, the fact is that each and every act of communication occurs in a flow of progressive and vital living which already has impetus and force.

Just as theorising is a political–ethical act which is not independent of history but occurs in the full flood of history's flow, bound by its urgency, and specifically, by the urgency of our current, global problems, so *all* communication is a form of political–ethical action, caught up in the flow of life and in turn, influencing it. Any adequate theory of communication will recognise this embedded, embodied, biographically and socially constitutive character of communication — its character as a form of action. One of the standards for judging theorising of communication is its adequacy with respect to the dynamics of action. The problem of *action* brings in its train a cluster of related problems. How conscious, how chosen, is a particular construction of social meanings? This is the problem of *agency*. There is a close relationship between the problem of action (and agency) and the problem of cultural membership. To what extent can members of cultures deliberately change them — through criticism, for instance. The role of postmodern intellectuals as critics of European cultures appears paradoxical when in some readings those same critics appear to assert the impossibility of agency.

But problems of theorising communication — the activity of making meaning (individually, interactively) — lead to problems of theorising meaning itself. Is meaning a mental phenomenon, a conceptual scheme, a set of images in the brain, or somesuch, or is it the structural situation of a text — a configuration of elements each defined only by its location relative to all the others, residing elsewhere than in the individual symbols, signs, or words? And in the action of communication, is meaning produced by the symbols uttered, written, inserted into social life's historical/biographical time/space? Or is it a broader process of which strings of uttered signs are only a pointer and a provocation? Does language = meaning? Or is meaning a fallible, revisable narrative, story or theory which interlocutors construct through inference, drawing upon many resources, including of course the sign strings uttered/read? This last account of meaning is a *pragmatist* one. There is room within it for a *structuralist* theory of meaning or rather, part-theory — that the meaning of signs does not reside in the individual sign but in its location in the *structure* of a system of signs — but it goes beyond the view that meaning is confined to signs. For a pragmatist, the sign, or even sign-string/sentence level of analysis of meaning is insufficiently holistic. With Foucault, pragmatists would argue that meaning resides in the reading and uttering of narratives (rather than in the narratives themselves) which, in turn, only make sense in something wider, like an *episteme* (roughly a set of institutions, roles and practices together with the narratives that prevail in it).

There are two general dimensions of theoretical difference here, the difference between pragmatist and structuralist (also post-structuralist) accounts of meaning, which fall roughly on a holistic–atomistic continuum, and the difference between a theory of meaning that is semiotic and one which recognises the active character of communication as not only ontogenetic but semantogenetic. Meaning doesn't reside in language or sign systems, not even as systems of difference, although such systems are essential to the intercommunication of meaning. The words and sentences of an utterance are a part of a wider process of insertion of semiological or semantic meaning in *history*. Meaning is made, not communicated and it is made socially not individually.

In analytical philosophy, the distinction between the dictionary meaning of words and their meaning as history has been called the distinction between 'meaning' and 'force'. However, in this book, 'meaning' is used in the wider sense and the narrow sense of meaning of a sentence or sign-string is called semiological, semantic or 'dictionary' meaning. The study of the relation between the *form* (semiological form) of a sentence which is uttered and the *effect* of its utterance is called *Rhetoric*, so the problem of theorising meaning as a part of life (i.e. as historically and biographically *real* utterances, creating social life itself) is called the problem of *rhetoric* in this book. Classically, the problem of rhetoric was deeply interconnected with the problem of truth, because all truths that could be recognised by humans had first to be rendered communicable. The problem in this was that the form in which truths were stated was always 'imperfect' and there was always a choice among alternative ways of communicating truth. One of the ideals of the study of rhetoric was to achieve a unity between the most persuasive form of communication and the most truthful.

Another difficulty of various theories of meaning is the difficulty that is created by the fact that people use language to direct each other to do things and somehow quite complex, technical performances can be coordinated this way, as when by radio in an emergency a surgeon instructs an amateur to remove an appendix with a pocket-knife. This has been called the problem of *reference*. Some theories of meaning tend to say very little about this relation of language to *concrete* action and objects, but the theorists concerned would probably not let the mechanic who fixes their automobile take out their appendix.

Derrida is quite clear about this function of language, but some Derrideans are less clear. Derrida's remarks about the absence of the object of the signifier (the signifier is part of a sign) and his critique of the notion that meanings of the marks-on-paper-which-signify are in no way simply present in the same way the marks (the occasion of the signifiers) are simply present, is not meant to apply to everyday writing about concrete processes, such as the instructions for setting up a new computer. But some followers of Derrida, seeking to adopt a radical pose, wish to treat all communication as if it was equally detached from a concrete context. They would be surprised to learn that some old-fashioned analytical philosophers adopt a position somewhat parallel to Derrida's. Davidson,[16] for instance, sees the idea of conceptual schemes (as sets of meanings which underlie language) as an unnecessary complication. One consequence of this is that cultural difference is not usefully theorised as conceptual incommensurability. Quine,[17] from a behavioural perspective on meaning argues that the reference of language is 'inscrutable' — we can never be sure (in the strict, logical sense) what objects people are talking about. Perhaps, but as Quine himself points out in a more pragmatist moment, this doesn't stop us being sure-for-all-practical-purposes. We will meet Davidson and Quine again in later chapters.

A corollary of the problem of reference is the *problem of relativity*. It would appear that the 'same' ideas can be expressed in different language. For instance, we can call someone a 'bachelor' or an 'unmarried adult male'. Conversely, the same language can express different ideas (in different contexts of utterance). The conceptual or semantic relativity-of-language does not appear to be as much of a problem in a pragmatist view, since the emergent, constructive, narrative and inferential character of meaning is stressed in a pragmatist view and language is seen in an instrumentalist light. But post-structuralist theory, notably Derridean theory, makes the relativity of meaning the centrepiece of its analysis — as signalled by Derridean terms such as 'différance' and 'dissemination'.

However, Derrida himself is very much aware of the problem of the constant surplus of meaning, its capacity to spill over beyond the text of what is written (or said). Whether we are talking in analytical terms about the problem of what 'force' adds to meaning or in Derridean terms about sedimentation and the violence of inscribing meanings *onto* people there are problems of the process whereby the cultural member accepts or refuses the meanings others would inscribe in them, the process of agency in the forceful creation of identity, nationhood etc., and the way in which interlocutors relate to each other *through* the production and reception of texts. In addition to problems of the activity of public meaning making, and the nature of meaning, there are *problems of interpretation*, of the relationship of agency to making meaning.

Some readings of Derrida take his famous remark that there is nothing beyond the text in an absolute way. This leads to what Rorty[18] has called textualism, the view that critique of texts is merely preferring one text over another. Pragmatist theory rejects textualism because pragmatism espouses a kind of transactional realism. Particular texts can be chosen or rejected because they help us live well or make us live badly. Our experience is of a reality beyond the text, and perhaps even beyond texts. By that is meant, that at the least our experience is an experience of being a unity of experience relative to many alternative texts. The reality beyond the text (singular) is our multitextuality. We can experience this even if we acknowledge our lack of inner unity, our inner division and ambiguity. Perhaps, too, we experience a reality beyond all texts, even if we must provide a textual account of it when we seek to communicate our experience. One thing is sure, pragmatism is not a textualist view and textualism robs itself of the possibility of intelligible talk about texts, because intelligibility depends on claims that texts make about other texts and the world in general and the fit or lack of fit between texts and a way of life.

Here, we can be guided by identifying[19] three broad problem areas in the theory of interpretation (or 'hermeneutics') — problems of *reproduction, emancipation from authority,* and *conversation.*

From a pragmatist perspective, the problem of reproduction is the problem of the conditions under which the narrative a hearer hears comes to resemble the narrative from which a speaker began. I have already made the point that even identical twins are not *perfectly* identical. Perfect reproduction or matching of meanings is not possible. What *is* possible is pragmatic concord. From this point of view, understanding is the same as reaching an understanding.

The problem of emancipation from authority is related to the problem of reproduction. As we have seen, meanings aren't simply neutral 'information' — they can be life-threatening or life-enhancing and they are not isolated from the rest of our bodily life in some purely cognitive corner of the brain, but are psycho-somatically connected with all the life circumstances of individuals who hear them. So reproduction of the meanings created and voiced by a person in authority is not the same as acting as a purely cognitive repeater station in an electronic network — it entails *becoming* the meanings in some sense. So authority is really being in a position to originate other people's meanings — to define their identities and so to make them *into* the reality of the new meanings. The apparently intellectual problem of whether or not meanings are reproduced by the hearer is also a social problem — an ethical/political problem. The problem of emancipation — literally, casting off the chains — is a problem of a specific kind of agency called critical agency. In the process of interpretation of a message, critique can, indeed must, come into play. If we always rejected the meanings others try to inscribe in us we would not be social beings at all. If we always accepted them, we would be slaves who were totally enslaved, mind and body. Neither of these extremes is possible.

The problem of conversation is the problem of how it is that critique can work in the process of interpretation and still in some sense be interpretation of a message. Can we respond to a message in part while rejecting it in part? Can we negotiate meanings? How do *agents* interact to produce mutually acceptable meanings which they are happy to allow to inscribe the identities of all agents? What role does dialogue play in reaching an understanding?

Summary

The problems of theorising intercultural communication (and communication in general) are the problems of the nature of cultural *membership, action and agency, rhetoric* (form and effect), *reference and relativity* (some-

times called indeterminacy), and the problems of interpretation (hermeneutics) — *reproduction* of meaning, emancipation from *authority*, and the
problems of *conversation*.

To all of these problems, a critical–pragmatic solution has been adopted.
The remaining chapters of the book are an extended argument for the view
that a critical–pragmatic approach offers a workable solution to these
problems. However, to simplify the discussion it is possible to sum up the
many different possible positions theorists might take in five general
theoretical approaches to the explanation of communication and culture.

The study of understanding and how it is achieved, including all the
problems discussed above and more, is called hermeneutics.

Systematising Differences: Five Theories[20]

Conservative, or traditional hermeneutics tends to see communication
problems as relatively (theoretically) trivial difficulties of categorisation
and coding. The essential preservation of intended meaning in the
interpretive event is seen as a real possibility. A common model here would
be something like the difficulty that arises in a classroom when the
cognitive schema of a student has no place in it for say, a mathematics
teacher's new concepts, with resultant misunderstanding. In this view
agency is unproblematic, meanings do not create social reality but merely
describe it, authority is based on truth and discourse merely fine tunes
truth. There is only one best account of the meaning of a text when the text
is flawed (i.e. ambiguous).

In the liberal or moderate view, we see the beginning of a recognition
that interpretation is creatively open, but there is still a strong orientation
to a notion of mutuality in meaning making and a view of dialogue as
sharing. Over time, under the right circumstances, connections can be
multiplied in number and kind so a situation arises where the hearer begins
to get a good general grasp of the speaker's concepts. The speaker, also
reacts to the hearer's difficulties by trying to understand the hearer's
concepts and to change the message so as to connect with them, just as a
determined teacher will try many ways to present a new mathematical idea
and will try to guess the nature of student's misunderstanding in order to
make the necessary connections.[21] To an extent, it is possible to share the
liberal insight that where more communication is possible, and circumstances permit, misunderstanding can be overcome. Where the liberal view
fails is in its theory of circumstances. There is an insufficient emphasis on
the fact that openness is differentially distributed by power.

The liberal picture is one-sided if applied to the colonial situation. The metaphor of teacher/learner is not very useful when we come to circumstances in which two or more communicators from different cultural backgrounds are faced with a communicative problem. The point about real, historical situations is that they are not even handed.

The descriptions of context in both conservative and liberal hermeneutics are a little 'thin', a little too 'cognitive' and cerebral to help us with many everyday communicative situations where politics, pride, economics and power are at stake. Conservative hermeneutics tends to ignore these dimensions. Liberal hermeneutics is not strong in them.

Certainly, the reasons for communicative misunderstandings have to do with a list of different things which might be mismatched in some way: definitions, situational goals or situation tasks, the status of culturally recognised categories of participants in respect of them, background assumptions about the task-relevant evidential features of the world and of people, expected (unfolding) structures of action required to successfully accomplish the situation task, and expectations about linguistic usage in these structures. But accidental mismatches, differences in perception of context, are not the only difficulties present in communication. We have to add the extent to which such situations, tasks and agent roles fail to realise basic existential needs of at least some participants. And, going beyond conservative and liberal hermeneutics, we would have to examine the reflexive dimension, where talk curls back on itself to regulate the meanings available to politically defined classes or categories of speakers.

Where these distortions are culturally and socially institutionalised we speak of the communicative *structures* as distorted and the *practices* as 'ideological', and the process whereby those whose interests are subordinated try to express them *despite* the structures and practices as 'resistance'. This resistance, which is essentially resistance to the structures and practices, to role definitions, allocation of tasks, and to the 'speaking parts' allocated in the drama of life, is often identified by the powerful as incompetence or as a manifestation of intellectual or moral deficiency. If it is to escape this to some extent it has to become more than mere 'resistance'. Critical hermeneutics is a hermeneutics in which the creativity of interpretation and the capacity of meanings to make human identity and ways of life is recognised and some attempt is made to provide a systematic account of strategies for changing this. That is, a critical hermeneutics has to go beyond 'liberal hermeneutics with politics added', but as we will see, not as far as a Marxist-radicalism, in which critique is seen to be historically objective, and certainly, it must stop short of the transformative suspicion of postmodern-radical hermeneutics, which effectively criticises every-thing, saying little that is positive or optimistic.

First, it has to stop short of postmodern radical hermeneutics such as that represented by Foucault's theory of the discourse of regimes of power/knowledge and his view that critique can come only from the margins of society. Critique can be found closer to the centre than that. And, as we will see in Chapter 4, it doesn't take a particularly optimistic reading of history to show that it sometimes is. For resistance to oppression to become a politics of liberation it has to be guided by an ideology critique of practices that goes beyond the framework of small-scale situations to uncover the macro-political structures through which the micropolitics of practices in many situations is maintained and supported and also to a critique of the culture associated with the view of the world which sustains the overall politics of ideology. Foucault's own work is an incomplete attempt to do this because it does not identify any possibility for large scale political action and it lacks the necessary values within which political progress could be defined. Perhaps the women's movement offers a better model of an attempt to change society at both structural or large scale and situational or small scale levels.

But a social-structural analysis and clear values are not enough, as a look at Marxism shows. Certainly, the self-assurance of either classical or neo-Marxist accounts of seeing through ideology and their accompanying radical hermeneutics of ideology critique must be regarded as more than a little suspect in the light of postmodern critique.

Ideology is more various and more fluid than Marxist structural analysis of ruling class ideology reveals. Meaning is always dynamic and changing. A critical theory of meaning concedes this much to the post-structuralists — a fixed view of meaning is a false one. Critical views of meaning recognise that it has a Heraclitan character. The river of meaning into which we put our interpretive foot is never the same river into which we put our foot a moment ago, just as it is not the same foot that it was a moment ago. All meanings are also claims we make against fate and the future, and they are claims on each other and on ourselves. Every response is an acceptance or a rejection, but the process can no more stand still than making love can.

It is clear enough that an understanding of communication requires both an understanding of the meaningful person and situation categories, practices and expectations of participants — their action frameworks — and an ideology critique that encompasses both critique of unjust structures and cultural critique. But it needs to go beyond this to a dimension of the body, desire and imagination. Post-structuralist emphasis on desire, the body and the aesthetic has been a valuable adjunct to critical theory here.

If Davidson is right, and we theorise interpretation as pragmatic participation in a whole way of life we must see that the pragmatic test of the coherence of our interpretations with the location of our utterances in the events and dilemmas of a way of life is an appropriate test of our interpretive practices. Here we reject simple empiricism or Quine's behaviourism and any reduction of meaning to a story about stimulation of the molecules of the sensory surfaces of the body. Rather, we see meaning as a form of action, which takes its place among other forms of action we enact in living *with others* in a way of life. But we also stop short of reducing interpretation to an adjunct of the history of the working class.

But the study of ways of life, and the way they cohere, fragment or change is called anthropology, and it seems reasonable to see what it can tell us about how meaning action is produced and suffered before we develop our analysis further. This will be done in the next chapter.

To conclude, let us set out the structure of the journey you are just about to embark on. In Chapter 2 you will look at ways of life and the concept of culture. In what way are we shaped by culture as members of it and in what way are we agents who are capable of distancing ourselves from our culture, deliberately changing it, and living in a cosmopolitan way?

In the next chapter, we move on from culture to meaning and communication. Several things come together in Chapter 3. First, the question of how reference works and how language might relate to empirical experience is examined. Behaviourist accounts of meaning are criticised but, through drawing on accounts of pragmatist philosophers, a practical empirical element is rescued. Second, useful insights are gleaned from empirical research. And finally, meaning and communication are defined pragmatically by practical concord among participants in a shared way of life. It is shown that the key issue for an optimistic theory of communication is its capacity to cope with the possibility of cultures learning from each other. Postmodern views are weak in this respect.

Chapter 4 explores postmodern views of culture and communication. While it is shown that postmodern thinkers have made an immense contribution to our understanding of cultural difference and cultural power it is argued that they have quite fundamental shortcomings when it comes to theorising human well-being and cultural harmony. The key to an optimistic and positive theory of intercultural learning is an account of dialogue as a process of mutual respect and mutual learning. Postmodern views are not strong in this, but a pragmatic-critical view is able to help.

Chapter 5 outlines a critical-pragmatic theory of intercultural communication developed from the philosophy and social theory of Jurgen Habermas. Habermas' work has been misunderstood but this discussion sets the record straight. Habermas' theory is a theory of intercultural learning through communicative agency. However, the acid test of such a theory is how well it deals with politics.

In Chapter 6 we see Habermas (aided by Dewey) in contention with his postmodern adversaries. Habermas' theory of politics is that most politics ultimately is about either coercion or ideological control and ideological control is about the control of meaning making. If we understand the process through which cultural exclusion and manipulation of identity of culturally different people is carried out in everyday communication and the way this process is embedded in social roles and practices we have a clear basis for an effective politics aimed at changing empirically observable mechanisms for the creation of ideology or the assertion of the reality of one culture over another

In Habermas' view, intellectuals must play a key role in promoting intercultural understanding through the politics of communicative agency. But the kind of intellectuals involved are not the old 'high' intellectuals. Now that the social processes of production have become information-rich, intellectual workers are found throughout society. Foucault would see teachers, social workers, health professionals, youth workers and the like as wielders of pastoral power in the name of the system of power/knowledge, but Habermas sees professional people as being citizens and critical intellectuals capable of providing democratic leadership, even if they are sometimes or even often forced into the service of existing structures and institutions. Habermas identifies 3 roles for intellectuals in intercultural learning. The first of these is the critical analysis of communicative agency or lack of it. In the next chapter, Chapter 7, three tools for the critical appraisal of structures of communicative agency are described: critical hermeneutics (from Habermas) genealogical critique (from Foucault) and deconstruction (from Derrida). Far from being in competition with each other, these three offer complementary methods for critique.

Finally, the book concludes by examining the wider role of critical but pragmatic professionals in promoting intercultural learning. Perhaps the primary location for critical work by professionals will be within their own culture, their own institution, their own role and their own practice and in interaction with the practice of those around them. In these places, they will work to make their own and their colleagues professional practice more 'interculturally friendly'. They will do so by a combination of intellectual work, employing the tools of critical appraisal of communicative agency and the politics of culture discussed in Chapters 6 and 7, and the skills of collective agency — the old fashioned hard yards of the politics of solidarity, persuasion and sometimes confrontation.

However, as stated earlier, the place to begin is with a concept of culture and cultural membership which leaves room for intercultural solidarity and respect, while allowing learning, agency and change. That is the subject of Chapter 2.

Notes

1. Derrida's work will be discussed extensively in Chapter 4.
2. Examples of extreme or one-sided readings of Derrida and others are not hard to find. Fortunately, as I write, the reception of postmodern thought is entering a more mature phase and recent work is more balanced.
3. G. Steiner, *After Babel: Aspects of Language and Translation*. New York: Oxford University Press, 1975.
4. D. Held, *Introduction to Critical Theory: Horkheimer to Habermas*. London: Hutchison, 1980.
5. J.F. Lyotard, *The Postmodern Condition: A Report on Knowledge*. Minneapolis: University of Minnesota Press, 1984.
6. T. Adorno, *Dialectic of Enlightenment*, with Max Horkheimer. New York: Herder and Herder, 1972; *Negative Dialectics*. New York: Seabury Press, 1973.
7. Toulmin, *Cosmopolis: The Hidden Agenda of Modernity*. New York: The Free Press, 1991.
8. A. Callinicos, *Against Postmodernism: A Marxist Critique*. Cambridge: Polity Press, 1989.
9. Foucault is discussed at length in Chapter 4.
10. Jurgen Habermas, often known as a critical theorist, is the theorist whose work most influences this book. His views will be discussed in progressively greater detail, chapter by chapter.
11. This is one of Derrida's words. It means roughly the view that words mean what they say and can describe reality, independently of cultural and other differences.
12. e.g. C. Norris, *Derrida*. Cambridge: Harvard University Press, 1987. Most of the general points made about Derrida in this chapter can be found in Norris' exposition and in many other discussions of Derrida
13. Many names will be mentioned along the way. I was in two minds about this, but it seemed appropriate to provide enough clues for readers who want to locate the discussion by understanding who each theorist sees themselves as arguing with. This list of 6 are Derrida's main interlocutors.
14. For a discussion of the linguistic turn and subsequent developments see D. Hiley *et al.* (eds), *The Interpretive Turn: Philosophy, Science, Culture*. London: Cornell University Press, 1991.
15. A. Tarski, *Logic, Semantics, Metamathematics*. Oxford: Clarendon Press, 1956.
16. See D. Davidson, *Inquiries into Truth and Interpretation*. Oxford: Clarendon Press, 1984. Davidson's views are discussed further in the next few chapters.

17. W. Quine, *Ontological Relativity and Other Essays*. New York: Columbia University Press, 1969; *Word and Object*. Cambridge: MIT Press, 1960.

18. R. Rorty, 19th century idealism and 20th century textualism. Pp. 139–159 in *The Consequences of Pragmatism*. London: The Harvester Press, 1982.

19. S. Gallagher, *Hermeneutics and Education*. Albany State University of New York Press, 1992.

20. By comparing the positions theorists adopt on the problems for theories of communication and meaning we have just discussed it is possible to categorise than into five broad categories: conservative, liberal, critical, Marxist, and postmodern. Gallagher identifies four general theoretical positions on these hermeneutic questions. But Gallagher's four need a little reworking if they are to be useful in the present discussion. Gallagher's four models can be placed on a continuum and it can be shown that the differences between Gallagher's 'moderate' hermeneutics and 'critical' hermeneutics, properly understood, are not great, except in one crucial respect — critical hermeneutics makes an explicit virtue of hope. Gallagher assimilates Habermas' critical hermeneutics to neo-Marxist hermeneutics, characterising it as claiming the capacity to see through ideology. However, this categorisation is based on a mistaken understanding of Habermas, the details of which need not delay us here. If we split off Habermas' critical hermeneutics, from neo-Marxist radical hermeneutics, and finally, postmodern radical hermeneutics, we can identify five points along the continuum — conservative, moderate (or liberal), critical, Marxist-radical and postmodern-radical.

21. It should be noted here that Davidson would reparse this discussion so as to leave out talk of concepts and stay with the public level of the linguistic meaning itself.

2 Culture and Difference

No anthropologist better suits the present purpose than Clifford Geertz.[1] Probably no anthropologist has had a greater influence on current thinking about culture than Geertz and certainly no body of work illustrates the theoretical contest between postmodern and modern thought better than his does. We retrace Geertz's journey from modernism to postmodernism and back and discover what is at stake in different conceptions of culture. It is an important journey to retrace different conceptions of culture because in many ways it is the journey of many if not most social scientists in the years 1960–1990.

First, we examine the debate about understanding other cultures carried out among social philosophers and anthropologists before Geertz's work began in earnest. We will look at different concepts of culture and their limitations. Geertz's postmodern-influenced thinking will be described and criticised. His move away from a view of culture that left room for intelligent human adaptation is pinpointed and its contradictions highlighted. Finally, through a series of critiques we move back towards a pragmatic view of culture, closer to the view with which Geertz began.

Geertz begins Chapter 6 of *Works and Lives* (1988) with a 1934 account of a French ethnographer supplying pen and paper to an Ethiopian woman, Emawayish, so that she could record her songs, particularly her love songs. The ethnographer records that at this request Emawayish asked:

> Does poetry exist in France?

and then:

> Does love exist in France?

Geertz makes of this a parable of the epistemological delicacy that has overtaken modern anthropology:

> This nervousness brings on, in turn, various responses, variously excited: deconstructive attacks on canonical works, and on the very idea of canonicity as such; *ideologiekritik* unmasking of anthropological writings as the continuation of imperialism by other means; clarion calls to reflexivity, dialogue, heteroglossia, linguistic play, rhetorical

32

> self-consciousness, performative translation, verbatim recording and
> first-person narrative as forms of cure… The Emawayish question now
> is everywhere: What happens to reality when It is shipped abroad?
> (*Works and Lives*: p. 131)

He identifies the tone of the ethnographers who recorded Emaywayish's
questions as a form of 'text positivism':

> …the notion that, if only Emawayish can be got to dictate or write down
> her poems as carefully as possible and they are translated as faithfully
> as possible, then the ethnographer's role dissolves into that of an honest
> broker passing on the substance of things with only the most trivial of
> transaction costs. (*Works and Lives*, p. 145)

Text positivism is, of course, the same as the conservative theory of
hermeneutics discussed in the previous chapter. We can agree with Geertz
that much more than this is involved. The modern ethnographer's task is
greatly complicated. The 'burden of authorship' is 'deepened', as Geertz
puts it.

What Emawayish's questions tell us is that all speaking is open, often
radically, to the future and to the possibility of the hope of new
understanding. In a world of change we speak ourselves into a future
reality that is always anticipated in the present. Speech is context
dependent, but context is created in the space between the weight of the
past, and the fact of its irremediable loss. We can agree with Derrida that
context is always fleeing away, retreating from our grasp. The positive side
of this loss is that there is always something new born in the moment of
speech. And the very presence of the culturally other is a problem to us and
a challenge to the myth of preservation with which we hide the openness
of living from ourselves.

Anthropology is the traditional disciplinary practice which has developed and reflected the cultural or holistic level of analysis and has
attempted to provide a methodological account of the study of cultural
difference. The goal of anthropology has been to understand cultures and
explain societies, and so to understand and explain human action and
action frameworks of culturally recognised conduct. As it has been usually
practised, and this is its strength as well as its weakness, anthropology has
attempted to understand and explain the culturally other. It has been an
intercultural enterprise.

But as Geertz tells us, it is a form of inquiry that grew up to meet the
needs of European colonial expansion. So, it is a tainted well from which
we are seeking to draw clear water; never an easy task. But the history of
anthropology is also the history of the attempt by the scholars of the

European culture area to understand the culturally other. That is, it is not simple imperialism. It has always been shot through with ambivalence.

We could start the analysis of intercultural understanding in the ancient (European) world, with Greek and Roman historians' understandings of exotic peoples. All peoples have their stories of the 'other' and literate civilisations develop literary traditions of exognosis, but systematic anthropology as a full-time profession is a modern phenomenon, as is an anthropology that began slowly to come face to face with its own latent ethnocentrism.

We could then, begin with some of the first, distinctively modern attempts to provide a rational understanding of non-European cultures, under the aegis of 'science', such as the early German ethnologies, or the systematic comparative anthropology of Frazer's studies of religion, or even Weber's analyses of the religions of Ancient China, or India. Unfortunately, there is not sufficient space for such a leisurely treatment. An arbitrary, but useful point of entry is the last, great, modernist debate about understanding a primitive society — the last, that is, before postmodernism and the *intellectual* resurgence of the colonised profoundly opened up the debate, and changed its basic terms. What I want to do in revisiting this debate, which 'began' with Alasdair MacIntyre's[2] response to Peter Winch's *The Idea of a Social Science*,[3] is to locate and describe 'a path not taken' in this discussion, the path of critical theory, and to show that more postmodern concerns with latent ethnocentrism and the denial of an intellectual politics of essence and universal knowledges can be accommodated and at the same time, the shortcomings of some readings of postmodernism overcome if we take this path.

Understanding Other Cultures in the Social Sciences

Peter Winch is one of the main post-war proponents of the view, which developed within modernist anthropology, that each culture has its own, unique way of seeing the world, and within this, its own, unique *form of rationality*. Winch's view is a useful place to begin because it represents the first breach in what might be called 'high' modernist views of the study of other cultures. It is a liberal view. Conservative hermeneutic views are represented by Evans-Pritchard, an influential early British anthropologist, who made scientific thought, as he understood it, the measuring stick for judging other cultures. For him, cultures were separate but not equal. Winch was a part of the 'linguistic turn' in social thought. He was strongly influenced by Wittgenstein, who has been called the (politically) 'conservative Derrida'. Wittgenstein's later work represented a break with modernist theory of knowledge and is credited with having a major influence on the linguistic turn in social theory. In this way, Winch himself is a transitional figure between modernism and postmodernism.

Following Wittgenstein, Winch sees social life as meaningful action (including using language as a form of action) and he sees the social scientists' task as being the interpretation of systems of meaning embedded in socially constructed 'ways of life'. Winch believed that this interpretative task *can* be achieved, and that it is achieved through a knowledge of the set of rules members of a society use in interpreting each other's conduct. Interpretation is just understanding which rules apply in a situation. In this view, social actions are just those acts which can be brought under one of the culture's rules. Insofar as most instances of human action are linguistic the social scientist's task may be said to be that of understanding the local cultural rules governing linguistic behaviour. The problem for intercultural understanding then becomes a problem of incommensurability between sets of rules.

Winch pointed to the double structure of social science (discussed in Chapter 1) as the basis for the methodological distinction between it and the natural sciences:

> ...whereas in the case of the natural scientist we have to deal with only one set of rules, namely those governing the scientist's investigation itself, here *what the sociologist is studying*, as well as his study of it, is a human activity and is therefore carried on according to rules. (*The Idea of a Social Science*, p. 87)

† Each culture has its own set of concepts and rules which its members possess, even if implicitly (i.e. in the way most people 'possess' the rules of the grammar of the language they speak). It is these rules which govern correct and incorrect action and, together presumably with the rules of grammar, correct and incorrect language use — that is, competent and incompetent communication.

It is in the light of this analysis that Winch accused Evans-Pritchard of a 'category mistake', when Evans-Pritchard made judgements about Zande witchcraft beliefs by comparing them with Western scientific beliefs.[4] Winch went on to argue that each culture had its own standards of rationality and that the standards of rationality are not universal, but local. Thus, there could be no rational basis for intercultural critique.

The Azande believe that some of their number are witches, capable through occult means of (unknowingly) harming their fellows. But a Western High Modern anthropologist studying the Zande way of life does not share these beliefs. In explaining these beliefs and associated practices it becomes a problem for the Western anthropologist to explain just how the Azande maintain these beliefs in the face of what to a Western observer is clear evidence to the contrary. Another objective is to explain what *latent* role such beliefs and practices play in Zande society (i.e. their role other than the role the Azande themselves believe them to play). Evans-Pritchard did this, but in the process he labelled the beliefs as irrational because the Azande maintain them despite disagreement with 'objective reality'.

Winch argued that it is just this notion of 'objective reality' which is a problem, since it is a category of Western culture, and while it might be irrational to continue to hold beliefs contradicted by 'objective reality' in that culture it is not irrational for the Azande because they have no concept of 'objectivity'. We need to know what Zande concepts of reasoning are like before we can accuse them of breaking the rules.

Winch's argument drew on Wittgenstein:[5]

The limits of my language mean the limits of my world. Logic fills the world: the limits of the world are also its limits. We cannot therefore say in logic: This and this there is in the world, and that there is not. (Wittgenstein, *Tractatus Logico-Philosophicus*, Para 5.6)

But Winch also argued that all worlds contain a logic. The Azande aren't simply non-objective or non-logical — they have their own logic and criteria of reasoning. Winch held much the same thing with regard to sub-sets of rules within our own culture. For instance, he held that religious thought and practice have their own set of rules, different from those of the language game of science. Winch held that it is possible to be illogical in religious thinking. It is not that he means illogical in the scientific sense; he is talking about being illogical in the sense of the logic of religion. For instance, a belief in witchcraft in a 'Christian culture' is 'irrational' and cognitively unorthodox, whereas among the Azande it is rational or orthodox.

Despite Winch's liberal hermeneutics, expressed in his belief in the equality of cultures and the pluralism of truths, his view actually makes it difficult if not impossible to see how interlocutors could begin to understand each other or how interpretation of one culture could occur in the logic/language/concepts of another and vice versa, in dialogue, because each culture is defined only in terms of its differences from others.

But perhaps the problem lies partly in Winch's (and Evans-Pritchard's) view of culture and cultures and of the skills ordinarily employed amid the ambiguities and contradictions regularly and ordinarily dealt with within any given, so-called single, 'culture'. Winch's conception of cultural membership seems to have no room in it for members to be distant from

WINCH racist

aspects of their own culture, or to have any means available for criticising it. This is a kind of subtle racism, since, in the defence of subordinated cultures, the members of them are not being credited with the possibility of having the same capacity for cultural auto-critique as members of modern cultures are credited with — or, at least, the authors of such views.

A number of problems are implicated here. When a member of a culture is seen as just an instance of that culture, there is no room for agency, since the culture is fully written upon the body/mind of the member. The meaning of members' activities is reduced to the cultural text that is inscribed in them. The members' utterances are not authored actions but mere instances of the culture. Both Evans-Pritchard's and Winch's Azande are representatives of culture rather than people. In this view, the rhetorical process that inscribes the culture is *ritual* rather than critique or inquiry, however unsystematic the inquiry.

In such a view, culture changes by processes other than authorial creation of new meaning. Not for the Azande the possibility of affecting their own fate. If the error of liberal hermeneutics when applied to modern society is to place too much faith in the independence of inquiry, its error when dealing with other cultures appears to be the opposite error to the liberal, individualist error. When dealing with other cultures, Winch seems to move away from liberal faith in mutual understanding to a postmodern view that each culture is entirely separate and entirely equal. Winch's Azande have no possibility of cultural independence at all. But members are neither all-powerful liberal free agents in creating meaning, nor are they mere repeater stations for the culture. Both extremes lead to a dead end. In a pragmatist view, cultural freedom is something people in all societies can struggle for against a horizon of the learned culture of particular times and places. This struggle is aided by the fact that inter-generational human development provides a constant marriage of convenience between individual development and the need for adaptive cultural innovation. Put crudely, the young make the new. What differs from culture to culture is the institutional structure of this learning and the environmental circumstances that the culture assumes. Even the most rigid tradition-maintaining institutions must give way to radically new circumstances, as the history of imperialism has shown all too clearly. However, the crucial point is that some definitions of culture appear to have little room in them for any story about cultural learning.

The Post-structuralist Ethnographer

Some anthropologists have defined 'culture' broadly, as the whole way of life of a people — including artefacts, practices, social structures, technologies, languages, myths, rituals, stories and economic systems. Others, like Geertz[8] feel such definitions to be so broad as to be meaningless. Certainly, something gets lost if we do not distinguish between what people do and the framework of ideas and sentiments through which they make sense of this. The distinction is something like the distinction between a language and speech within it. For Geertz, at least in his early work, it is the language which is 'the culture' and speech is the social life which the culture 'frames'. Something like this would appear to be necessary if we are to be able to attribute good intentions to the culturally other, despite actions which may decode in our cultural framework as dubious or even negative. For instance, one way of dealing with a breach of protocol by a cultural stranger is to attribute the conduct to ignorance rather than malice.

To put it another way, we need to recognise the distinction between sense and force — the problem of rhetoric. One version of this is the distinction between intentions and attempts to carry them out. In addition, a distinction between concrete circumstances and ideology would seem necessary for certain sorts of social learning.

Post-structuralist critics of Geertz were not content with this dialogic view of culture and sought to push Geertz right to the end of the textualist path. In the course of twenty years, Geertz moved steadily towards the textualist terminus, but as we will see below, remained ambivalently attached to the notion of dialogue. One of the burdens of the argument in this book, is that it is possible to remain within a pragmatic, dialogical perspective yet meet criticisms made by textualists.

Conservative and liberal views of culture fail to identify the tensions between culture and society, treating the two as either a harmonious whole, as in the case of conservativism, or as an aggregate of individual satisfactions, as in the case of liberalism. Both cope poorly with change. No doubt conservatives would see this as nothing more than desirable and liberals as inevitable, but not problematic, since in a liberal view, change is generally tacitly equated with progress. When supposedly radical views — textualist versions of post-structuralist views — adopt a narrow view of culture, and reduce culture to text, thus banishing any realist moment in the dialogue, they also reduce their capacity to cope with change. But they still claim a radical relevance to the real political world. These issues will be explored more closely in the next two chapters.

The broad view of culture has other difficulties. For a participant in a way of life intercultural communication involves attempted understanding between oneself and a participant in a different way of life — someone with different experiences, beliefs, feelings, expectations of conduct in different repertoires of significant life events and different sets of familiar situations and even different languages, habits of speech and rules for speaking. Who could succeed in understanding under such circumstances? If everything is different and no distinction can be made between dimensions of living, no seam of comparison can be opened up for the logic of cultural discovery to begin to operate.

The broad formulation conceals something crucial. Where we conceptually distinguish what people do from their frameworks of sense-making, we allow for the development of experience other than the harmonious, homogenous experience of a 'way of life'. I refer to the experience of frameworks not working, failing to deal with circumstances, and being modified and developed through experience of more or less successful 'doing'. This is a universal limitation of all frameworks, all 'traditions'. This formulation permits us to identify the 'evolutionary' tension between language and speech. Speaking always in some sense goes beyond or 'stretches' language, because speakers are creative, and in greater or lesser degree, *have* to be creative to cope with changing circumstances, new problems, indeed, even the problem of communicating with a member of another culture. Speakers within a culture are always already partly autonomous with respect to it. That is one of the main reasons why languages change over time. And speakers are aware of the tension between experience and language. They are not simple rule-followers or mere 'instances' of cultural rules. This awareness can serve them when they reach out to the culturally other.

In turn, this tension is incorporated in new forms of speech so that language is changed and new ways of speaking become 'traditional'. Even intercultural communication can be institutionalised and traditional, as anthropological studies of 'traditional' trading relationships in Melanesia or studies of Iroquois diplomacy reveal. In both cases,[7] the problems of intercultural communication were solved by so called 'unsophisticated' peoples because political necessity and trade opportunity made it imperative to do so. The beginning of this is lost to memory, but there must have been a time when the first steps were taken. It *was* possible, the question is *how*.

But we must be careful not to provide too linguistic a formulation of the concept of culture. When the analysis is confined to language, and what is spoken *about* is improbably banished, we move from a dialogic position to a textualist one. In Geertz's hands this has led, over time, to a new kind of cultural relativism in which individual agency is submerged. In the hands of his textualist critics, even the sunken hulk of agency is lost in the deeps. Geertz's early view (in *The Religion of Java*, for instance) was that individuals operated as *creative* agents within cultural rules, choosing, in conditions of ambiguity, between one rule and another, playing the loopholes of the cultural system of rules and concepts to create new political opportunities and in turn, have a dynamic effect on the culture itself. In Melanesia and the Iriquois Federation someone must have taken the same first steps of departure from past ways of interpreting the rules. Over time (1960–1988) Geertz moved from this conception of cultural actors and action to a more 'textualist' understanding in which the cultural text creates the actors and their purposes. This is the very opposite of his earlier view that purposive action is both constituted by culture and at the same time reconstitutes it, a process which Giddens[8] called 'structuration' (and which is closer to the view adopted in this book).

As Diane Austin-Broos[9] has argued, in his early work in Java, Geertz was concerned to emphasise the creative and dynamic possibilities of culture over against the more usual view of it as an essentially unexamined 'way of life' or 'tradition'. He employed Talcott Parsons' view of symbolic interaction to develop a model of culture which departed from the relatively static view of it as an unconsciously learned and inherited way of life. Whatever the reasons for the static character of the anthropological view of culture before 1960, the situation of rapid change in Geertz's field work situation in the newly independent Indonesian nation, involving as it did deliberate attempts by the leadership to create a new, national culture, was not a fertile field for the older view.

The problems Geertz found demanded he come to grips with the tension between tradition and the course of events in Javanese life. Situations of this kind were not uncommon in the ex-colonial 'third world' in the immediate post-war period.

The apparently conscious manipulation of cultural symbols, the bending of tradition to new purposes, led Geertz to adopt an 'action-theoretic' understanding of culture as a set of publicly observable symbols and rules, forming a relatively loose, sometimes ambiguous system, which purposive actors could 'employ' to give meaning to new lines of action. The tension between culture and structure, language and speech was employed theoretically to explain purposive change and cultural learning.

The old view that culture was in some sense a possession of individuals and that it should be studied by a kind of comparative psychology was associated with the view that it was a learned tradition. But Geertz rejected this view as incomplete. While culture involved a set of ideas and dispositions, it was not simply private or 'psychological' but public and social. For Geertz, it was,

> ...a set of loosely connected (language) games each with its own symbolic system, bearing only Wittgenstein's 'family resemblance' to other such systems. (Austin-Broos, p. 147)

It was beside the point to ask to what extent such games consisted of ideas and what extent of deeds, since culture was a public process of meaningful doing — that is, of action in the sociological sense, rather than a dualistic interaction between mental events and raw external 'behaviours'. In this, there is a convergence between Geertz and Davidson.

However, it is clear enough that the assimilation of the theory of culture to Wittgenstein's epistemological discussion[10] and of language to 'language games', which Wittgenstein's own analysis encouraged, can create a 'value-slope' towards cultural relativism that Wittgenstein himself may not have intended.

Whether we interpret language games as occurring *within* a culture, as Geertz did to begin with, or whether finding some family resemblance among a set of such games we compare this with a similarly general construction of another culture as a whole, it is still necessary, if we are to avoid cultural relativism, to find some basis for comparing and judging such games. If we over emphasise certain parts of Wittgenstein's argument there would seem to be little purpose for such comparison because all meaningful criteria of comparison operate from within some particular language or other. Thus, judgements of any meaningful kind between one culture and another would amount to a form of cultural imperialism or ethnocentrism.

As will be argued in the next chapter, despite the many failings of empiricist and post empiricist behavioural theories of meaning, and the always problematic nature of extra-linguistic relationships of text, we *can* get some extra-linguistic purchase on language games. Geertz rejected this, at least in regard to social reality, because he argued that social reality was creatively, even 'artistically' constituted by a kind of poetry of metaphors. Those metaphors or images whereby a society created the meaning of its sense of social order he called 'ideology'. The fact that this insight is not incompatible with the view that some form of reality constraint might operate in the context of texts, even, minimally, in the fact of the presence of other texts, seems to have escaped him. His textualism (which fortunately remained ambivalent) also deprived him of the possibility of delineating any sense in which anything emergent in culture could be said to be less ideological than anything else. I say that it was fortunate that he was ambivalent, because this meant he did not consistently apply his definitions to his own work, which consequently makes claims to see through ideology, and does so in valuable ways.

He came to view the nature of politics, the self, and even of social interaction as metaphorically defined and culturally specific. In his study of Balinese 'person definitions', Geertz rejected some of the categories which European phenomenology had considered universal. The 'subject' was culturally constructed, and there could be no universal categories of the subject. But this shifted the creative origin from the subject, in some sense universal, and in some sense, therefore, outside any particular culture, to the culture itself.

For instance, he adopted the argument[11] that a Balinese cockfight isn't a construction of the players, nor is it explicable in terms of purposes of actors or their intentions. It is a 'display' in the 'medium' of blood, feathers, crowds, money and excitement of the status system of the Balinese village. This display confirms and inscribes the culture in individuals who participate in such emotion-charged, ordered inscriptive events, dramas or 'rituals'. In a sense, the culture defines a space for actors to act in — not a generalised structure of identity — and history if there is such a thing, is the history of changes in this space, not something made by actors stretching or manipulating cultural elements. There is no 'psychic unity of mankind', no common phenomenological structure of the self or 'the life-world', and therefore no sense of reality to set against the particularity of cultures. Only within a specific culture is the social, the non-social, the personal and the interpersonal defined. Geertz's journey towards a form[12] of post-structural postmodernism is now complete and on the way the possibility of the creativity of the individual over and against tradition is somehow lost sight of.

An Alternative View

How can we respond to this reduction? The theoretical separation of culture and society, language and speech, was not intended to lead to the reduction of one to the other. The static, museum specimen conception of a culture as *the* way of life of a people was unsatisfactory because it couldn't cope with actual change and offered no conceptual purchase for action as a mechanism of change. The dialogic view of culture/society did offer such a mechanism — structuration — but it involved a balancing act between a process in which culture defined human possibility and human social creativity defined culture. The reduction of society to culture seems to again make history and agency redundant.

Perhaps both the traditional anthropological error and Geertz's spring from the kind of small-scale, homogeneous societies they typically studied. As Diane Austin-Broos points out, had Geertz spent more time in Java later in his career he might not have so easily abandoned his sense of dynamics of change which played off *the lack of unity* of 'a culture'.[13] And whatever may be said of Bali, the sense in which *modern* cultures can be said to embody a 'text' which writes our identities and subjectivities *for* us seems to dissolve in the empirical pluralism of male, female, Hare Krishna, Catholic, drug addict, teetotaller, homosexual, heterosexual, new-ager and scientific rationalist — a range which contains a plurality of concepts of everything from subjectivity to the scope and nature of common sense.

Geertz's journey has begun and ended in static, homogeneous, totally opaque or taken-for-granted CULTURE, only he has replaced an ontology based on the eternal sameness of the diurnal and annual round of 'a way of life' with one based on the 'mere' textuality of the same.

Perhaps the weakest point in the later work of Geertz is his reliance on some mysterious alchemy whereby cultural texts are 'inscribed' in human psyches and in the public interaction of them. As Austin-Broos shows, Geertz's model for this agentless process of inscription appears to be that of 'following a rule', specifically what Geertz takes Wittgenstein's account of following a rule to be. The weaknesses of this account are also among the weaknesses of Geertz's account, but Geertz, in misunderstanding Wittgenstein's adds some of his own. And, as Austin-Broos points out, the various parts of Geertz's analysis sit uneasily together. The creativity and flexibility of metaphors and associated rules, the precisely 'loose' character of their denotative power, which gives them much of their cultural power, can scarcely be denied, which makes metaphors a poor vehicle for any macroscopic analysis of culture which simultaneously seeks to deny agency and intention or to subsume these under a textual rubric.

First, Geertz's apparent misunderstanding of Wittgenstein. As Wright[14] has pointed out, Wittgenstein's reflections on following a rule actually appear to be directed towards a rejection of the everyday, common sense notion of it and to arguing for the view that there can be no determination in advance of just what a successful following of a rule would consist of. That is, following rules is extra-cultural and extra-textual. Further, Wittgenstein appears to argue that our conception of understanding of meaning should not be confined to the notion of interpretation of an act or an utterance.

This seems to preserve a role for the agent to be an active, appropriator of culture. Austin-Broos picks up Kripke's[15] argument concerning Wittgenstein and uses it to make a point about Geertz's limitations. She cites Kripke when he says 'What is really denied is...the "private model" of rule-following, the notion that a person following a given rule is to be analyzed simply in terms of facts about the rule follower and the rule followers alone, without reference to his memberships in a wider community' (Kripke, cited in Austin Broos, p. 188). That is, Wittgenstein's purpose was *not* to emphasise that rules created their own followers. Equally, however, it was *not* to emphasise that the community was just the culture writing itself.

While it is the members of that community who judge whether or not a rule is being followed, conversely, because of the contingency of judgement, from the standpoint of members of that community (or an anthropologist's) almost any course of action can be construed as being in accordance with or in breach of a given rule. How is it then that the member or anthropologist is able to deduce, abduce or induce a cultural text or make a judgement of conformity or breach from the externally observable utterances and physical behaviours of individuals?

This is a problem for Geertz, but it is one that he does not adequately deal with. If he did, he would have to provide a more reflexive account of the construction of the ethnographic descriptions that are the very object of his own theorising. Perhaps an anthropologist constructs an account of rules in the same way as members do — by developing a narrative or 'theory' related at many points to experience and making 'sense' of it in some at least semi-holistic way, despite the ever present possibility of error or a kind of obsolescence.

However, as McDowell[16] cogently argues, it may be more appropriate to reject the view that the philosophical dilemmas in the conceptualisation of meaning (of rules) can be overcome '...only by locating meaning in a framework of communal practices' (p. 344). Meanings do not 'take care of themselves' permitting human activities of judgement to 'fade into insignificance' (p. 352). On the contrary, McDowell argues, an adequate account of how language means, following Wittgenstein, has a central place for human meaning-action and judgement in it. Kripke's interpretation glosses over this. To paraphrase McDowell: It is not the case that cultures as texts are the way they are in themselves, utterly independent of us and determining our subjectivity and judgement. Conversely, human nature is necessarily implicated in every formation of judgement but that does not mean that texts are thereby utterly dependent on perspicuous individual judgements either. The truth is somewhere in between (McDowell, pp. 351–358). That is to say, McDowell wrings from a close analysis of Wittgenstein a view of following a rule which is quite consistent with the concept of structuration. Following rules and what constitutes following a rule is learned by individuals in interaction with the community of which they are members through a process of constant formative feedback of signs of approval and disapproval. The psychic inertia of learned behaviour in the sheer mass of numbers of others, relative to ego's small innovative movement at any one point, is the component in the feedback loop that prevents human creativity resulting in excessive volatility.

If this is a valid view, we may well part company with Geertz on his journey towards a structuralist, even textualist understanding of social life and away from a balance between structure and agency/desire. We can take up the neglected question of cultural ambiguity and of interpretive pluralism within cultures, as well as attempt to reinstate a sense of the internal politics of cultures, of the interplay between strategy, purpose and culture (whether we speak here of agency at the level of individuals or derivatively, at the level of status groups, castes, classes or clans etc.).

Only with such an understanding of culture do we escape Geertz's cultivated exoticism and come to the realisation, tacitly denied in Geertz's formulation, that modern societies also possess 'cultures', yet these societies are undergoing *internal* cultural change, exemplified by self-conscious culture changing 'movements', such as the environmental and women's movements. What is at stake is the very possibility of engaging in a cultural politics that is meaningful. For textualists, being a feminist or an environmentalist is a form of self deception rather than a struggle for cultural agency. Indeed, it is this complex possibility for change, coupled with mechanisms of resistance to change, that makes politics a form of *work*.

The problem with what Geertz's analysis of culture offers us, at least until his most recent books (1988) is that the only circumstances he offered us were those of his ethnography and even there he ignored the manifestations of processes of global change in favour of a certain selectivity which could at times be equated with cultural antiquarianism and a certain, latent objectivism. Geertz's own cultural context — the context for which he was writing as he himself later admitted (1988), was not fully factored into his work. To give his own postmodern turn an extra, reflexive twist we can say that Geertz's analysis of the (common) process of textual (cultural) formation of subjectivity in Morocco, Bali and Java was produced from the standpoint of his own, formed-in-America subjectivity. The very analysis claimed objectivity of a kind, since that is what anthropologists do, and, as Geertz pointed out in a recent (1988) discussion of this very question, they cannot unilaterally abrogate the cultural meanings of what they do, since these are a given. Of course, Geertz can as he does in his recent work, acknowledge the fact that he produces his text as a product of a Western subjectivity, and so relativise it. But can he at the same time deny that such texts *work* precisely because they make universalistic claims? He admitted as much when he recently(1988) sought to shift his ground, decisively undercutting his earlier (1983) post-structuralist analyses.

He claims for anthropologists, in the framework of modern culture at least, and driven by the pressures of political critique from dominated peoples, a capacity for intercultural communication, based precisely on the politics of ambiguity in Western culture which are at last affecting anthropology itself:

> Like any cultural institution, anthropology…is of a place and in a time, perpetually perishing, not so certainly perpetually renewing… Since the Second World War, the dissolution of colonialism and the appearance of a more realistic view of science have rather dissipated [the energies that created anthropology]. Neither the role of intercultural middleman, shuttling back and forth between the Euro-American centres of world power and various exotic elsewheres to mediate between the prejudices of the one and the parochialism of the other, nor that of transcultural theoretician bringing odd beliefs and unusual structures under general laws, is anywhere nearly so available to anthropologists as they once were… The next necessary thing…is to enlarge the possibility of intelligible discourse between people quite different from one another in interest, outlook, wealth, and power, and yet contained in a world where, tumbled as they are into endless connection, it is increasingly difficult to get out of each other's way. This world, is one of a gradual spectrum of mixed-up differences… The Theres and Heres, much less insulate, much less well-defined, much less spectacularly contrastive (but no less deeply so) have again 'changed their nature… (*Works and Lives*, pp. 147–8)

I share his hope, but do not understand Geertz's grounds for it, given his conceptual and methodological relativism. For how can members of different cultures understand each other if cultures are incommensurate and if there is no basis on which the modern anthropologist can understand them or mediate between them?

Unless, that is, we admit, as Geertz tacitly does with the words 'gradual' and 'less insulate' that the degree to which a given culture defines the subjectivity of its members is a variable, and any account of culture must stretch to include the account-giver — the modern, sophisticated (?) possibly bi-cultural narrator. The relativism that Geertz is given to can be extended downwards, as he himself tended to do in his earlier work, right to the level of the small group, the specific village, the particular clan. Culture writ as large as Java is, in fact, a set of family resemblances between language (culture) games of regions, religious, villages, clans. The presence of groups, layers, localities is not unremarked *within* the culture itself. Folding back on itself, culture observes its own internal differentiation, maps its own inner struggles, its social contradictions, limitations and dissonances. Few cultures on the world today entirely lack an awareness of the fact that they are 'cultures' and this is conceptually crucial.

It is rather like recognising that you have been speaking prose all your life, or that your particular brand of Physics isn't the real 'nature of the universe' but just a theory of it. Almost 100 years after relativity displaced Newtonian mechanics it has become an unremarked commonplace to think of it as 'relativity theory'. We have forgotten how revolutionary it was to move out of a transparent Newtonian world into a world removed from our direct gaze by the veil of 'theory'. Something like that has happened to all the cultures of the contemporary world.

> The transformation...of the people anthropologists mostly write about, from colonial subject to sovereign citizens, has...altered entirely the moral context within which the ethnographical art takes place... One of the major assumptions upon which anthropological writing rested until only yesterday, that its subjects and its audience were not only separate but morally disconnected...has fairly well dissolved. The world has its compartments still, but the passages between them are much more numerous and much less well secured... The entrance of once colonialised or castaway peoples (wearing their own masks, speaking their own lines) onto the stage of the global economy, international high politics, and world culture has made the claim of the anthropologist...increasingly difficult to sustain. (*Works and Lives*, pp. 132–3)

But there appear to be two possible responses to this new world of multicultural complexity, a postmodern relativism, which while privileging cultural diversity, robs us of critique, and a view which while acknowledging the dangers of ethnocentrism recognises the cultural reality of critique. (To see what the difference between the two consists of we will examine postmodern ideas more closely in the fourth chapter.)

Too many discussions of this problem hypostatise cultures. No doubt this is, in part, an artefact of the sources from which most philosophers obtain their examples — ethnographies. The trouble with many ethnographies, as the 'early' Clifford Geertz pointed out, is that they tend to reify processes and freeze this reification into a fixed, organic whole, whereas the reality is internally contradictory, uncertain in outcome and changing. To some extent, this is a product of the limited time and resources available to individual ethnographers. Few are able to spend more than a year or two in the field, and many never go back. There is also a certain sort of antiquarianism in much anthropology and *a fortiori* in its use in such debates. In present debates about rationality, Evans-Pritchard's pre-war Azande are frozen in time, culturally complete, culturally enmeshed, culturally perennial, whereas the real Azande today are driving around in four-wheel drives listening to Sony Walkmans. The question we must ask is: How did they get this way? Presumable, they coped with change. They changed their ideas, their 'culture'; they absorbed new ideas from other cultures, and this all happened through a process of interaction during which some sort of critique of the old culture occurred. Individuals, perhaps influential ones, took first steps to change, to abandoning an 'old' custom, to advancing a new hypothesis of theory about the world, influenced by the new, technological culture of the Europeans. Part explicit dialogue, part change by default, part changed substance without changed names, nevertheless, it happened. Intercultural communication happens in somewhat the same, imperfect way.

Fundamental Cultural Differences?

It may be appropriate, too, to be more than a little suspicious of ethnographic (and ethnolinguistic) accounts of 'fundamental' logical and epistemological differences. After all, there is a certain quixotic quality in using ethnographic evidence to argue for the practical impossibility of understanding other cultures. Sometimes differences in logic or epistemology celebrated in the anthropological literature dissolve on closer acquaintance. A celebrated example, which must stand here for many, is that of the Fang concept of truth and the purported lack of 'Western' logic in Fang thought.[17] Early ethnography of the Fang reported that the Fang word for 'true' translated roughly as 'simple' and the word for 'false' as 'complicated'. On the basis of this a relativistic argument about the lack of universal criteria for rationality was constructed. More recent and more thorough ethnography reveals what the Fang mean by their terms. If someone tells you something that doesn't fit your existing beliefs, and they speak with conviction or authority, it makes thinking complicated, because the new information can only be accommodated by much elaboration of old ideas. Apparently the Fang have anticipated Habermas! Or perhaps they have just adopted a different focus than the drive for certainty of High

Modernity. Life gets complicated if someone tells an untruth. Simple, isn't it?

The early ethnography also made much of the absence in the Fang language of equivalents of the 'logical particles' — 'or', 'and', 'if' etc. It was argued on the basis of this that they employed a different logic from 'Western logic'. Again, a closer inspection reveals that the Fang manage the functions of the logical particles quite well without them. Not surprising when it is quite easy to do this in English, if somewhat convoluted.

The concepts and ways of speaking of other cultures can create difficulties, but some of these are of our own making. We forget the differences of interest and focus common within our own cultures. We take the abstract, universalised and disembodied categories of High Modernity and expect to find them in other cultures. Even among philosophers in our own society such concepts vary greatly. The concept of truth in Dewey, for instance, is quite a far cry from the concept of truth in Tarski (or Calvin, if a theologian can join in). Only with further explanation can we see what is common among the various ideas — for one thinker knowledge is absolute and we can be said to know when we possess just that which is absolutely true, for another, truth is a temporary and probabilistic assignment of 'warranted assertability', and thus a constantly emerging and changing product of higher and higher levels of learning (Habermas and Dewey), for Tarski truth appears to be a property of the relationships of statements in a logically well-formed object language and other statements in a meta-language and has nothing to do with the relationship between statements and states of affairs in the 'real world'. Why must we assume that members of other cultures are irrational because they focus on the effect of a statement on the rest of our thinking, rather than its relationship with experience? Would we want to label such differences evidence of irrationality? I have by no means listed the more bizarre notions in Western culture (Nietzsche, Heidegger, Rudolph Steiner). I would prefer to say that what we are often dealing with are differences in and around a shared and complex 'problem'. There is no prima facie reason to suppose that within culture differences are any less great than between culture differences in this matter. Of course, Wittgenstein was aware of much of this. He was the critic *par excellence* of the failure of High Modern philosophy to be aware of its own limits.

Neither Incommensurable nor Transparent: A Pragmatic View

There is an irony that Davidson[18] points to — the irony that talk of incommensurability between theories or cultures already supposes that something about the other theory or culture is so different from the speaker's own as to be incommensurable with it but that the other's theory or culture can still be recognised as a theory or culture. This irony surfaces in the debate about cultural relativity in the form of reliance on ethnographic evidence for relativity of meanings, logics etc. But perhaps the greater part of the problem of incommensurability (and its corollary the fully immersed member to whom the culture is totally transparent) is a logical one rather than one of evidence. It may be possible to restate the problem in less dichotomous terms. Certainly, that has been Davidson's strategy. The central burden of Davidson's argument has been that it makes no sense to assume that other cultures are not similar to our own. Talk of difference only makes sense against a background of similarity. Davidson endorses Wittgenstein's view that conceptual problems are at stake in this kind of debate more so than substantive ones. It makes no sense to start from the assumption of cultural relativity. That assumption may have made *political* sense in a context where the debate was within the colonial structure of power, because it permitted rejection of the colonial assumption that all cultures could be judged by the standards of one, but it makes for poor theory.

As Winch tells us:

> Wittgenstein says somewhere that where one gets into philosophical difficulties over the use of some of the concepts of our language, we are like savages [sic] confronted with something from an alien culture. I am simply indicating a corollary of this: that sociologists who misinterpret an alien culture are like philosophers getting into difficulties over the use of their own concepts. (*The Idea of a Social Science*, p. 114)

For Winch then, the social sciences proceed by a method of conceptual analysis and clarification — sociological knowledge is a more explicit and systematic form of *the same kind of knowledge* that participants in a society possess in a more implicit and unsystematic way. In this, he is reacting against a High Modern conception of social science (such as Popper's). But perhaps he is overreacting when he undercuts this idea of the social scientist's understanding in the intercultural context by adopting a strict relativist view. The truth may lie in the middle ground.

Davidson would argue that when we see social actions take place and explain the interpretation of these as the mapping of actions onto conceptual schemes underlying language, we fall into incoherence. This couldn't possibly be how we interpret action or utterances. The idea of the meanings of language being relative to an underlying set of conceptual meanings is incoherent. Such a set of concepts would just be another language. It would either be a private language, which we cannot speak about, and which would not be able to be connected to public language in an intelligible way, or it would be redundant, since it would be as shared as public language, and require no discussion. It is not that something we might describe as 'conceptual schemes' do not exist in people's heads. Nor is it that these might not be a proper object of study for psychologists. Nor is it that we should not hypothesise such things as intentions poorly realised in actual rhetorical devices. Davidson's point is a logical one. Postulating these schemes does not help us give an account of interpretation, either within a single culture or across cultures. If you are looking for a final explanation of meaning, there is no point going past the public utterances themselves, since concepts still stand in need of interpretation. They do not provide a layer of magic language whose meanings are objective, transcultural, and interpretation free. Indeed, the problems of talk about inner conceptual states are generally greater than those arising from making sense of public linguistic events. It follows that trying to explain intercultural misunderstanding in terms of different underlying concepts (assuming that members of different cultures are speaking with each other in a third language, patois or pidgin) adds nothing to our account of that misunderstanding.

Four Logical Difficulties for the Postmodern View

MacIntyre also finds several problems with Winch's line of argument, although insofar as it is a departure from those functionalist views in which it was held to be possible to understand a society without understanding the meanings of its members, he is in accord with it, as a starting point. The *first* basic problem is that Winch's view seems to assume that the only options for social scientific work are provided by a dubious dichotomy — the dichotomy between the notion that there are universal norms for the intelligibility of actions (which Winch rejects) and the notion that ways of life are constructed entirely out of unique meanings and are thus incommensurable with the conceptual frameworks of other cultures (Winch's view. Davidson would speak of the meanings of other cultures).[19] The *second* problem is that Winch seems to believe that understanding a society and culture is confined to a more systematic version of the present level of understanding of the participants and/or it precludes the use of other, extra-cultural explanatory categories employed by the outsider. I might add here that Winch also seems to believe that participants themselves have no reflexive awareness of the non-meaningful, systemic dimensions of their own societies — that they are, as it were, totally mythologised. What is missing from the account, because it tries to take us back to a kind of intercultural language of concepts in which we can speak about misunderstanding, is the connection between utterances and the concrete, public way of life. A behavioural (or other realist) dimension is entirely missing from his hermeneutics, so the possibility of making sense of meanings by seeing what work they do as actions which are part of a way of coping with the common tasks of human living is lost sight of. While each culture copes with human needs differently, and each culture works with its own technology and knowledge, each culture copes with our sexuality, our need for companionship, our need for food and shelter, play and aesthetic pleasure, and so on.

MacIntyre also rejects the universalist thesis of conservative hermeneutics. He does so because it is not possible to agree on the *identity* of the objects under study without reference to the particular meanings of a culture, because the objects of social life (situations, statuses, rituals etc.) are meaningfully constituted by participants stories about the way they participate in the way of life. In this, he is in agreement with Habermas, who argues that our 'objective' or external observer view of social life is unable to fully comprehend the meanings things have for participants. To get an *adequate* grasp of these you have to be so far inside the meaningful action of a social situation that for all intents and purposes you are a participant (even if an ambivalent and ambiguous one). This leads us to Macintyre's *third* point.

He points out that participants themselves display a capacity to reject the alternative, relativist view, in which the local meanings are absolutised. He gives three reasons for believing this. First, with Malinowski he prefers to recognise that it is not possible to understand society if we see behaviour as entirely governed by cultural rules — there is a gap or tension between language and speaking, between culturally given rules and the actual course of conduct. This leads to an awareness of the limits of understandings of life. As discussed earlier, following a rule is not a simple idea but is itself a creative process and a product of communal judgment and negotiation. Second, rules and criteria of their application have a history. Further, the criteria employed in a culture, whether explicit of implicit, may not be coherent and so may not yield a clear answer. Under such circumstances 'the people themselves may start questioning their own criteria'.[20] If we tend to see the rules of a culture monolithically and as frozen in time, we make historical transitions within a culture unintelligible:

> In 17th century Scotland, for example, the question could not but be raised, 'But are there witches?' If Winch asks, from within what way of social life, under what system of belief was this question asked, the only

answer is that it was asked by men who confronted alternative systems [of meaning] and were able to draw out of what confronted them independent criteria of judgment [RY: Independent of the old culture]. Many Africans today are in the same situation. (MacIntyre, 1976, p. 129)

The third reason is that rules involve judgements and judging is not only influenced by cognitive criteria but also by needs, wishes and desires. Cultures are not desires or needs, nor do they have them. Human agents would be dynamic relative to culture for this if for no other reason.

MacIntyre's *fourth* point is that, while always difficult, imperfect and incomplete, our experience is that translation is possible (and more will be said about this below). In addition, there are features of social life which an outsider can notice and which an insider can also, in principle, learn about. The possibility of doing sociology of the sociologist's own society rests on the possibility, even within Winch's account, of noticing systematic connections that everyday participants do not themselves usually notice, *but could recognise*. For instance, I may interview a sample of men and women and *successfully* show *to participants* that women's opinions are not the same as men's in an area of opinion that, hitherto, men had generally thought them the same. With Weber and Malinowski, we may also accept that causal regularities which are unrecognised in a culture can be learned about and their reality intersubjectively established through dialogue and argument with, and giving evidence to, members of a society. Something like this occurs when we learn about the aggregate unintended result of a whole lot of individual actions — such as we have become aware of in recent years in the areas of traffic management or the environmental and ecological effects of behaviour. However, it is fair to say that MacIntyre's liberal view almost entirely lacks any reference to the distortion of communication by power.

Taylor's Critique of Winch

Charles Taylor[21] has also taken issue with Winch. He takes up a similar stance to MacIntyre, arguing that an understanding of participant's own categories and concepts is a necessary starting point for analysis and that it cannot be dispensed with, even if an extra layer of analysis may be added which goes beyond participants' common sense. From Davison's viewpoint we would speak of understanding participant's meanings, and see any reference to their concepts as at least as problematic as the question of meanings, and not as somehow giving us understanding of the meanings at some level deeper than the way the meanings are used in daily life. But Taylor also goes further. He makes the point that this going beyond common sense is often felt to be praiseworthy (from a critical point of view) when it is done in the social scientist's own culture but ethnocentric if attempted cross-culturally. The Winchean thesis that participant's perceptions and values are incorrigible seems to offer protection against such ethnocentrism, but the price that has to be paid is that it rules out critical cultural analysis within a culture as well. It also rests on the notion that it is only modern cultures that are aware that something like 'common sense' is not sufficient to explain everything that goes on.

But there is a middle road:

> The error in this view is to hold that the language of cross-cultural theory has to be either theirs or ours... But, as a matter of fact, while challenging their language of self-understanding we may also be challenging ours. Indeed, what I want to argue is that there are times where we cannot question the one properly without also questioning the other. (Taylor, 1983, p. 125)

Taylor speaks of a language of 'perspicuous contrast' in which the alternatives of different cultures are described. He gives an extended example of a discussion of whether magic should be seen as a deficient form of means/ends action relative to our more effective technological means or as a primarily expressive/symbolic activity, for which means/ends criteria are simply inappropriate. He argues that we can describe magic as a form of life incommensurate with our own because it is one in which means/ends and symbolic dimensions of action have not been separated. However, he argues, this doesn't mean what Winch appears to think it means. Certainly, it offers some protection against the simple ethnocentrism of rejecting magic on the grounds that it is poor 'science', but it is still open to members of different cultures to open up a dialogue about which way of thinking is most valuable and for what purpose. Incommensurability, properly described, is not the end of the issue, but the beginning, since it describes alternative ways of living and organising reality and, *unless you rule out cultural criticism on a priori grounds*, it is available to members of each culture to in some sense reconsider their own culture and consider the view of the other. In further opening up the dimension of critique, Taylor moves towards a critical hermeneutics.

It is more than a semantic quibble to say that the traditional Azande does not have the critic's role available to him or her and that adopting such a role must mean the culture is no longer Zande culture. Such a view appears to assume that traditional cultures never underwent change (except by unnoticed drift). It also flies in the face of the reality of a changing world. The real issues concern the circumstances under which such reconsideration may take place and the conditions under which they can be anything other than a form of cultural oppression. And of course, the language and speech in which the inquiry could take place.

Put together, it would seem, as MacIntyre argues, that the statements by, say, one of Evans-Pritchard's Azande, or King James VI of Scotland, that 'There are witches!', and by a modern person 'There are no witches!' would be in a very peculiar relationship to each other were we not to accept the foregoing arguments about perspicuous contrast, translation etc. This is how MacIntyre puts it:

> Unless one of the statements denies what the other asserts, the negation of the sentence ['there are witches'] could not be a correct translation of ['There are no witches']. Thus if we could not deny, from [a modern person's] standpoint and in our own language what the Azande or King James assert in theirs, we should be unable to translate their expression into our language...' (MacIntyre, 1967, p. 129)

But, to coin a phrase, this view has a corollary, the translatability of statements rests upon some cultural common ground such that the relevant cultures have at least some common general meaning-action tasks when they need to indicate the existence or non-existence of everyday objects (however they may do this 'existing'). This level of common ground provides a basis for *contextual* coordination of meaning. It also presupposes a common, behavioural level of functioning. That is, in Quine's terms (see next chapter), that they have in common a behavioural substratum of speech and language that would make possible at least a minimal form of translation (which, in circumstances of wide cultural difference, Quine calls radical translation).

To Conclude

In this chapter, we saw that Geertz was unable to give a satisfactory account of cultural change and the concrete role of agency in it when he lost sight of the action dimension and the public process of behaviour (acts, utterances) which is the stuff that interpretations are made of. If the flaw in conservative hermeneutics is a misplaced realism, the absence of any kind of realism in some readings of post-structuralism results in the same political quietism as afflicts Winch's liberal hermeneutics. Or would do if post-structuralist writers did not smuggle politics in by fiat (as we will see in Chapter 7). It is just such a minimal realism that is absent from post-structuralist-influenced intercultural theory. We must look more closely at the flaws in this theory if we wish to avoid a theory of intercultural communication without political implications in a real world. The question of the concrete character of situated communication must be addressed. This will be done in the next chapter and we will then go on to examine the other strengths and weaknesses of post-structuralist thought as it is found in Foucault and Derrida.

Notes

1. C. Geertz, *Local Knowledge*. New York: Basic Books, 1983. *Works and Lives: The Anthropologist as Author*. Stanford: Stanford University Press, 1988.
2. A. MacIntyre, The idea of a social science. Pp. 112–130 in H. Lewis (ed.), *Contemporary British Philosophy*. London: George Allen and Unwin, 1976. See also MacIntyre's, *Whose Justice? Which Rationality?* London: Duckworth, 1988, Chapter 19.
3. P. Winch, *The Idea of a Social Science*. London: Routledge and Kegan Paul, 1958. See also 'Understanding a primitive society'. Pp. 8–49 in P. Winch, *Ethics and Action*. London: Routledge and Kegan Paul, 1972.
4. E. Evans-Pritchard, *Witchcraft, Oracles and Magic Among the Azande*. Oxford: Clarendon Press, 1937. Where I write of the Azande people in this chapter, it is Evans-Pritchard's constructed 'Azande' I write about, rather than the 'real' Azande people.
5. L. Wittgenstein, *Tractatus Logico-Philosophicus*.
6. C. Geertz, *The Interpretation of Culture*. New York: Basic Books, 1973.
7. T. Dutton (ed.), *The Hiri in History*. Canberra: Australian National University, 1982.
8. A. Giddens, *The Consequences of Modernity*. Cambridge: Polity Press, 1990. For 'structuration' see *Sociology*. Cambridge: Polity Press, 1989.
9. It should be obvious that I am indebted to Diane Austin-Broos for a good deal of the interpretation of Geertz upon which this chapter relies, however, it should also be recognised that I expand and develop that criticism and, effectively, give it a different emphasis to Austin-Broos' emphasis. D. Austin-Broos, 'Clifford Gertz: Culture, sociology and historicism'. Pp. 141–59 in D. Austin-Broos (ed.). *Creating Culture*. Sydney: Allen & Unwin, 1987.
10. L. Wittgenstein, *Philosophical Investigations*. Oxford: Blackwell, 1953.
11. C. Geertz, 'Deep play: Notes on a Balinese cockfight.' Pp. 412–53 in *The Interpretation of Culture*. New York: Basic Books, 1973.
12. Ricoeur's form.
13. Austin-Broos, p. 157.
14. C. Wright, *Wittgenstein on the Foundation of Mathematics*. London: Duckworth, 1980.
15. S. Kripke, 'Wittgenstein on rules and private languages: An elementary exposition.' Pp. 238–312 in I. Block (ed.), *Perspectives on the Philosophy of Wittgenstein*. Oxford: Blackwell, 1981. Cited in Austin-Broos, *op. cit.*
16. J. McDowell, 'Wittgenstein on following a rule.' *Synthese*, 58 (1984): 325–63.
17. P. Boyer, *Tradition as Truth and Communication: A Cognitive Description of Traditional Discourse*. Cambridge University Press, 1989.
18. D. Davidson, *Inquiries into Truth and Interpretation*. Oxford: Clarendon Press, 1984: pp. 180–90 *et passim*.
19. P. Winch, *Idea of a Social Science*, p. 88.
20. MacIntyre, 1976, p. 128.
21. C. Taylor, *Philosophy and the Human Sciences*. Cambridge: Cambridge University Press, 1985: p. 125.

3 Translation and The Reality of Social Life

When it comes to driving your car on the right side of the road, or planting rice after the monsoon breaks, everyone is a realist. But everyday realism is not the same as metaphysical realism. The fact that social life is able to be understood through notions of language and writing/speaking, and that, in a certain sense, there is only the texts of our writing/speaking, because nothing talk-about-able lies beyond them, should not blind us to the sensuous concrete experience of our lives. We experience conduct in a manner which constantly plays off a distinction between what our senses tell us and what that which we feel *means*. All cultures have to deal with the problems of this divide. Our texts are uttered into the concrete flow of sensible, public events, themselves interpreted, but interpreted in the context of each other and the satisfactory or unsatisfactory experiences of growing rice, running red lights, loving, failing and succeeding. There is nothing that is social that is not meaningful, and when the concrete is endowed with meaning it becomes a text. But, equally, and this is often forgotten, there is no text that cannot be related to the sensuous, bodily experiences of pleasure/pain, pride, excitement/arousal, and so on. Indeed, the separation of text from context, of symbol or sign from the body, is at best a tool for analysis of particular problems of experience, since there is no body perceptible to us but that we make a text of our experience of it when we attend to it.

In this chapter we show that behaviourism makes a mistake in its attempt to build an intelligible account of conduct on the artificial splitting off of one part of the text/experience whole from the other. Equally, some readings of post-structuralism make the same mistake. The difference between the two lies in the part of the whole that they discard. Behaviourism retains only the bodily experience, split off from the structures of narrative meaning that accompany it. Beyond a basic language of an elementary sensuous kind, language is said to give rise to illusory meanings. Textualism retains only the text, separated from the sensuous immediacy of biography, relationship and history. All trace of the concrete

57

conditions of the emergence of texts is expunged, robbing analysis of the *living* context of text. What we need is both text and context, figure and ground, each inexplicable without the other, but in the flow of making meaning in adapting to change and in the movement of life itself, slipping against each other in political friction. But this chapter tries to rescue something of value from the concrete emphasis of behavioural approaches to communication. Later, in the chapter this concreteness will be rejoined to its lost other, text. Texts not only get brought into being by concrete persons and have concrete if sometimes short lives, they are brought into being in the presence of concrete circumstances. Yet, somehow, their meanings are themselves also active historical realities.

Behavioural Approaches to Culture and Communication

Strangely enough, although the central idea of behavioural and behaviourist approaches to the study of human conduct is that we should place a premium on studying overt, outwardly observable behaviour, the concept of culture in most traditional behaviourist research in intercultural communication is resolutely mentalistic — culture is a set of conditioned inner states of belief and feeling, reference to which 'explains' overt or outer conduct of categories of actors. While the behaviourist view must sometimes be distinguished from the behavioural approach, there is a great deal of common ground. Both approaches fail to be open to recognition of the reality of culture as a public, group phenomenon. In both, the public, constructed character of cultural symbols, and the significance of this for their role as the medium of interaction (e.g. language), is not emphasised, but plays an inert, passive role in theorising, as do the accompanying public symbols, rituals, 'situations', and institutions. So the approaches usually employ an individualistic level of analysis and the group level is represented by some notion of disembodied, self perpetuating rules or contexts.

In this view of culture it is not possible to make the mistake of viewing it in the postmodern manner as an extra-individual text by which the form of individual subjectivity is itself 'written'. That could be an advantage if it led to a balanced view, but it doesn't. We have already seen that the extent to which individual consciousness is written and the extent to which individuals are innovators who write new culture, and the way in which both processes are embedded in group life, is a matter for empirical study, and varies from situation to situation. Whatever the limitations and exaggeration of the structuralist (and post-structuralist) view, surely something is lost when the relative mutability of, say, language and speaker of a language, is lost sight of, so we can no longer find any value at all in saying that the language speaks or at least, constrains the speaker. Or even less tendentiously, that to a great extent speakers have to make do with the language they inherit and cannot single-handedly remake it without falling into incomprehensibility. Equally, the behaviourist view loses something because it fails to explore the converse side of the individual–culture relationship. Behaviourisms' individuals fail to have authorship too. Conditioned by the mysterious 'environment' of rewards and punishments, they lack conscious agency, but equally, because their conduct is a product of conditioned responses to seemingly random environmental events, they lack culture, in the sense of inscribed stories about how life should be lived.

An unbalanced view like this one leads to a certain conceptual and terminological confusion. A study of culture which bases itself not only in methodological individualism (to study society you have to study individuals because they are the 'carriers' of the social processes), but also in conceptual individualism (a culture is just a shared set of beliefs and feelings and their expressions due to shared environments), is unable to cope with change in social structures and institutions except as the more or less accidental fallout of individually motivated behaviour. Often the analysis of change is ignored and culture is presented as an amorphous product of many contingencies.

In the first section of this chapter we will discuss a typical behavioural science approach to intercultural communication. It will be seen that such a view oversimplifies the relationship between members and cultures. The theory of communication and meaning provided by behaviourism is defective. It is particularly inadequate when describing the translation process of intercultural communication. In the second section we examine what is generally agreed to be the most sophisticated behaviourist theory of meaning, that of the philosopher Quine, and show that while it makes some valid points, it falls short of an adequate view of translation.

In the next part of the argument, pragmatist views are shown to make the best of both worlds, allowing for a rich view of meaning and translation. Finally, the positive contributions that empirical studies can make are demonstrated.

Individualistic Cultural Adaptation: Political Quietism and Behaviourism

Many of the problems of traditional behavioural science approaches are illustrated in a theory of the role of intercultural communication in the cultural adaptation of immigrants developed by Y. Kim.[1] In this approach to the problems immigrants meet in a new cultural setting we see that the way behavioural theory treats culture and communication leads to a one-way view of cultural learning.

Of course, the situation of immigrants arriving in relatively small numbers in a host society is only one general situational type in which intercultural communication (IC) may be studied and any critique of conceptual strategies should take this into account. The question we must ask then is this: How well does the behavioural theory perform in this context. It will be assumed, but not argued for in detail, that Kim's approach epitomises behavioural science approaches to IC.

Kim's strategy for dealing with the conceptional and terminological confusion, and disciplinary fragmentation of the study of IC, and the failure to integrate different levels of analysis (group and individual, short term and long term immigrants), is to provide a new, systems-theoretic stipulative definition of the field.

She aims to integrate group and individualist foci of study and the findings from studies of both long and short term immigrants, to criticise perspectives of different disciplines and create a clear and defensible set of definitions of terms, concepts etc. She sums up her purpose, following a critique of existing approaches in this way:

> The line between theory and ideology must be much more clearly drawn so that scientists may approach the reality of cross-cultural adaptation with maximum clarity and objectivity. (Kim, p. 30)

This statement shows her allegiance to the traditional paradigm of behavioural science as continuous with the methodology of the natural sciences, separating fact from value to maintain objectivity. The ideologies she has in mind are those of both cultural assimilationists and pluralists. Her approach is to see these as 'two sides of a coin'. From the standpoint of intercultural communication these ideologies translate into either an absence of such communication (because assimilation means achieving membership in the dominant culture by learning to communicate within it) or a presence of intercultural communication in the relationships of a plurality of cultural groups, but a presence which is unexplained. Unfortunately for Kim, ideology is not as easily side-stepped as she thinks, and pluralists would almost certainly see Kim's approach as 'assimilationist', as an examination of her stipulative approach to theory-building will show. The interesting problem of how communication might be possible under conditions of cultural pluralism is never tackled.

The theory-building strategy adopted by Kim has four levels, 'metatheory', 'assumptions', 'axioms' and 'theorems to be tested'. These levels are occupied by

(1) General Systems Theory (metatheory).
(2) A stress-reduction model of the individual's adaptation and a sociali-sation model of the acquisition of the inner states that form the individual's cultural identity and a somewhat deterministic view of these processes (assumptions).
(3) An axiomatic model of the cultural adaptation process.
(4) A set of associated theorems of the 'the greater the immigrant's development of communicative competence in the host culture, the greater the participation in interpersonal communication within it' variety.

An examination of the boundary definitions of Kim's theory shows that the explanandum (dependent variable) in this theory is the individual's degree and type of adaptation to the host culture. The explanans (inde-pendent variables) are drawn from social and cultural factors, features of the environment and internal predispositions of individuals. Psychological change and learning in individuals can lead to better adaptation of the individual but the host culture cannot learn because it is *defined* as the independent variable. By conceptualising culture as a fixed background for individual psychological change and enshrining this in the logic of the analysis, the behavioural approach legislates for the political passivity of immigrants and the incapacity of the host culture to learn from them.

The reasons Kim gives for this focus on the individual's adaptation, rather than on the politics of the relationship between minority culture and dominant culture, are methodological:

> Whatever change occurs in a group through contact with another culture, it cannot be understood without understanding the changes among its individual members. (Kim, p. 37).

But many philosophers of social science would quite flatly disagree with this. Even were it accepted, it is incomplete. The reverse might equally be true — many changes to individuals cannot be understood without studying changes to the group!

A second reason is also given:

> Also, because individuals operating in a given environment are influenced by sociological and cultural factors..., these factors must be taken into consideration as well as environmental and predispositional factors' (Kim, p. 37).

But this is not an additional reason at all. It is simply a corollary of the first reason. Once you decide on an individual explanatory focus, social and cultural factors are defined as external or independent variables. The problem is partly a deficiency in the conceptualisation of culture and partly a product of the way multivariate studies substitute mathematical relations of co-variation between variables for substantive models of actual processes. Words like 'influenced by' stand in for correlations which are otherwise unexplained.

The stipulative process continues in this way:

> In addition, the theory limits its focus to the adaptation of individuals without specifically dealing with possible changes in the host environment. (Kim, p. 37)

and the reason for this limitation is:

> Although both the individual and the host society undergo adaptive changes as a result of prolonged intercultural contact, the influence of *the individual* on the host society is incomparably smaller. (Kim, p. 37; emphasis added)

The circle is now complete. The structural and public level of analysis was relegated to the status of a extraneous variable, and this analytical stance so quickly absorbed that a few lines later the possibility of an influence on the host society of the deliberate cultural priorities of the immigrant society or group has entirely disappeared and with it any possibility of examining the role of *politics* on the adaptative process or the response of the host society. The powerless individual, with no choice but adaptation, is legislated into the theory at the very beginning. In a curious way, this methodological and conceptual slight of hand has the same effect as textualism. The individual agent is trapped again in a web of determination. The standards for theorising that Kim has adopted have led to a theory which supports a *particular* kind of accidental and privatised cultural politics and all in the name of objectivity.

It is no surprise that later, at the level of assumptions, we find a one-sided model of the individual immigrant as a homeostatic, stress-reducing system, forced into learning and adapting by the environment. Kim approvingly quotes Dobzhansky (1962): 'evolutionary change *comes from* the environment' (p. 17). But this is a model of the human being as a homeostatic system not an autopoetic or self-aware system. Homeostasis is quite simply not true of human learning, as we have all known since Piaget and the critical response to Piaget. There is little or no room in this model for 'metacognition' — awareness of and reflection on one's own learning — only for adaptation as an environment driven process. Any practical recommendations derived from this theory are likely to be in the form of a magisterial manipulation of subjects rather than any process of 'consciousness raising' or 'conscientisation'. There is little to choose between being written by the postmodern cultural text or being conditioned by the behavioural environment.

Behavioural Views of Communication

Despite the fact that Kim's work is often described as theory of intercultural *communication* the fact is that the actual process of communication is treated as a black box in her theory. The closest she gets to a theory of communication is a theory of learning an inner language of concepts and appropriate feelings which outer language in some sense could be said to translate. Perhaps enough has been said in Chapter 2 about the inadequacies of this inner language view when it comes to explaining communication. The main objections are simple ones. First, the problems of giving an account of the translation of the inner concepts into outer language are just as great as the problems of giving an account of the translation of one language into another. And if such an account can be given, and the meanings of the words of outer language explained in terms of inner concepts, the problem of meaning is not solved, because you would then have to give an explanation of the meaning of the concepts, and what language would you give that in? Second, an inner language view shifts our attention away from the public dimension of language and from the dynamic or action centred view of language as a way of doing things as part of a public way of life.

What the empiricist Kim has tacitly relied on, the post-empiricist Quine[2] makes quite explicit — a behavioural theory of meaning, a logical/objective account of language and a reproductive or conservative hermeneutics. To understand why this theory too fails empirically we will have to examine Quine's ideas more closely, difficult though they are. This is a necessary step towards rescuing the notion of the empirical (or the concrete) from its empiricist and post-empiricist (behavioural) distortions.

It is appropriate to look at Quine for a second reason. His argument presents something of a hard case for the argument in this book. For Quine argues that translation from one language to another is, *in principle*, indeterminate, and by extension, that intercultural understanding is problematic. There is no 'best translation', and no 'fact of the matter' with regard to the translation of meanings or, indeed, synonymy in general. If we can use Quine and still argue our case that IC is at least possible, it may well be reasonable, if we reject some of Quine's assumptions to go on to an argument that IC is, if not easy, eminently practical and that it can be learned.

However, it must not be forgotten that intercultural communication occurs in the language of one party or one culture, or in a creole or a third language. So the problem of intercultural communication is often found in a form where the difficulties of translation manifest themselves indirectly. Often enough in today's world members of non-English speaking cultures find themselves conversing with *each other* in the third language, English. In such situations the problem is for interlocutors to find a way of expressing themselves and understanding the other in a language which engages both parties in some translation. Just the same, the task of translation, considered broadly, raises many of the same questions as the task of social scientific interpretation, in a more demanding form.

Quine's Argument

A Quinean answer to the problem of translation is to say that the expectation that there is a single, determinate meaning of native utterances (or actions) is mistaken. The problem is not one of the difficulties of settling on one particular best translation out of several possibilities but of supposing that there was a particular meaning in the first place.[3] This view of the problem of translation is a simple extension to the IC context of Quine's behaviourist doctrine of the indeterminacy of all meanings beyond the level of behavioural stimulus meanings. In Quine's view, even within a single culture it is impossible to determine the meaning of any sentence beyond the degree to which we can point to the behavioural concomitants of utterances.

This situation contrasts with Quine's realist view of reference in Physics. There Quine holds elementary particles to be real referents of Physical theory, which is reducible to talk about particles and their interactions. Such talk has clear referential meaning and the fact of the matter with regard not only to states of affairs but also to meanings can be determined. Clearly, if Quine is right about meaning, the translational model of social science is in difficulties from the start.

Now I think Quine's view of meaning, and his associated view of language, which is roughly that learning a language is nothing more than learning to coordinate utterances with certain behavioural stimuli (which themselves are explicable in physical/physiological terms), is a mistaken view of learning a language and of the nature of meaning. But before taking Quine to task in this respect, I think it is worth saying that even in such a narrow conception of meaning — a view that construes all higher meanings, such as we might invoke in metaphysical or religious talk, as constructions built up over a lifetime from simpler behavioural components, or as not being clear meanings at all — it is possible to provide a reasonable account of translation. Quine distinguishes between the extent of translation possible with direct reference only to behavioural criteria — radical translation — and translation manuals (roughly guidebooks to full translation) which attempt to translate all the meanings of a culture. He argues that a given radical translation might be compatible with several translation manuals because many meanings in a culture are indeterminate (i.e. behaviourally equivalent).

Quine's view here, like Kim's, approaches that of the textualists. There is no truth, only the would-be truths of regimes of power. There is no reference in language, except, as some Derrideans say, in the trivial everyday physical/phenomenal world of 'The grass is green'. Indeed, Quine could have no general methodological quarrel with the deconstructionists, since the texts that they are deconstructing possess no determinate meaning, only an illusion of meaning due to their enmeshment in each other.

However, contrary to some critics of Winch who seek to use the resulting indeterminacy of translation as a stick to beat Winch with,[4] and contrary to a textualist reading of Derrida, a close reading of Quine indicates that he did not believe that translation actually would be indeterminate in most instances. As Quine argues, behavioural criteria permit complex and powerful discriminations because they are public. After all, he sought to build a theory of meaning on them which was to be commensurate with the most sophisticated scientific talk: in fact, Quine believed 'radical translation proceeds in the light of observed behaviour, and behavioural criteria will ordinarily decide in favour of one translation manual rather than another',[5] that is, he believed translation would often be possible in practice. As Quine admits, we have no significant or developed examples of indeterminacy of translation to underpin his case about in principle indeterminacy.[6]

Nevertheless, he wants to argue that even though full translation can contingently occur under favourable circumstances, providing enough detailed behavioural evidence is available, it isn't always possible (in principle). But this point cuts two ways. It allows the practical feasibility of Winch's interpretative project, and it suggests behavioural criteria have a great deal of power in sorting out alternative possible meanings and permitting some meanings to be seen as incompatible with evidence. The evidence at stake in determining success, here, as Quine elsewhere argues, is of the same logical order, in relation to the theory in question, as the evidence which functions, albeit loosely and contingently, to allow us to sort out good from bad scientific theories — sensory or observational evidence based ultimately in the interaction of physical particles . While we may have to avoid jumping straight to higher order hypotheses about meaning equivalence between utterances and build up our interpretations behaviourally, if we could, it seems, we could also turn Quine's own remarks against him, namely that '…translational synonymy at its worst is no worse off than truth in physics…'[7] But Quine is systematically ambivalent on precisely this point, as we will see below.

As is clear from the above reference to 'truth', it is Quine-consistent to hold that the same testing process that is available in Physics is also available to the ethnographer or intercultural communicator, and to members of the 'other' culture, and it may be employed to engage in a critique of higher order meanings within a culture, always supposing institutions and roles would permit it. In a Quinean view, the point is not that such a critique is likely, just that it is, sometimes, even usually, possible. It would rest quite simply on the notion that some differences in meaning make a behavioural difference and others do not and it is possible to distinguish between the two. In itself, however, such a critique would be a necessary, but not sufficient, condition for cultural learning — a possible candidate for rational common ground. What are we to make then, of the weight some critics of social science's claims to intercultural validity give to Quine's point that, *in principle*, it is not always possible to decide between one translation manual and another?

Quine's Limitations

The core of Quine's 'in principle' argument is an extension of his view of the logic of scientific theories. Scientific theories are said to be *underdetermined* by evidence because the same theoretical statements may be compatible with more than one collection of bits of evidence and vice versa. For example, you can draw an infinity of mathematical curves through the same set of data points (although some curves will be convoluted) and you can often draw the same curve through different data points. For Quine, evidence is roughly that which is reducible to observation statements referring to stimulation of the sensory surfaces of the human body. That is, systems of logically incompatible theoretical statements can exist which are compatible with the same evidence and that no amount of evidence can be accumulated which uniquely determines one theory rather than another. The meanings of the terms in a theory are also *under*determined in the same way. One of the reasons for underdetermination is expressed in the form of the Quine/Duhem thesis, or the holist argument: that you cannot test a single hypothesis but only the whole network of hypotheses. That is because the process of testing involves instruments and assumptions of various kinds, and you must rely on some understanding of how your instruments work etc. The same is true for establishing the meaning of terms by identifying the objects they refer to. In any real life situation there is an array of objects. When Galileo's opponents quibbled about the notion that Jupiter had moons, they attacked the idea that the new-fangled 'telescope' was a reliable instrument. They argued in effect that Galileo's evidence was a product of his method, not of what was actually the case with Jupiter. They argued, quite rightly, that he would need to show his theory of how the telescope performed was reliable before you could trust its evidence. Similarly, they might well have argued that you would not know what Galileo meant by his terms if he could not point unambiguously to the objects they referred to. You can never test just that part of physics that deals with Jupiter, you also and unavoidably test your theory of how light behaves and telescopes. But these, in turn, will be dependent on other tests and associated assumptions. If we knew that Jupiter had moons, we could demonstrate the telescope by seeing them…but…

In much the same way, you cannot be sure what a term is referring to, because the process of pointing itself uses instruments like fingers, and telescopes.

The only way to choose between two theories is to introduce considerations other than the evidence. As observations accumulate, the adjustments that must be made to one theory may make it more and more byzantine. Eventually, you may employ the value of simplicity, and choose the simplest theory, but simplicity isn't evidence, it is a preference, and there have been times in the history of science where employing it would have led you astray. And values like parsimony, clarity and elegance are themselves culturally derived and do not help much in the case of translation from the language of one culture to another.

Quine makes two associated logical points about translation. The first he calls 'inscrutability of reference'. If you point to something, he argues, a foreigner doesn't know whether or not you are referring to its colour, shape, speed or spiritual significance. If a native speaker points to a rabbit, Quine explains, and says 'Gavagai', you do not know whether he or she is saying 'rabbit', 'Good to eat', 'fluffy tail' or 'Look at that critter go!'. You need to know the language to know its reference, but, if so, how can you learn the language in the first place? Or so it seems to Quine. The second point concerns the *under*determination of meaning in a natural language by evidence. At first sight this would seem to leave translation of language no worse off than scientific theory — meaning would be underdetermined, but rules of thumb and preferences built up by experience would allow the best theory of meaning to be chosen. Such underdetermination would explain the uncertainty learners of a new language experience in the very early stages. But Quine wants to argue in the case of language that *under*determination thereby renders language meaning *indeterminate*. He says that there is no truth of the matter with regard to meanings, no equivalent of the particles of Physics to provide the equivalent of observation statements, and this means that underdetermination becomes full-on indeterminacy. That is, learning a new language should be, in principle, impossible. But that is nonsense.

How does Quine work this sleight of hand?

> In being able to speak of the truth of a sentence [in Physics] only within a more inclusive theory [which is itself underdetermined], one is not much hampered; for one is always working within some comfortable inclusive [physical] theory, however tentative... (Quine and Ullian, pp. 75–6)[8]

And that inclusive theory, at its most inclusive, is Physics itself, which by an earlier fiat Quine has quite simply *declared* privileged. Translation is indeterminate because '...translators do not supplement their behavioural criteria with neurological criteria...' so they have no basis for asserting that their translational preferences correspond with '...any distribution of elementary physical states better than [another]...'[9] (Quine and Ullian, p. 167). Here, it is ultimately the *success* of Physics that is the warrant for using it to provide the world view within which other theorising is judged. In this, Quine is a pragmatist, but a crude one, since there is no reason to suppose that Physics can provide a model for *all* knowledge, even when it may provide a useful basis for physical science. Since theories about what some words mean do not of themselves make reference to physical states, they pass up the only prophylactic against indeterminacy.

But, as Rorty points out,

> Quine...thinks there can be no 'fact of the matter' about [meaning] states of affairs because different such states can be attributed without making a difference to the elementary [physical] particles... But surely all that such irreducibility shows is that one particular vocabulary...is not going to be helpful for doing certain things with certain [things to be explained], e.g. people and cultures. (Rorty, p. 201)[10]

And, as Davidson argues, we always do have a comfortable inclusive theory — our own culture modified by our experience of the other.

Consequences of Pragmatism

Feleppa[11] adds another argument against Quine. Quine assumes that it is possible to have alternative translations that make sense in the new language but which are logically incompatible with each other while at the same time being compatible with the empirical behavioural or situational evidence provided by observation of the usage of the original language. This assumes far too much similarity between the way scientific theories are expressed and the way language is used in everyday life. We are not dealing with mathematical sets of points. In social life, some curves are too improbable. To this I would add Habermas' query: 'How do Physicists agree among each other, cross-culturally, that they are talking about the same things?' If you answer, they have all acquired the same culture, that of physics, it is necessary to ask: 'How did they understand each other in the first place?' If to that you answer in terms of the relationship between physics talk and elementary particles it is necessary to ask: 'In what language were such things first referred to?' I think the manifest difficulty of Quine's position is clear.

What is at stake here is Quine's grand style of reasoning about theories and his arbitrary (he himself admits its arbitrariness) privileging of Physics. His manner is metaphorical and vague. As he admits, he can point to no actual examples of rival translations that meet the criteria he outlines. It is entirely speculative to speak, as Quine does of our theory of nature as a whole in terms of '...a single big tandem theory consisting perhaps of two largely independent lobes and a shared logic...',[12] meaning, of course, Mathematics and Physics, and logic.

One way out of the Quinean problem is to assert that translation theories *are* on a footing with physical theories — underdetermined but not indeterminate. It can be made at least as plausible as Quine's alternative, as Feleppa shows.

Another solution is to regard it as mistaken to regard translation manuals as descriptions i.e. descriptions of a language. They are, Feleppa argues, '...*pre*scriptive elements of theories'[13] similar in function to rules of inference in hypothesis testing or rules of thumb about simplicity or elegance, 'Occam's razor' etc. In other words, there are grounds other than stimulus meanings upon which rival translations may be compared because languages may be used in contexts where it is possible to get behavioural feedback, *not* about the entities etc. to which the language

refers but feedback of a prescriptive kind through expressions of puzzlement, or comprehension — about the adequacy of language use — from
other language users. For instance, it is accepted among empirical linguists
that there are universal or species wide similarities in the way mothers
respond to successful or unsuccessful infant language use.

Davidson's Alternative

Donald Davidson, whom we met in earlier chapters, is a philosopher
who in many ways is quite close to Quine. In fact, he has sometimes been
labelled a post-Quinean.[14] It is interesting that he has come to quite different
conclusions to Quine when it comes to problems of understanding
culturally different people. Davidson shares many of Quine's starting
points, but the crucial difference is that he doesn't share his preference for
Physics. Davidson has made the 'linguistic turn', but he doesn't simply
reverse Quine by privileging language in the same way Quine seeks to
privilege Physics. For Davidson, there is no fact of the matter with regard
either to meaning or physical states, just a pragmatically workable process
of coherence between our language and what we do. All interpretations are
fallible just as all physical theories are fallible. Davidson is a pragmatist
philosopher of meaning.

It doesn't matter that in principle we can never be absolutely, deduc-
tively sure of meaning because, pragmatically, we can be. Fallibility has not
been an obstacle to the progress of science and there is no reason why it
should be an obstacle to the progress of human understanding.

Quine's physicalism, which is the touchstone of knowledge for him,
connects language to the world via its relation to behaviour and behaviourally established stimulus–response links within the brains of organisms.
But Davidson thinks this is altogether too simplistic an account.

Davidson may be a post-Quinean but he is also a philosopher who is
quite close to Derrida. He has been labelled a deconstructionist: 'Davidson
and Derrida emerge from traditions which have had little contact over the
past century. That they reach similar positions from analogous considerations and analogous predecessors indicates that...they are getting
something right.'[15]

However, for the moment we will concentrate on Davidson's critique of
Quine. Later we will try to show how Habermas' Davidsonian theory of
communication can complement Derrida's theory of texts.

Davidson offers us an alternative to Feleppa's critique. He shows that
Quine's concession that we ordinarily can translate is crucial. The 'in

principle' arguments Quine gives us are shaky. Once they are out of the way Quine's pragmatic recognition of our translational success takes on greater significance. Inscrutability is a problem, not an absolute barrier. We do not encounter a language in a world where life stands still while we point at an isolated rabbit. Far from being a source of difficulty due to confusion and complexity, the enmeshment of our actions in a whole way of life is an advantage, because, unlike mathematics, we cannot keep constructing more and more convoluted curves to fit events. After we have caught the rabbit, dressed it, cooked it and eaten it, all accompanied by language, we may be able to place the various interpretations of Gavagai that occurred to us in an order of probability. For instance, when skinning the rabbit (here readers of delicate sensibility may skip a paragraph) the tail may have been cut off and handed to us with a word other than Gavagai being said. Similarly, on eating the rabbit, a dish of it may have been placed before us with an utterance other than Gavagai, accompanied by lip smacking, and smiling. Over time, and many such experiences we try out our hypotheses, that there first of these new words means fluffy tail and the second utterance means good to eat. Some of our attempts evoke laughter, others apparent acceptance. Later we pass some rabbit droppings on the ground and we utter the sound we hypothesise means 'good to eat'. This evokes hysterical laughter. Another piece of evidence. Their sense of humour is not unlike ours. Of course, all this is fallible. But the coherence and success of becoming a part of the way of life of a people over time gradually confirms us in our interpretations. Not many of us have had the kind of experiences that are described above, but field linguists often do, migrants do, and the author, working in Papua New Guinea has also had such experiences.

However, Davidson agrees with Quine's view of the logic of theories. Theories are complex webs of statements that touch experience only obliquely at their outer edges. But unlike Quine, who tends to confine this view of logic to physical theories while discussing meanings in an atomistic way, Davidson argues that meanings too are like locations in a *web* of significance rather than a set of one to one pointers to things in the world. Where Quine confines his holistic view to the testing of theories against experience — the logic of theory testing distributes the test over all the statements in the network that makes up the theory — Davidson argues that meaning works the same way. Where Quine provides for the sense of this web to be provided by the contact of the outer edges of the web with physical observations (themselves explained by a physical account of how particles behave in the human sensory apparatus), Davidson provides for the sense of a linguistic web or *text* to be provided by its immersion in an historical and cultural context at every point. Individual signs may be arbitrary relative to their notional objects, but they occur in situations. Where Derrida and Davidson would probably agree is that the art of writing allows the separation of written texts from their situation of origin, thus increasing the underdetermination of the meaning of particular signs and sign strings, and even, under circumstances of radical separation from context, creating a practical indeterminacy.

Another point of resemblance with Derrida occurs when Davidson argues that there is no final, objective meaning to a text. Texts mean as part of a way of life, but ways of life are not fixed. They are in movement. Thus, meaning is also in movement and its finality is always deferred (or as Derrida would say, characterised by *différance*). If, by meaning, we mean something like 'trajectory', we may reasonable speak of meaning. If, however, we mean something fixed or defined, we are failing to recognise that meaning is a verb, an action and that *to mean* is to transform something, and in the case of a way of life which is a flow of meanings, to mean is to re-direct the flow, not to stop or freeze it.

For Davidson, the intersubjective field of action in a culture is like the life of an individual — always moving and changing, but not necessarily in an arbitrary or senseless way. Meanings and rules of thumb for effective communication grow up in a culture and slip against each other like geological faults. The flow of first level meanings (roughly the conventional dictionary meanings of words, as in e.g. the English language) has a rate of change different from the flow of second level or specific meanings. I can change my identity, while the first order or public/conventional meanings of the English words I now use or once used to describe myself change only a little. First order meanings are in movement, but their movement is much slower than the rate of change of second order meanings. If this were not so, we would have no relatively stable linguistic resources to utter specific sentences in. The distinction between first and second order meanings in Davidson is related to the distinction between language and speech.

Davidson's view is that we know the meaning of a sentence at the first level of meaning when we know the conditions that would have to prevail for us to count it as true or valid. This is not the same as the process of coming to regard a claim as true or valid. It is merely the business of recognising what is at stake — what aspects of the way of life are being spoken about. Indeed, if language could not do this for us, we could not have a linguistically-mediated, and therefore *social* way of life at all.

Conventional meanings are not arbitrary. They can be uttered satisfactorily in any situation. Utterances get their first order meanings from the overt features of a way of life and are only meaningful if their claims can be related to features of that way of life — i.e. we can see what the speaker is talking about. But the second order meanings of utterances are derived from the nature of the claims being made. First order meanings tell us a claim is about, say, the order of precedence at a ceremony. Second order meanings tell us that the claim, say, for a member of one race to get precedence over another, is a political move of a particular kind, with a certain moral and political weight. It is at the second order level that we can make judgements about the validity or otherwise of the claim as a claim that is or is not a part of the moral order of the world we inhabit or wish to inhabit. It is the second order meaning problem which is most acute in intercultural communication. You can take a course in the language and culture of a country and get a reasonable grasp of the first order meanings.

Davidson makes a further point. To assume that the second order meanings of another person are so different from our own that they are totally incommensurate is incoherent. Here, for the sake of discussion we must assume that the problem of first order meanings has been overcome by conducting the conversation in some highly malleable lingua franca. Davidson argues that we cannot intelligibly talk of difference or even recognise that a way of life is a human way of life if we did not have much in common and acknowledge this. This is what Davidson calls the principle of 'charity'. Of course, when we begin to communicate we find problems, and we seek to overcome these by finding some common ground where we seem to understand each other and working out from there. Davidson calls this common ground a 'passing theory' or temporary theory of meaning. When you think about it, it is the only reasonable stance to take. While being aware of the probability of difference, even surprising difference, we must do the other the honour of starting from the assumption that their claims are as valid as they can possibly be in *our world*. Derrida speaks of respect for the other. What else can this respect be in its initial stages but attribution to the other of what we have already experienced as worthy of respect. An abstract enough point, you may think. But there are more concrete reasons for rejecting an expectation of incommensurability as a starting point.

Translation and Realism: First and Second Order

No doubt a behavioural dimension is important in learning a language (we point to a fat quadruped and say 'pig', and only over a number of behavioural instances do we individuate 'pig' to the porcine organism rather than to something that would translate as 'good to eat' or 'curly tail').

But we may have access to more information than the behavioural connections *between terms and their reference* — more, that is, than the juxtaposition of observable things and language performances. First, as already mentioned, there is the response of other language users — puzzlement, confusion amusement etc. Then there are additional factors. For instance, it has been argued that we usually name things which are detachable from and move or are moved within a relatively fixed background. Hence when we point at a running quadruped and say 'oink' we will, more often than not, be taken to be naming it rather than some undetached part or property of it. This is, of course, a rule of thumb. Its usefulness could be viewed probabilistically. Across a large sample of cases it may lead to error, say, 49% of the time. Now the philosophical point can certainly be made — it is not a determinate method of translation — but if we consider an interpretation of an utterance chosen at random from the large class of possible interpretations and we can identify five features of the situation that have associated rules of thumb, the probability of a randomly chosen analytical (meaning) inference meeting all tests is quite small. Conversely, if we use the rules of thumb to construct a possible meaning, the probability of that meaning being appropriate is not likely to be small.

The question is, do such tests exist? One plausible possibility has already been mentioned. A number of others suggest themselves. Human variability is not infinite. While some societies have residential groups which are not kinship groups, most residential groups *are* kinship groups. While mother and father roles differ culturally, most societies have mothers and fathers, and the physical and emotional needs of the dependent human child are not completely dissimilar. While some societies practice approved incest, most societies have an incest taboo. Most societies have a form of exclusive sexual and parental bonding between one male and one or a number of females. Colour vision is subject to only a limited cultural variation in naming (of which too much has been made). Gestures of rubbing the stomach and pointing to the mouth will most often be interpreted as a sign of hunger, especially if accompanied by imploring gestures (gestures which will most often be interpreted as imploring). More generally, we all use speech to communicate. We have a common experience of languaging. Research on early language acquisition has identified general cross cultural non-verbal indications in mother's voices which babies respond to before they acquire words and which signal success or failure, positive or negative response from the mother.[16] As any logician will tell you, if, in the context of experience of the world you add to 'yes' and 'no' the logical operator 'and', you can build up all other specific meanings.

We all have a need to be aware of and deal with the universal fact that we cannot have everyday access to the inner states of others, that self and others are separate in some degree, and that self and the world of others and objects in the world must be distinguished in some way (not necessarily by Western notions of animate/inanimate etc.) Certainly, identifying such common ground may be problematic when cultures differ profoundly, but that, clearly, is a matter of degree. It is methodologically dubious to suggest that a theory of intercultural understanding should be judged by the hardest possible cases, and in human terms, disastrous. The point is a simple one. Similarities and connections do not have to be universal to be useful.

In addition, as Davidson points out, the information we receive in face to face communication does not consist of the rather abstract utterances of sentence-meaning beloved of philosophers.[17] We normally communicate *in* the context of reference of the talk. When we communicate *about* an absent context, we usually attend to the construction of its features, as a part of the new context. We constitute the absent context virtually. Of course, this is less true of writing. In face to face communication we have facial expression, posture, gesture, tone of voice, cadence as well as choice of words and syntactical structure. Again, while there is coding variety, I suggest that there is also some common ground. A full-faced, open smile may not mean *exactly* the same thing in different cultures, but nowhere does it mean unhappiness (as contrasted with say, a small embarrassed grin). There is variation. There is room for much misunderstanding. But variation has a limit and there is much common ground. While values such as those of parsimony and elegance may themselves be culturally derived, it is also possible to point out that a theory of the meaning of a text compatible with all of the sources of evidence (behavioural, rule of thumb, non-verbal responses and more) could quickly become byzantine beyond capacity for belief of members of any culture. The fact is, theories of text meaning, as expressed in translations of it, must have a human scale of complexity.

There is also 'situation'. While situation is constructed, not all aspects of it are constructed from higher-order interpretations — situations have reference features. Some situation types have cultural common ground. We are usually not involved in the abstract, rational attempts to translate what philosophers talk about but in real situations with a history and referentially specifiable features. And concrete features of situations have inherent potential meanings, unlike physical particles. While cultures differ in their cuisine, the need for food is universal, as is a high degree of overlap in the class of *inedibles*. Shelter from the driving sleet or rain, even if only a rock overhang, is universally meaningful for those out in the rain, and so on.

Of course, it is possible for a concrete context to be deeply read. For a rock or a river to be much more than a rock or a river. In the 'dreamtime' of the world's origins, as traditional Australian aboriginal beliefs have it, the landscape was shaped by cosmic events. The depth of interpretation of concrete features of the situation may be much greater for one culture than another — the concrete features may be more 'significant'. This imposes an interpretive load for both cultures. For members of the one, to see in the other the depth, the richness of cultural connection, of something which in their own culture lies more on the periphery of the cultural network or web of experiences/meanings. For members of the other to somehow bracket that richness and see it, for interpretive purposes, as 'just another river or rock'. What remains common is that the things talked about are there, otherwise it would not be possible to have a conversation about a 'sleeping spirit being/large red monolithic rock' or raise the issue of difference of significance at all.

In constructing meaning we ordinarily take hundreds of inferences into account and produce holistic interpretations consistent with all or most of the 'evidence' at hand, including the evidence of the responses of our interlocutors to our tentative interpretations. We are ordinarily familiar with puzzling situations, situations where we lack information or where an interpretation consistent with all the information is difficult to find. We have ways of dealing with these difficulties.

In addition, Quine takes his holism too far when he asserts that the whole of our scientific theories face the 'tribunal of experience' at one time and that we are unable to tell which bit of them, higher order meanings (e.g. metaphysical assumptions) or auxiliary beliefs about our method of measurement, are at fault when experience tells us something is wrong. If we took this holism too seriously, we would be unable to account for the history of science. Ordinarily we do not lack reasons for isolating some parts of theory rather than others — we are in practice at worst in a part-holistic situation, whatever is the case 'in principle'. Much the same might be said about the logic of translation. From a logical point of view the situations are the same. Particular sentences are interpreted in the light of a part-holistic theory of meaning. Ordinarily this begins as our own culture modified by our expectations about the culture we are dealing with. Later, we develop what Davidson calls a 'passing theory', a theory about meaning that seems to work for the time being. Within that theory there are parts which we (fallibly) feel we have more reason to be confident about than others. Other parts are more tentative. But we do have ways of narrowing down the problem when the evidence we are getting about the meaning of utterances doesn't seem to fit our interpretation of them. Some of these are vicious and some constructive.

It would also appear that a respectable case can be made out by linguists for some *semantic* common ground among human languages. The case for a set of semantic *near* universals is strong:

> Every language is a self-contained system and, in a sense, no words or constructions in one language can have absolute equivalents in another...however, as soon as we abandon the notion of absolute equivalents and absolute universals, we are free to investigate the idea of partial equivalents and partial universals; and if the former notion is sterile and useless, the latter idea is fruitful and necessary. (*Cross-cultural Pragmatics*, p. 10)[18]

If we have so many (admittedly partial) aids to translation, the probability of error may be minute. But even were it to remain significant we would also have available the remedy of further communication. All languages have strategies for such situational difficulties. All languages have question forms. All cultures have modes of inquiry. The non-verbal aspects of question-asking also have some degree of common ground. We are familiar, in our own culture, with the processes involved in stopping an interaction's progress temporarily while sorting out a communicative problem. All cultures have linguistic practices which reflect on ongoing communication and keep it 'on track' — formulating practices, alignment practices and the like. All cultures employ such strategies for normal communicative reasons.

There is a growing field of research into these interlanguage strategies.[19] Speakers *have* strategies of simplification, tactful overlooking of errors, special ways of correcting error, register simplification, increased levels of redundancy and the like whereby they cope with cultural difference and related linguistic shortcomings.

The necessary conditions for sorting out communication problems include the availability of means of sorting out meanings, behavioural or otherwise. When these conditions are coupled with a desire to understand, a willingness to make allowances, to live with uncertain interpretations, to proceed tentatively, to respect the difficulties of the other, we reach the level of *sufficient* conditions for sorting out communication problems, given enough time. The emergence of such conditions is, of course, a political matter. And, no doubt, these conditions are always only incompletely present. There is never enough time. The desire to understand is never strong enough to overcome any and every demand of time, energy, patience or good will.

It would seem that we are talking about a counterfactual 'ideal', which brings us into Habermas' territory, since the major tool employed in his analysis of language is just such an ideal notion of the political and cultural openness of communication. This point will be taken up in Chapter 5.

The Positive Contribution of Empirical Studies

If I were to summarise the last page or so, I would do it this way: understanding relies on extra-textual characteristics of language, objective characteristics of texts, and conventional intertextual relationships to limit and guide the construction of meaning by readers/listeners. While these are often weak guides, the creativity of interpretation is not always undisciplined, a form of mere open play. It is primarily for this reason that we need an empirical component in our account of IC, although not a behaviourist one.

We must be oriented to the material medium of languages (and other sign systems), since readers/hearers are oriented to this simply in order to be hearers of sound, readers of print. Sound, print etc. are material expressions of a 'language' of some kind. However arbitrary or conventional, the relation of this language to the conventional marks on paper and vibrations in the air must be empirically reasonably reliable or we would spend much more time mishearing than we do. Shorthand writers get high levels of agreement as to utterance of conventional sign strings (the words spoken, for instance). But we must also find a kind of meaning at a high level of reliability, too. Otherwise we might be able to reproduce the words spoken but would typically experience them as if they were the words of an unknown, but phonetically transparent language. Shorthand writers with a few simple phonetic rules can happily transcribe phonetically transparent or regular languages without understanding a thing (e.g. Esperanto). Human experience is experience of reasonably reliable access to the primary or conventional level of meaning of words/signs, and their grammatical combinations. Whatever else it means when someone tells you 'Jack won't be coming tonight' it means 'there is a proper named person, time tonight, who is not coming'. Of course, what *that* means at the second level is anyone's guess. It is when we come to the level of the meanings beyond *the primary, conventional or dictionary meanings* that we begin to have to do a lot of inferential work.

That inferential work is work of many kinds. It is the stitching together of a plausible account of meaning from many different bits of old cloth. Perhaps Jack's non-arrival is bad news, perhaps good. Eventually we make a kind of motley that the world around us seems content to wear. This is a kind of meaning-realism, or pragmatism, if by pragmatism we mean the kind of active, constitutive pragmatic realism that Dewey practised. This has been called 'transactional realism'. It is not only a kind of realism but also a kind of metaphysics, if metaphysics is an understanding of the way a fluid cultural reality is created and changed.[20]

The Yield from Empirical Studies

As cultures change and grow, new elements, new patches are stitched into the old. Often the colours clash. The stitches that hold contradiction together are of several kinds. Some are rationales, accounts or myths that explain contradiction away. There are always seams of contradiction between the conventional level of meaning and the second order level of commitments and claims.

Sometimes it is the temporal and spatial separation of the patches that permits contradictions to remain unperceived. Out of sight is out of mind. We are quite capable of being a devout believer in Church on Sunday and one of the more pagan 'boys' or 'girls' at the office through the week. But the fragmented and contradictory character of culture also presents opportunities for agency because culture fragments along the fault lines of rhetoric — the line between what is claimed and the cultures sedimented store of accepted past claims. When cultures are contradictory, and their meanings ambiguous, as they must always be under conditions of change in the context of the realisation of cultural meanings, they are less able to write the subjectivity of individuals in an unchallengeable way. Their rhetorical success is reduced. The force of their texts — the ontogenetic force — is incommensurate with their sense. Inevitably, this failure forces fractures in sense too.

When society (not culture) is characterised by structures of inclusion and exclusion, economic advantage and exploitation, wealth and poverty, privilege and deprivation, power and powerlessness as *all* societies we know about are to some degree, daily life *and culture* become shaped by the dilemmas, limitations and deprivations that result. We *live* superiority and inferiority, winning and losing, no matter what the particular set of rules we play by. At the very least, there are prizes (concrete and symbolic) for winners and, perhaps, dis-prizes or expropriations (concrete and symbolic) for the losers. At least, this is true for all scarce 'goods' and for 'positional' goods. One of the major functions of social institutions and their rituals is to help us to live *within* contradictions. The fact that such reinforcement is needed not only points to the rhetorical failure of oppressive texts, but it also points to the fact of opportunity for critique and agency.

The point I am making is not that the rules of the game should be fair, nor that cultures become repositories of beliefs, attitudes, identities, justifications, and expectations about the nature and behaviour of winners and losers but that cultures are themselves necessarily 'contested'. If a society is characterised by a set of social arrangements where there is some unfairness and injustice etc., then the price that disadvantaged members of it will have to pay in both concrete and symbolic terms always creates various forms of resistance to the existing social order. Foucault makes much the same point but, as we will see in the next chapter, what he doesn't show us is the source of this resistance — the inevitability of rhetorical failure.

If power and wealth in a society is concentrated in an elite, and this elite is able to pass on power and wealth to its own offspring, and members of the non-elite are relatively deprived of the goods that are valued in the culture (vacations, automobiles, housing, household appliances, health care, jobs) there will be dissatisfaction and protest. Unless, that is, this state of affairs can be hidden, or the attention of the masses distracted. Critique will arise, including critique of the values as well as of the rules and practices — this is cultural and social critique. Such critique often exposes the key ideas and values of a culture as deeply ambiguous and, at their very centre, signs of contradiction, whose function is to legitimate existing practices and obscure their actual nature and results. There is no shortage of examples of the contested, ambiguous and problematic nature of much in, say, mainstream European cultures, but it is also possible to find the same processes at work in ancient China, India or pre-colonial Africa. This critique arises because oppressive cultures are always adaptively deficient at the rhetorical level, since oppression always rests on a contradiction mediated by ambiguity.

Some of the most illuminating examples of these ambiguities are provided in a series of British empirical studies of the ideological dilemmas of everyday life (*Ideological Dilemmas*, by Michael Billig *et al.*)[21]

In a chapter of ethnic prejudice, they describe the attitudes of some British schoolchildren towards West Indians:

> Wendy and her friend had been expressing their support for the unambiguously racist political party, The National Front. They had been justifying this support with tales about the violence of West Indians, the shortages of jobs caused by immigration, and the differ-

entness of Asians. In outlining these tales, Wendy and her friend had been displaying the signs which psychologists normally associate with prejudice. They were advocating discrimination against non-whites, for both believed that non-whites should be expelled from Britain. Both made free use of stereotypes, as they described West Indians and Asians in simple terms. No doubt a standard attitude questionnaire might have been given, and these supporters of The National Front would have provided the answers which psychologists would have little difficulty defining as prejudiced. (*Ideological Dilemmas*, p. 100)

But Billig *et al.* reject the simple equation of prejudice with something like an authoritarian personality and lack of prejudice with egalitarian and liberal attitudes. Rather, prejudice is a complex, ambiguous and dialectical phenomenon. The simple, stereotyped *concept* of prejudice is an ideal type. The authors call it 'a product of Enlightenment thinking'. Wendy and her friend themselves use this ideal concept of prejudice *and accept that it is morally wrong*, but at the same time as they affirm this and also state that they are not 'really' prejudiced, they speak of circumstances and details of context that make the desirable ideal 'impracticable'. At the pragmatic realist level, they recognise the failure of their racist claims — the fracture between the racist sense of their texts and the impracticality or unreality of the associated force or claims.

Naturally, Billig *et al.* detect an ambiguity within the prevailing racist ideology itself. In the way language is used, in the attempted rationality and justification of racist views and in the easy movement from anecdotes about racial clashes to abstract generalisations about 'us' and 'them', there is evidence of a struggle between a belief that some of *them* are 'OK', that hating people who are different is wrong, and a belief, even a fear, that these people whose skin colour and customs are different represent a threat, a wild or extra-cultural element which threatens orderly (i.e. cultural) interaction. The culturally stereotyped or first order content of racism makes unacceptable claims.

> Complaints about 'immigrants' or 'foreigners' would be made, only to be followed by concessions. Blame would be mingled with sympathy, as tolerant themes followed on those of prejudice. Seldom in the discussion groups of Cochrane and Billig would there be direct confrontation between those who only voiced tolerant sentiments and those who clung to unalloyed prejudice. More common were discussions in which all shared the contrary themes, and all chipped in with remarks which added the 'but...' qualifications to previous assertions.

> Nor did it matter whether it was the same or a different speaker who had made the previous statement that was in need of qualification...
>
> This form of agreement by disagreement occurred when all shared the contrary themes of 'reasonable prejudice'. Nevertheless, this form of discourse must be prepared to argue with those who express 'unreasonable prejudice'. If one of the themes of reasonable prejudice is the rejection of 'prejudice', then it needs a symbol of 'unreasonable prejudice' from which to distance itself... In other words, the reasonable discourse of prejudice needs its unreasonable prejudiced Other. (*Ideological Dilemmas*, p. 114–15)

A little later in his argument, Billig reminds us of the essential ambiguity in Voltaire's claims to rationality in his attitudes to other races, particularly the Jews. Billig helps us to recognise that the ambiguity, indeed, the contradiction, between racism and humanism is deeply embedded in many European cultures. The fundamental contradiction between the enlightenment's recognition of the unique value and rights of the individual, and the rejection of whole categories of individuals has been present in Western culture for a long time. But this ambiguity cannot be present in the culture at the same time as its members possess an inner unity in respect of it. The ambiguity runs *within* cultural members too. Their identity as 'fair-minded people' is at war with their racist beliefs.

> Time and time again, Voltaire went out of his way to castigate the supposed primitive irrationalities of the Jews... [calling them] ...the most contemptible of all nations... [and] ...vagrants, robbers...abhorred by men... (*Ideological Dilemmas*, p. 122)

Curiously, Voltaire was also adamant that he did not hate the Jews and at the end of a diatribe against them, in which he calls them ignorant, barbarous, avaricious, sordid, detestably superstitious and haters of those who tolerate them, he nonetheless opined that we ought not to burn them.

As the example of Voltaire makes clear, the ambiguity of Billig's working class adolescents is shared more widely. If we confine our analysis to talk of cultures in the abstract and shy away from actual cultures in their historical detail, we can easily miss this contradictory character and so fail to see the opportunity it represents.

Rules of the empirical game are also necessary, whether in guiding genealogical critique (Foucault) or deconstruction (Derrida). Such rules, or, better, sensitising methodological notions, are ultimately pragmatically derived, and so are themselves fallible, but they are essential if we are to be able to identify the fractures between ideological sense and circumstantial force of cultural utterance or ontological claim. Sufficient to say here that

Foucault's own history fails pragmatic empirical tests of adequacy as history on these grounds. For instance, significant simplification, and omission of confounding historical data can be identified in Foucault's work. There is little sense of the continually contested character of ideology, despite Foucault's discussion of the permanent character of resistance, because, for Foucault, resistance is inevitably 'marginalised'. That this is not so is clear from Billig *et al.*'s studies. Resistance is within each fractured self.

The Middle Path

An appropriate rule of thumb is to take the middle path between textualism and realism, both in our view of the nature of social reality and in our view of the way we make languages mean. As we will see in subsequent chapters, this middle path, or pragmatic realism, need not be a 'philosophy of presence', nor need it involve 'essentialism' or 'universalism'. The very multiplicity of meaning possibility of which Derrida writes is the condition of cultural agency. The ambiguity, pragmatic success and failure, transactional reality and situationally-engaged, experienced character of communicative action is the key to understanding culture.

Ambiguity runs through all cultures not just modern ones because all cultures are a result of historical accretion, accidental blending, and aggregation of political solutions to particular, local cultural and social problems. They are not rationally planned, or conceptually coherent constructions. However, I hesitate to press this point too far, because that would lead to the opposite error to textualism — from the loss of the agent we would move towards the loss of cultural coherence and hence all possibility of a shared, public character of culture. We would not even be able to explain the conventional character of the marks on the paper you are now reading. Some behavioural studies of intercultural communication typically fall into this error. They somewhat improbably banish the public, textual dimension of culture, dissolving it completely without residue into the purposive, acting individual agent. It is in the tension between the public, mythical or ideological sense and the particularity of circumstantial selves that the rhetorical problem emerges and the politics of culture is played out. That is why education is so crucial and learning so important.

In an embodied, historical, view of culture identity and agency, the resolution of cultural differences is not merely an aesthetic game, but something measured in suffering or freedom from it. Conversely, the more we make such judgements, the more uncomfortable most of us become.

But while cultures can be absolutised when a minimal realism is lacking, they can also be absolutised by methodological fiat. A typical structure for empirical studies involves the observation and analysis of communication episode or episodes between members of different cultures. Problems of communication are then traced back to different communicator assumptions derived, of course, from cultural differences. But it was on the basis of stereotyped attributions of cultural membership that the subjects in the studies were selected in the first place. The identification of differences in communicator assumptions, speaking rules, coding devices etc. — culturally specific communicative competence — is only a part of the story of intercultural communication, as is the interaction of individuals with given levels of 'acculturation' etc.

Typically, there is no attempt in the behavioural approach to see that the communicative problems which arise during inter-ethnic communication are only an extension of the problems which arise on a daily basis in intra-ethnic communication. In all communication situations there are always different assumptions etc. The issue is one of degree, and of participant's understanding of interethnic situations as differences of kind. That is, it is an issue of the phenomenology of ethnic 'essentialism' in participants' definitions of ethnicity and race. Ethnic essentialism (the belief that members of racial or ethnic groups differ from each other in some essential way, possibly with a biological basis) is the ideological core of racism. But defining racism in terms of the racial essentialism of participants is not a problem, providing this essentialism is not reflected methodologically at the level of the 'second order' structure of the research method used to study it. Unfortunately, this essentialism is often reflected methodologically in empirical studies. The whole thrust of empirical methods such as scale construction, the survey questionnaire and observation schedules is to push for the construction of types, for main effects, for generalisation. In the case of this research, types become stereotypes all too easily. Again, similar methodological assumptions are made about the inner world of individuals — that individuals have an opinion, a single viewpoint, as if we never experienced ourselves as divided against ourselves.

The communicative skills we use in daily life, when faced with misunderstanding, can be brought into play to bridge the cultural gap. But studies which focus on stereotyped group differences, to the exclusion of all else, leave us with a rather one-sided understanding of communicative problems and subtly reinforce participant essentialism. They fall short of the educative level that interethnic communication research can reach, even within an empiricist understanding of knowledge. Much the same effect occurs in a great deal of speculative theoretical writing, or in studies of colonialism or post-colonialism. While it is beyond the scope of this book, similar points could be made about methods of psychotherapy.

The virtual failure to focus on empirically rare, but theoretically important strategies for intercultural communication produces a kind of methodologically induced pessimism — a focus on the source of intercultural communication difficulties rather than on sources of hope for overcoming them. This limitation of empiricism in particular and what Horkheimer called 'traditional theories' in general, is nothing more than a failure to recognise that the forms which dominate in a given social situation are not the only possible forms. In some cases, a greater attention to ambiguity, play, humour and the poetry of subversion might help us to break out of the straitjacket. In others, a greater political seriousness coupled with realism might be valuable.

The possibility of genuine intercultural understanding rests on distinguishing between the experience of most research subjects under present conditions of intercultural understanding (on which most empirical studies concentrate), and rare behaviour, which points the way to as yet unrealised possibilities. The danger of all empiricism is that the drive to simplify and generalise runs the risk of mistaking the whole of human possibilities for the given, historically specific forms in which they presently appear.

The irony of textualism is that, coming from the opposite analytical pole from realism and denying all realist intuitions, it manages to reproduce the same behavioural closure as extreme realism. In the theory of interpretation it tacitly allies itself with traditionalism or conservative hermeneutics — as its opposite, although the traditionalism of textualism is latent. While seemingly opposing and deconstructing all traditional meanings, textualism leads to political-historical quietism, since it espouses no alternative meanings, except quite arbitrarily and in contradiction of its own positioning. It posture is one of authority but its message one which denies the intellectual pretensions of its speaking position. This is precisely a rhetorical failure.

We need research which attempts to identify the common capacity of speakers in all cultures to engage in critical contextualising of utterances and which explores the possibility of extending this awareness to the intercultural communication context. Rhetorical success, ontologically defined, is when there is harmony between sense and claim, because what is claimed is sensible and true. That is why Aristotle connected the study of rhetoric with the search for truth. If so-called 'modern' cultures differ from some others in any respect, it is in their relatively high level of potential for a certain cosmopolitanism, an awareness of cultural diversity and of the non-absolute character of culture. It is from this awareness that the context for successful intercultural communication may be created. Paradoxically, we can only communicate between cultures when speakers are prepared to admit the possibility of change in their own culture — the possibility of a two-way cultural learning process. The greatest weakness of post-structuralist thought is its relative incapacity to provide a theory of just such change or learning.

Notes

1. Y. Kim, *Communication and Cross-Cultural Adaptation*. Clevedon: Multilingual Matters, 1988. The discussion of Kim's work here is taken largely from my review of her book: R. Young, 'Intercultural communication and criticism'. *Journal of Multilingual and Multicultural Development*, 12 (4) 1991, 301–308.
2. W. Quine, *Word and Object*. Cambridge: MIT Press, 1960. See also Roth, pp. 64, 65.
3. Quine, *Word and Object*.
4. e.g. C. Williamson, 'Witchcraft and Winchcraft'. *Philosophy of the Social Sciences*, 19 (1989), pp. 445–60.
5. W. Quine, 'Fact of the matter'. In R. Shahan and C. Swoyer (eds) *Essays in the Philosophy of W.V. Quine*. Norman: Oklahoma University Press, 1979, p. 167.
6. Quine, *Word and Object*, p. 72.
7. *Word and Object*, p. 75.
8. W. Quine and J. Ullian, *The Web of Belief*. New York: Random House, 1978.
9. Quine and Ullian, p. 167.
10. R. Rorty, 'Method, social science and social hope'. Pp. 191–210 in *Consequences of Pragmatism*. London: Harvester Press, 1982.
11. R. Feleppa, *Convention, Translation and Understanding*. Albany, Suny Press, 1988.
12. Quine, *Word and Object*
13. Feleppa. *op. cit.*
14. B. Martin, 'Analytic philosophy's narrative turn: Quine, Rorty, Davidson.' Pp. 124–43 in R. Dasenbrock (ed.) *Literary Theory After Davidson*. University Park: University of Pennsylvania Press, 1993.
15. S. Wheeler, 'Truth conditions, rhetoric and logical form: Davidson and deconstruction.' Pp. 144–59 in R. Dasenbrock (ed.) *op. cit* and D. Davidson. *op. cit.*
16 B. Whiting, *Children of Different Worlds*. Cambridge, MA: Harvard University Press, 1988.
17. See M. Walzer, 'A critique of philosophical conversation.' *The Philosophical Forum*, 21 (1–2) 1989–90, 182–203.
18. A. Wierzbicka, *Cross-Cultural Pragmatics: The Semantics of Human Interaction*. Berlin: Mouton de Gruyter, 1991.
19. e.g. C. Faerch and G. Kasper (eds) *Strategies in Interlanguage Communication*. London: Longman, 1983.
20. See my 'Postmetaphysical discourse and pedagogy.' In P. Atkinson, P. Davis and S. Delamont (eds) *Discourse and Reproduction. Essays in Honour of Basil Bernstein*. New Jersey: Hampton Press, 1995.
21. M. Billig *et al. Ideological Dilemmas*. London: Sage, 1988.

4 Postmodernism and Conversation

In Chapter 1, the twin necessities of intercultural communication and critique were identified. Like all problems which our species has to adapt to, the global problems which create this necessity have been thrust upon us by circumstances — by history. If we are to escape the pull of blind history and begin to gain some sense of direction in our species' affairs we must find some way of solving both problems together. Exaltation of difference may have acted as a circuit breaker, allowing us to move out from under the historical weight of imperialism but it is not enough if we reject belief in the possibility of some essential human nature and universal features of our humanity just to employ this rejection as a stick to beat history with. While remembering the oppressed and repressed may be an appropriate response to the suffering of past generations, it is an insufficient response to their hopes. Perhaps paradoxically, the resources of postmodern thought may be no more valuable than High Modern Marxism as tools for the criticism of modernity.

Certainly, political relevance in a real world cannot be relevance of the kind that High Modernity dreamed of. There can be no political master narrative, whether Marxist or liberal, that provides justification, direction and technical guidance for politically foolproof action. Since the linguistic turn in social theory, politics has been seen to be about the politics of culture, about meaning-action and power first of all over meanings rather than bodies. Of course, bodily power over bodies is still in some sense ultimate, but the organisation of concrete power is linguistic. Bodily coercion requires armies and armies march on their symbols (once their stomachs are full). In the day to day shaping of social life, in the long marches of stable structures of power, bodily power over bodies is secondary.

But power over meanings — meanings which we now recognise are inscribed in our bodies — has material implications. Such power is ontogenetic. It creates cultural realities. These realities are a changing flux

87

rather than a fixed structure, but they are realities nonetheless to those caught up in them. However, it is necessary to be careful not to adopt too textualist an understanding of this ontogenesis. Bodily reality and the facticity of other texts gives us an experience of constraint, of the limited malleability of meanings. We do not experience ourselves as free meaning creators, but as involved in a struggle for the capacity for meaning. While we make meaning, we do not always make our own meaning. Ontogenesis — the making of the form of things — is often better described as meaning making us. In part, this is because meaning-action is not the uttering of meanings in a private language but in a public language. This intersubjective dimension is the source both of constraint on what we can 'say' and is the grounds of any possibility for uttering the new. Ideas of free self-uttering and of constraint must be retheorised if we are to make sense of this. A degree of constraint and lack of autonomy is unavoidable, if we are to utter things in *a language*. The language, and the wider meaning-repertoire of the culture existed before us, lives around us (in others) and will go on after we depart the scene. Autonomy in the old liberal sense is impossible. A fully autonomous person would have no language to speak and no way of life to live.

But relative autonomy does appear possible. Life and language are moving things. They are not static. Nor are they monolithic, they are flawed and ambiguous and the art of dealing with circumstances, whether conceived of on the model of following cultural rules or in some other way, involves adaptation of the resources of the system in innovative ways. The real political question is how do we relate to others in the inter-making of this reality. Do we enhance the space for life, joy, love, and pleasure for all or only for ourselves? To put it another way: Is it possible to have a form of human flourishing to which the oppression of others is *intrinsic* rather than accidental? That is, is oppression of others constitutive of a human good for those who are able to do it? Or does it diminish the oppressor as well as the oppressed, as Hegel tells us in the master/slave dialectic?[1]

The differences among the forms of intersubjectivity are politically crucial for a new politics of culture. Both Foucault and Derrida have recognised this, each in his own way. But each has displayed limitations when it comes to providing an account of the politics of intersubjectivity. Both are surefooted when they follow the tracks of ideology but their feet slip when they try to climb to the higher ground of the ontogenetic conversation in which we may learn to speak our flourishing to each other. Habermas, for his part, has written a great deal about conversation, and, perhaps has said too little about the negative. Davidson, too, has some useful things to say about these questions. In this chapter, we will explore the strengths and weaknesses of various accounts of meaning-action, beginning with Callinicos'[2] Marxist critique of postmodernism. While we may not agree with the positive elements in Callinicos' theory, he is, as a Marxist, in a good position for critique. Marxism at least promised a coherent and balanced theory of how we may make meaning (politics), as well as how we are made by it (history and culture), even if it was a deeply flawed one. Postmodernism appears to have confined itself to the way we are shaped by culture. It is a theory of passivity rather than politics.

However, we will need to do some translating. The issues just identified show up under many different labels. Some theorists, like Callinicos, speak of power, resistance and political action. But these can be parsed as inscriptive agency, active cultural membership (rather than passive), and the politics of ontogenesis. Sometimes writers, such as Foucault, use the 'formation of the subject' to refer to the largely passive process whereby (they believe) individuals have their identities inscribed in them.

Most of the writers we will examine talk of 'freedom'. But talk of freedom, rationality and critique is complex talk indeed. Much talk of freedom boils down to the notion that our species can have a kind of freedom from bodily or mental limitations of any kind whatever. But to speak of a malleable nature within wide limits, is not the same as speaking of a fixed, essential human nature. Freedom must be conceptualised *within* the field of human variability and possibility. Our best guide to the range of this variation is the range it has already taken across human time and space.

Similarly, while we may no longer accept High Modern notions of the rationality of scientific method, or of the complete independence of science, even Marxist dialectical materialism, from cultural and historical limitations, we may reasonably acknowledge the expression within science and elsewhere of a capacity for pragmatic, rational calculation. All human societies display a capacity — a critical capacity — to learn, to identify and reject errors, and to accept innovations that work. Conservative societies differ from those in which innovation is institutionalised only in degree. However, critical capacity, like agency, is hard won, relative and always compromised to some extent. That much we can learn from the post-structuralists.

In the first section of the chapter, the Marxist critique of postmodern views is examined. While the Marxist account of meaning may itself be flawed, its critique of postmodern thinkers consistently accuses them of failing to outline a possible politics. In the next two sections the critique of Foucault and Derrida is extended, but this critique is not total. Much that is of value remains. Richard Bernstein attempts to rescue that which is of value and to relate it to the work of Jurgen Habermas and the early critical theorist Adorno.

In the final section, the limits of a postmodern concern for the local, particular and culturally distinct are probed, and a distinctly postmodern argument which nevertheless connects with critical theory in the manner Bernstein suggests is explored in some detail. In this argument, Niranjani criticises Bhabha and Spivak and moves towards a synthesis of critical theory and postmodernism. The ground on which this synthesis is built is our common recognition in all cultures of hope and love. Hope and love provide the grammar of common meaning on which frail bridges of common purpose may be built.

Callinicos' Marxist Critique of Foucault and Derrida

Callinicos identifies three gaps in postmodern views — in the account of rationality, resistance and the subject. He deals with these for the most part in relation to the views of what are arguably the most influential postmodern thinkers, Foucault and Derrida. I think it is fair to say that Callinicos' reading of these thinkers is unsympathetic and one-sided. He misses much that is valuable, but his criticisms do not lack force for all that.

Callinicos points out that Derrida's theory of meaning is derived from Saussure's. It is an anti-realist theory of meaning, as is most semiotics. The focus of interest in Saussure is on the relation between the signifier (roughly a symbol or word) and a signified (roughly a concept) rather than on the relation between word and object or behaviour. This relationship is called a sign. In this focus it recapitulates phenomenology's bracketing of questions of the existence or non-existence of the objects to which the concept is taken to refer but unlike phenomenology it does not concern itself with the intentional basis of concepts but examines their location in a network of differences among signs. Subsequent structuralists, such as Levi-Strauss,[3] tended to focus on the structure of relation among signifiers and move even further away from the bracketed reality.

Derrida developed Saussure's ideas in two directions, first, in his critique of the idea that meaning derives from the relation of words to experience, the critique of essence or presence, he moved even further away from the possibility of any coherent discussion of the relation between signified and object, bracketing also the relation between signifier and signified (roughly 'concept'). Second, he abandoned the notion of an orderly network of mutually defining signs in favour of an infinite and changeable web of relations of difference and deference among signifiers. He labelled this dual relation *différance* — a combination of the French words for differing and deferring. Put simply, if meaning can only be attained by looking at the relationship of one word to others (e.g. by looking up a dictionary) then you continue deferring the completion of meaning because each looking up leads to more words which, in turn, must be looked up.

Certainly, the simple view of words as a representation of mental objects or concepts, either Lockean sensations of objects or perceptions of experiences of some kind, has many problems. Some of these have been mentioned in earlier discussions of Davidson's views. Similarly, the notion that language consists of a grammar for articulating a set of words-for-objects which are as independent of each other as the concepts (and objects) they name — semantic atomism — also has many problems. To some extent this is a difficulty for Derrida himself, to the extent that he follows the semiological pattern of analysis which tends to be the analysis of individual signs rather than whole texts.

However, as developments in the theory of meaning which Habermas draws upon have shown, it is possible to accommodate a non-atomistic (holistic) theory of meaning, and, indeed, a pragmatist-realist theory of meaning, without falling into the problem of either a metaphysics of presence or empiricism, as Habermas' appropriation of Davidson shows.[4] This is accomplished by a validity-conditional semantics which is socially anchored in dialogue or discourse. In its more fully developed form, this pragmatist-realist theory of meaning is more holistic than Derrida's, since it locates meaning more firmly in a context of human social creativity and history, rather than detaching it so that, in some hands at least we seem to be dealing with an infinite network of signifiers. In this it meets Foucault's objections[5] to Derrida's grammatology as a form of analysis unanchored in history and context. However, it is still consistent with a non-reifying (or non-essentialist) view of human possibility in which there is no reliance on the notion of a fixed 'essence' of humanity, but an open-ended possibility of becoming. For this reason Habermas calls it 'postmetaphysical'.[6] Of course, it is only a theory of meaning. At best it can have a certain plausibility. But faced with the alternatives of a pragmatist-realist theory of meaning, anchored in definite social relations, and Derrida's at times absolutist theory, in which the very possibility of social relations seems to recede, there is clearly little reason, apart from a desire to be thought avant garde, to prefer Derrida's. The pragmatist-realist theory of meaning is discussed further in Chapter 6.

Derrida's 'method' of deconstruction is simply the exploration of the web of signification from some standpoint or other, usually with a purpose of displaying the violence through which meaning is distilled out of the latent differences that define the signification of a text. This may be useful as a method but its use is dubious when attempts are made to inflate it into the whole of methodology. To give him credit, Derrida makes this very point. In a number of places he discusses the limits of deconstruction.[7]

From the standpoint of problems of intercultural understanding, one of the main difficulties with Derrida's formulation is captured by Dews:

> Derrida…is offering us a philosophy of *différance* as the absolute in the manner of Heidegger. While not denying the reality of the world outside text, its knowability is denied. (quoted in Callinicos, p. 77)[8]

But an unknowable world can provide no leverage upon which we can rely to move cultures closer to each other, no 'external-to-culture' basis of interpretation. The fact that Walkmans seem to work for Kalahari 'bushmen' just as well as they work for anyone else tends to give the rather high flown idealism of some of the more absolutist readings of Derrida the lie. While Derrida himself has been at great pains to refute suggestions that he has no account of context, pointing out that its attenuation is a characteristic of metaphysical writing rather than everyday life, the same cannot be said of many interpreters. As we have seen in Chapter 3, the common, concrete knowable world is a resource, up to a point, for overcoming cultural differences.

Foucault's approach presents a different set of problems for any account of social relations. Like textualist readings of Derrida and like functionalist social theory, it too seems to have no logical space for an account of social change or ontogeny. But unlike Derrida, Foucault tends to solipsism — a solipsism at the level of social orders of power or, for that matter, cultural orders of power, each of which has its own truth regime, incommensurable with the truth regimes of other orders of power/knowledge. (The habit of creating portmanteau words appears as confirmed among post-anythings as it is among the inhabitants of Wonderland.):

> It seems to me that power is 'always already there', that one is never 'outside' it, that there are no 'margins' for those who break with the system to gambol in. (Foucault, *Power/Knowledge*, p. 85 quoted in Callinicos, p. 83)[9]

What is at stake in all this is the simple possibility of action. True, the intolerant imposition of theoretical dogmas, whether by a Church Absolute, or the Communist Party or even the self-confident Victorian colonialists in their Indian Raj, has marred European history. (More will be said about colonial distortions in a later chapter.) But the possibility of action against these excesses rests on a humane and tolerant, dare I say humble, but still rational hope, not upon a relativism or a scepticism run wild. The latter can guide no action. It is recipe for acquiescence or withdrawal, as we will see below.

Foucault

As Charles Taylor[10] shows, Foucault's method is often more interesting than his analysis. His analysis of discursive regimes of power/knowledge provides useful *distopias* — negative utopias — but they are very suspect if taken as sociological descriptions. Their value lies in the mechanisms and connections they reveal, not in their reality disclosing power. They are relatively static 'thought experiments'. Although drawn from history, they are virtually silent about the processes of historical change.

Foucault's critique, as Nancy Fraser[11] also agrees, is a critique of modern humanitarianism. But unlike other critics, who find both gains and losses in the shift from, say, the public torture and slaughtering of criminals to the modern penal institution, with its psychologists and rehabilitation programs, Foucault seems to find no good in it. In such matters

> Ultimately, as is well-known, he wants to take a stance of neutrality. (Taylor, 1984, p. 156)[12]

This involves reading the modern, humanitarian system as just another system of domination:

> The picture is drawn, in both *Surveiller et punir* and Volume 1 of *Histoire de la sexualité*, of a constellation combining modern humanitarianism, the new social sciences, and the new disciplines [such as psychology, social work, and teaching] which develop in armies, schools, and hospitals in the eighteenth century, all seen as the formation of new modes of domination. (Taylor, 1984, p. 157)

The shift is from the public exercise of power and the great gap between ruler and subjects to a process of universal surveillance and socialisation, in which public space disappears into computerised data banks and cradle-to-the-grave internalisation of the values called forth by the system:

> The new technology brings about the modern individual as an objective of control. The being who is thus examined, measured, categorised, made the target of policies of normalisation, is the one whom we have to define as the modern individual. (Taylor, 1984, p. 158)

In the new system of domination it no longer makes sense to think of power as the capacity of some individual or groups to get others to do as they are told whether they like it or not. The new power is productive of order from within the subjectivity of the modern person, but it is not imposed by another subject. It is not interpersonal power but an unnoticed effect of a system whose overt aim is to give everyone a better life. This is, if you like, the negative side of Hannah Arendt's positive conception of power — the opposite of the power of solidarity against oppression. It is a useful adjunct to the critique of culture because it goes beyond culture and those struggles that participants recognise in terms of the culture's categories. The connection between this account and Habermas' discussion of the colonisation of the lifeworld will be explored further in Chapter 6.

But apart from its distopian excess, Foucault's critique here can't easily be seen as an *internal* critique of modernity. If it could be seen in this way, his speaking location would be within the culture as a critic of its dominant themes and classes. This *was* the position of the Frankfurt School thinkers, who produced a similar analysis. Following Schiller, they argued that a mistaken understanding of the relation between humankind and nature involving an attitude of domination, rather than respect, would sooner or later spill over into human–human relationships. An instrumental paradigm of reason led to the instrumental management of human affairs, insofar as there was an attempt, through social work, psychology, sociology etc. to manage these rationally:

> Seen in this way, Foucault offers the Frankfurt school an account of the inner connection between the domination of nature and the domination of man [sic] which is rather more detailed and more convincing than what they came up with themselves. It is a measure of the great richness of his work that this 'gift' is not at all part of his intentions. On the contrary, Foucault will have nothing to do with this romantic-derived view of the oppression of nature and our 'liberation' from it... This seems ultimately to be a matter of his Nietzschean refusal of the notion of truth as having any meaning outside a given order of power. (Taylor, 1984, p. 160)

The notion of liberation (or emancipation) seems to centre on some sort of tension between our own nature or potential and the actual state of affairs brought about by society and culture. A central theme of the modern project of liberation has been the theme of sexual liberation — freedom from culturally derived 'repression' of our authentic sexuality. But Foucault regards the notion that we have 'a nature' as a deep illusion. Many would agree. He also rejects the idea that we can uncover it through psychoanalytic methods or socio-cultural change. But he rejects both an essentialist reading of it as 'a nature' *and* a plastic reading of it as a range of possibilities in which some are better than others. All such ideas of better or worse are part of the new means of domination, or, at least, Foucault does not make it clear how they can escape implication in power/knowledge. It is here that we may wish to part company with him. As a pragmatist, I am committed to the possibility of a middle road. There is an internal connection between the way power is realised at the system level in a society and the way one class or group exerts power over other groups within a society. The cultural features that make pastoral and governmental power possible also underpin the class structure of society. The connection between power and knowledge is not mediated solely by the cultural connection and by institutional links, but by old-fashioned connections between the 1% who own 90% of the wealth and the large 'middle class' of knowledge workers whose power/knowledge is so important to Foucault. In a way, Foucault's error is a common one for French intellectuals and those who read them. He overestimated the power of the knowledge class to which he belongs and inflated its characteristic mode of domination. (Nevertheless, his account of institutions of the expert culture is revelatory.)

And, as Taylor rightly points out, such a wholesale repudiation of the modern project of liberation '...approaches absurdity', whatever insights it may contain into the way in which the themes of liberation can sometimes become oppressive. Its absurdity rests on a holistic, even totalistic and one-sided logic of analysis which, as Callinicos points out, can be seen clearly when we examine the relationships between culture, power, resistance, subjects and truth in Foucault's work.

For Foucault, history is not a product of the strategies of subjects but of the impersonal growth and development of contexts. In a way, Foucault's work can be read as the notion of unintended consequences of human actions extended to systematic, even paranoid absurdity. Foucault holds that the pattern created by these consequences is not the product of any class, but he still wishes to see it as a pattern of domination. He seems to accept the view that individual actors act in terms of their projects, but provides no account of the concatenation of their actions with the patterns he describes.

Charles Taylor again: '...much is made of the discovery...that any act requires a background language (culture) of institutions and practices to make sense' (p. 173), but there is no account of the way in which the problems of acting within a culture feed back to culture change.

> ...we can question whether we ought to speak of a priority of language over act. There is a circular relation. Structures of action or languages are only maintained by being renewed constantly in action/speech.

And it is in action/speech that they also fail to be maintained, that they are altered. This is a crashing truism that the fog emanating from Paris in recent decades makes it necessary to clutch at as a beacon in the darkness (Taylor, 1984, p. 173)

What Foucault[13] is arguing is that culture as a text is constituted by practices (discursive formations), and that in turn, it constitutes the subjects of culture, not only as participants in, say, a status displaying Balinese cock fight but also as participants in a modern society that needs and uses up great quantities of power/knowledge:

> ...we are forced to produce the truth of power that our society demands, of which it has need, in order to function: we *must* speak the truth; we are constrained or condemned to confess or discover the truth. In the last analysis we must produce truth as we must produce wealth... (Foucault, *Power/Knowledge*, p. 93)

In his mature work, Foucault redescribed his purpose as the study of the way our culture produces 'the subject' rather than the study of power itself,[14] but, notoriously, he provides no account of the way the particular subject, Michel Foucault, is produced in such a way as to be able to speak something other than the power/knowledge our culture calls 'truth'. This omission is not simply a reflexive one. It is a general omission or underplaying of the oppositionary or resistance culture (s) of European societies. Foucault himself stands in the position of a member of this 'critical' culture within culture, yet there is no real room in his account for it, only a kind of residue of resistance and escape from power which is 'local' and 'subjugated'.[15] This is the same over-determined conception of social life which we found in the work of Geertz. In it, the possibility of intercultural understanding is submerged because there seems little possibility of an interlocutor from such a procrustean situation being in any sense a subject-open-to-learning from another culture or in possession of any degree of autonomy of judgement which could be a resource for understanding another culture. For to possess such a capacity would imply the possibility of a kind of awareness of one's own culture that bespeaks a subjectivity at least partly autonomous with respect to it and the possibility of agency, even critical agency. There is little sense of this when the individual, as such, is seen as a product of a power/knowledge regime:

> The individual is not a pre-given entity which is seized on in the exercise of power. The individual, with his identity and characteristics, is the product of a relation of power exercised over bodies, multiplicities, movements, desires, forces. (*Power/Knowledge*, pp. 73–4)

If we are to rescue the possibility of intercultural understanding and communication we must rescue subjectivity from the overdetermined understanding of it at the same time as we rescue the concept of culture from the totalistic or over-homogeneous understanding of it. We must also assert, contra some interpretations of Wittgenstein, that no two language games are totally incommensurable with each other; it is a matter of degree.

As Charles Taylor points out:

> ...the idea of a manufactured or imposed 'truth' inescapably slips the word into inverted commas, and opens a space of a truth-outside-quotes, the kind of truth, for instance, which (Foucault's) sentences unmasking power manifest, or which the sentences expounding 'a general theory of regime relativity (of truth) themselves manifest (a paradox). (Taylor, 1984, p. 178)

The overgeneralised or total character of Foucault's (and the middle Geertz's) argument creates a false incommensurability:

> Because of relativity, transformation from one regime (of power/knowledge) to another cannot be a *gain* in truth or freedom, because each is redefined in the new context. They are incomparable. And because of the Nietzschean notion of truth imposed by a regime of power, Foucault cannot envisage liberating transformations *within* a regime...' (Taylor, 1984, p. 178).

We can also recognise that what is said here of a regime of power/knowledge can be said (indeed *is* said) of cultures. It would be said that cultures cannot improve or 'progress' by transformation (i.e. into a better culture) because any criteria of progress are culture specific. Not only that, cultures are seen to be so self-bound, so absent of any internal agency, that it is difficult to see *how* they might evolve into a better form of themselves.

Taylor argues that this combination of monolithic analysis and relativism is unfruitful. We need to admit of the possibility of gradual change — movement towards greater freedom or greater truth — but this implies that '...the form before and the form after the change cannot be seen as incommensurable universes' (p. 180).

Taylor points to biographical changes such as 'falling in love' or deciding not to take a particular job. The 'before' and 'after' of these are held together by a perception of our continuing 'identity'. He argues that there are comparable processes in history: 'The American revolutionaries called on their compatriots to rise in the name of the liberties which defined their way of life... This claim is always contested... But is it, by its nature unacceptable? Is it always a sham? Foucault would have us believe so' (p. 180–1).

There are discernible gains and losses in our history, and sufficient continuity for some sort of culturally internal weighing up of these, whatever may be said of attempts to make more distant comparisons (e.g. modern America versus Ancient China). Foucault seems to want to stand outside all culture as well as each culture considered individually but does not relativism imply that at least within the continuity of a broad cultural tradition judgement of worth might be possible? And whatever may be said of distant cultures, are there not cultures close enough to our own, with sufficient sharing of subjectivity, to permit some commensurability to be identified (e.g. within the European 'culture-area').

> The reality of history is mixed and messy. The problem is that Foucault tidies it up too much, makes it into a series of hermetically-sealed, monolithic truth-regimes, a picture which is as far from reality as the blandest Whig perspective of smoothly broadening freedom... Foucault's monolithic relativism only seems plausible if one takes the outsider's perspective, the view from Sirius... [But] Questions of truth and freedom can arise for us in the transformation we undergo or project. In short, we have a *history*. (Taylor, p. 182)

Ironically, Foucault's position tends towards the same kind of political privatism as his critic and rival Baudrillard. Such a view can cope with neither the moral requirements of action *in* history nor the political imperatives of minorities and culturally oppressed groups:

> ...withdrawing into the private... (says Baudrillard) ...could well be a *direct defiance of the political*, a form of actively resisting political manipulation. (Baudrillard, *Forget Foucault*, p. 39)[16]

or, an admission of defeat. Even in his final works, Foucault himself offers us little more — that in this privacy we make our lives 'a work of art'. Tell it to the child-workers of the third world!

It is possible to go on to admit that the choices we are presented with in our history, the alternatives, are sometimes sharply sometimes obscurely visible. At their strongest, they resemble the sorts of differences that intercultural understanding faces, as MacIntyre's discussion of the final repudiation of witchcraft beliefs in 17th century Scotland reminds us.

In his final interviews and in his last major work, *The History of Sexuality, Vol.3*,[17] Foucault began to make some acknowledgment of the limitations of his earlier work. When asked about Hannah Arendt's[18] communicative understanding of power as solidarity, he accepted that it represented another form of power and that the avoidance of one-sidedness in communication was essential to critique. When speaking of Greek thought, he found that the Greek classical emphasis on moderation, even in critique, was a desirable emphasis.

The lesson for Foucault, and for us, is this. If we attempt to stand outside a given tradition, or between traditions, in a context-free 'non-context' we run the risk of eventual incoherence. Nevertheless, an intercontext is possible, a liminal position in which communicators recognise that they stand between two possibilities, the past and the future, even if they stand there in the presence of the culturally other in the context of a future which includes him or her. This future cannot be realised through cultural extremism or relativism but only through a moderation characterised by a degree of cultural detachment.

We have already seen in a previous chapter that Geertz felt that the burden of modern anthropology had become — '...to enlarge the possibility of intelligible discourse between people quite different from one another...'.[19] But Geertz does not foreground the mutuality of that project, or the hope we should have *because* of Emawayish's capacity to ask: 'Do they have poetry in France?' and 'Do they have love in France?' If Emawayish could ask such questions, when asked to write down her love songs, it is clear that she was ready to learn about another culture and so, to learn about her own, in a way that would inevitable deepen her own reflective grasp of it. She was already moving into a new context, which her questions both presupposed and constituted — a context of intercultural understanding. In that context, the universality of love would be explored and perhaps demonstrated in its cultural and personal uniquenesses, thus relativising the modern, romantic, European form of it.

Derrida

Derrida's post-structuralism presents a different problem.[20] Derrida, as a number of commentators have noted is a more ambivalent figure than Foucault. As Norris has argued, Derrida has been read infelicitously.[21] Parts of his work on the nature of meaning, speech and writing appear to lead towards an irretrievably local even personal uniqueness of the meaning of the sign in the communicative event. Other emphases, such as the emphasis on the metaphorical and literary character of all genres of speech and writing, even scientific or philosophical writing, seem to reinforce the tendency towards a fragmentation of meaning, in that they undermine the universal, supra-regional intention of philosophical discourse. Yet elsewhere, Derrida appears (ambivalently) to defend the genre distinction, at least at the level of intention or project. Derrida, too, seems to seek to adopt a writing position that is simultaneously *inside* a culturally given speaking position and outside it, in some abstract space from which deconstruction becomes possible — a deconstruction that in some sense knows no cultural boundaries.

Derrida's ambiguity is attested by the variant readings which informed scholars have made of his work. Gasché[22] reads it as a radicalisation of Kant, but still a part of the enlightenment project. He takes seriously Derrida's protestations in the essay 'Of an Apocalyptic Tone Recently Adopted in Philosophy',[23] that the use of deconstruction in purely negative ways leads to '...a poetic perversion of philosophy'. In this essay, Derrida continues his critique of Foucault, amplifying earlier remarks[24] in which he accused Foucault of adopting the form of argument while denying the force of argument. He accuses those who would entirely abandon the genre distinction between Philosophy and Literature (rather than recognise the interplay between metaphor and argument in philosophical discussion) of 'overloading' their 'argument' with an apocalyptic tone raised to such a pitch that the possibility of rational discourse is abandoned. With Foucault, and American philosophical compradors in mind, so Norris argues,[25] Derrida paraphrases Kant to say '...They do not distinguish between pure speculative reason and pure practical reason; they believe they *know* what is solely *thinkable* and reach through feeling alone the universal laws of practical reason...',[26] seeking through the (Norris now) '...*performative* power...of an oracular, 'inspired' or prophetic style of speech...'[27] to overturn rational argument altogether.

Rorty,[28] among others, reads another Derrida. His reading is inspired by the Derrida who at times seems to wish to end philosophy altogether. It is this Derrida that Habermas appears to pit himself against. As Norris shows, in an even handed discussion,

> ...it is unfortunate that Habermas takes his bearings...from a wide-spread but none the less fallacious idea of how deconstruction relates to other symptoms of the so-called 'postmodern condition'. What Derrida gives us to read is *not* philosophy's undoing at the hands of literature but a literature that meets the challenge of philosophy in every aspect of its argument, form and style. (Norris, p. 445)[29]

It is against the Rortyan reading of Derrida, and those who follow it, that the present argument is directed. It is beside the point to note there that Habermas' reading of Derrida is also influenced by his discussions with Rorty, with the consequence that some of his early critique of Derrida was wide of the mark. However, it is not at all sure that Norris' attempt to rescue Derrida's rationality from the frenzy of the avant gardeism of his English-speaking fans has been successful. Foucault makes the point that

Derrida tends to grant some kind of autonomy to texts, setting them quite apart from the social practices that gave rise to them, including the texts produced by deconstruction itself. Derrida's late reassertion of the limits of his critique must weigh against the implications of the performatory dimension of earlier works, such as *La Carte Postale*.[30] This separation from history is a concomitant of Derrida's essentially anti-epistemological method of deconstruction — his focus on the impossibility of texts representing the world, through an analysis of the intertextuality of meaning. Because of this, the referential and communicative functions of texts drop into the background. Thus Derrida's hyper-contextualism led him to a trivialisation of the idea of truth and of the role of concrete contexts of discourse in favour of an ever multiplying set of possible webs of meaning, becoming, ultimately as numerous as possible interpreters (or deconstructors!). When Derrida discusses intercultural communication, which he does largely under the rubric of translation,[31] his exaggerations of the ways in which language escapes context and history, lead to a thinning out of the possibility of any understanding between interlocutors. The absolute conception of understanding is like the absolute conception of truth — a straw man (sic). If we set our sights higher than a pragmatically judged 'working understanding' about which we can construct warrants of some kind we are asking for something that members of a single family cannot have. If we implicitly focus our critique on such a target, it makes great negation but it creates a kind of mirror image of Sartre's 'bad faith' — in which the impossibility of identity has the same freezing effect as the complete reification of it.

Derrida's own speaking position is relentlessly abstract and appears at times to address all texts and *all cultures* indifferently. The semiotics he produces is clearly intended to be a universal semiotics. All signs are said to mean by virtue of the set of their systematic differences with other signs and in a way biased by power/difference. All texts are said to be interpretable only in a web of relations with other texts, previous texts, contemporary texts, other sections of the text in question etc. Up to a point, this is a 'natural' development of semiotics, and does not differ greatly from conclusions reached more prosaically by other semioticians and linguists, except insofar as it tends to treat all contexts as equally valent and all readings as equally probable and fails to fully theorise the concrete context of situation, due in part, perhaps, to Derrida's emphasis on writing rather than speech.

When applied by many 'Derrideans' to the process of interpretation, this abstract position produces a curious *inversion of concreteness*. The unique position of each interpreter, the essential arbitrariness of interpretation, and the uniqueness of the web of signification for each interpreter tends to relativise interpretation in a way that makes the notion of actually 'understanding' someone else seem highly improbable and abstract. One may begin to wonder why anyone would bother writing or speaking.

In the political domain, where we all must act or abstain, Derrida's relativism seems to distil a morally dubious preference for abstention. As Callinicos points out, Derrida, in a discussion of an exhibition of anti-apartheid art, seemed to take the view that it was useless to attempt to respond to apartheid with a political program or strategy.[32] When all is text, and all genres are collapsed, there is no distinction between politics, philosophy and fiction. We reduce life, or rather our capacity to act knowingly in it, to an aesthethicisation of ourselves and our lives considered as texts. Derrida's own political activism does not rescue his theory however much it attests to his integrity and courage. Indeed, Derrida makes a point of denying any connection between his work and political strategy. Answering political questions is '…incommensurate with my intellectual project.'

Perhaps a more sympathetic reading of Derrida might rescue him from these difficulties. Hoy attempts one.[33] In doing so, his reading of Derrida brings him closer to Habermas than Rorty's does:

> Deconstruction is best construed, I believe, by suggesting that theories must always be on their guard against themselves, since they may close off themselves from possibilities to which they should be open… The deconstructive operation puts…quotation marks around the theory in question by suspending the application of the theory and interrogating it instead. (Hoy, p. 451)

Hoy also argues that Derrida limited deconstruction to 'metaphysical texts' such as social theories:

> Deconstruction is not thereby claiming to be able to dissolve all texts, for instance, non-metaphysical ones. Radical deconstructionists might believe that all texts are metaphysical, but I do not know how they could argue that. (Hoy, p. 458)

Bernstein's Rescue of Treasures from the Wreckage

But Hoy's reading of Derrida makes one ask in what sense, apart from the focus on texts in social isolation which Foucault deplores, and a penchant for decoding metaphors, could deconstruction be said to differ from Adorno's notion of 'immanent critique'? This is a part-theme for R.J. Bernstein's[34] analysis of the relationship between critical theory and post-structuralist thought. And, as we will see below, it is also Benjamin's theme. Bernstein's work may be characterised as an attempt to reconcile critical theory and postmodern thought *from the critical theory side.*

Bernstein construes the debate as hinging on the problem of critique. It is a common ground between the two 'traditions' that at any given historical time the available thought and theory will be imperfect and in some sense characteristic of its age. Albeit the theory and social institutions of our time may have advantages compared with a previous age, they are not thereby rendered pristine. They do not represent the end of ideology, of the contamination of theory and practice by power, or the end of the practice of ideology via false universalism or false naturalism.

In this regard, Adorno[35] argues, the aesthetic dimension of life represents a drive for autonomy. Aesthetic ideas are able to express a provincialism — a unique and located complex of sensibility — to oppose to the neutrality and abstraction of universe-claiming theory.

Bernstein argues that the post-structuralist enterprise produces a set of 'concepts' which are non-concepts — permanent contradictions, named paradoxes — such as Foucault's power/knowledge or dispositifs (as social, embodied, concrete, power/knowledge formations) or Derrida's *différance.* These have the effect of always localising discourse and forcing us to 'work through' the relation between the universal and the particular in our discourse. Thus they have an essentially aesthetic and performatory role.

However I go beyond Bernstein when I say that what is at stake here is a hidden absolute which is at the same time a particular rather than a universal absolute. It is my personal preference to read the post-structuralist enterprise as a protest against the relativisation of the individual in the name of determining social theory — an assertion, however cryptically, of the irreducible uniqueness *and value* of each specific human being. That is, to read it humanistically. Unlike many observers, then, such as Nancy Fraser, I would assert that the only way to make sense of, say, Foucault's apparent attack on humanism and humanitarianism is to recognise that he is attacking the prevailing theoretical and conceptual bases of these attitudes because they *fail* to safeguard the integrity of the unique and absolute value that is intrinsic to each intelligent being. Humanism is attacked because it fails, in its present form, to preserve and defend that which it purports to safeguard — the possibility of genuine agency.

But post-structuralists are far from being the only ones who have concerned themselves with '...local reason and rationality, sensuous particularity (non-identity [of concept and object], alterity, otherness, the body), and judgement' as Bernstein puts it.[36] In his later work Habermas recognised the limitations of the specific areas or islands of rational discourse created within Western modernity, even in their critically reformed, dialogic version within his own theory of communicative action. Recognition of the discursive character of rationality provides no easy road to reconciliation of the various areas of rationality — no automatic connection between, say, on the hand, science and means/ends rationality and, on the other, political/ethical rationality. For this, judgement had to enter in, and particularity.

But Habermas' recognition of the elements which, arguably, some radical followers of postmodernism have elevated to a series of fetishes, was not without precedent. Before him, Adorno had developed a conception of critique in which it was advocated that philosophy should concern itself with '...nonconceptuality, individuality, and particularity...'[37]

Adorno recognised, before Derrida, '...the determinable flaw in every concept [that] makes it necessary to cite others...' (Bernstein, p. 53) and that philosophy rested, in part, on the construction of what he called 'compostions', complex 'constellations' of the general and the particular, whose construction was an art unsupported by logic or foundational evidence, resulting in a philosophy to be judged only on '...the consistency of its performance, the density of its texture...' (p. 35).

However, Adorno also recognised that, however localised and unique philosophical texts were, in their historical and cultural particularity they made *claims* which depended on the possibility of universal validity. Thus philosophy is always suspended in historical and intercultural 'becoming' that is simultaneously a moment in the overcoming of philosophy's own finitude.

Bernstein argues that, while Habermas doesn't pay sufficient attention to this paradoxical connection, he is right in saying that communication, like all action, presupposes an overcoming of particularity and that one of the necessary forms of critique, the particularly modern form of critique, has been to burst asunder all provincialisms with their restrictions and silencings.

Bernstein concludes by paraphrasing Kant:

> ...faith, love, judgement without universality is blind; universality without love and recognition is empty. This statement is not the prelude to a philosophical synthesis, but the recognition of the fate of subject and substance in modernity. (Bernstein, *New Constellation*, p. 232)

Perhaps Bernstein is reaching here for the same kind of reconstitution of humanism as I suggested Foucault may have intended. If so, it may be difficult to avoid the view that we need to recognise, with Raymond Gaita,[38]

that there is something profoundly wrong with the current terms of debate
in political and ethical philosophy. It certainly brings us again to the brink
of views of the human person which evoke a metaphysics long in disfavour
with modern philosophers.

Our Common Humanity in Hope and Love

Gaita argues that Bernard Williams[39] has misunderstood the nature of
human love when he seeks to characterise it (i.e. to show in which sense
one particular love is like another and so able to be conceptualised precisely
as an instance of love in general) in terms of the presence of a certain kind
of relationship between persons, even if this is not the kind of relationship
that some think it is. Williams is rejecting the view that to love someone
necessitates finding in them traits of personality and character which we
generally recognise as good and desirable (even if that is not a *sufficient*
reason for or cause of our love for them). He argues that we might well
admire and value these in the one loved without having a general
commitment to them, or even a personal one. In other words, you don't
have to be an honest person or even an admirer of honesty in general, to
love another because of their honesty etc. Gaita argues that this attempt to
reject universal categories misses something essential and so fails to
safeguard the very thing it seeks to preserve against the damage the critique
of universalism can do — the possibility of the ethical.

In Gaita's view this is a misidentification of that which is necessarily
present in loving another. The focus should be on how a person '...has to
see his (sic) beloved in order for her to be an intelligible object of his love'
(p. 157). Gaita goes on to say:

> She is an intelligible object of his love only if he sees her as subject to
> the requirements of love, the claims which are internal to our sense of
> what counts as real love and what merely appears as love... To love
> someone is to be unable to tolerate the thought that one day we might
> be entirely indifferent to what should happen to them. Exactly that
> happens often enough, but it is condemned as much by love as it is by
> morality... (*Good and Evil*, p. 157)

What is as stake here is, if you like, a basic ontological commitment
concerning particular persons. Gaita makes the same point about the kind
of remorse a murderer might feel. One dimension of this remorse has
nothing to do with the fact that the murderer may have broken a rule or
commandment or killed a 'human being' — it has to do with the particular
loss of *this* person, and the irretrievability of their particular 'window on
the world'. The same is true of the loss of species or cultures. Conversely,

a recognition of the character of loss and its possibility with regard to each and every person permits us to reconnect real meaning with the formerly empty rule. Much the same might be said about compassion. When we hear of a disaster on the other side of the world in which many have died, it may touch us only lightly; even the images of dead children sometimes awaken only an abstract compassion. Unless, that is, we bring to mind that *this* child was the particular apple of *this* mother's eye, played with *these* sisters and brothers, in the unique and intimate events of that family's important and humdrum days — until disaster broke the bonds. To put it another way, we need both universal and particular elements in our understanding. If we remain fixed in the particularity of our love, we cannot talk intelligibly about love at all. But if we lose sight of particularity, our generalisations, which are ultimately tools with which we move from site to site on our world, lose their force.

Particularity has many dimensions, and is philosophically little explored. But it complements rather than displaces more general thinking. Far from being antihumanistic it is the essence of humanism. Far from being antithetical to universality, it is logically necessary to universalist talk. Gaita explores many examples of the grammar of particularity, of which one more must suffice. In a moving discussion of just what we can say when we say that a pregnant woman 'loves her unborn child', Gaita exposes a part of the grammar of what he calls 'the language of love':

> We love what is precious to us and things are precious to us because we love them. The contrast between inventing or making and discovering cannot be applied...here. (p. 125)

The contrast between the particular and the universal is of the same order.

But we cannot explore this further unless we are part of a living culture in which we are able to learn our identity through a cultural conversation in which a grammar, or set of general terms, is available in which we can talk of our own identity as possibility.

Reconciliation from the Postmodern Side: Postcolonial Conversations

These concerns are also somewhat tortuously honoured in Tejaswini Niranjana's analysis of translation and colonialism.[40] Niranjana develops her argument partly as an expression of post structuralist ideas and partly as a critique of them. Post-structuralism's relation to materialist historicism is problematised through a discussion of the critical theorist Benjamin's conception of history.[41]

One of the key themes of this aspect of the analysis is Bhabha's[42] notion of 'hybridity'. In Bhabha's view, the basic ambivalence of colonial power, its valorisation of the master culture and its need of an understanding of the subaltern culture, actually produces the conditions for its own demise. That is why the better the colonial administrator, the greater the danger of 'going native'. The result of this hybridity is what Niranjana calls 'living in translation' — a process of change in which we are carried beyond *both* colonial and oppositionary cultures, towards a new, liminal zone. This process, however, stops short of a global homogenisation of cultures. Such a globalisation could only be based on a new essentialism. Niranjana's analysis seeks to find its way between essentialising colonial and subaltern cultures and total global cultural convergence.

Before further exploring Niranjana's argument, it is necessary to make a number of points about the limitations of Bhabha's work, which it is fair to say epitomises a textualised post-structural analysis of post-colonial situations.

Bhaba's analysis of cultural difference emphasises the 'incommensurability' of cultures rather than exploring the possibility of common ground. It is no doubt true to say that nations and people are constructed:

> The people are not simply historical events or parts of a patriotic body politic. They are also a complex rhetorical strategy of social reference where the claim to be representative provokes a crisis within the process of signification...' (Bhabha, *Nation and Narration*, p. 297)

But it is a mistake to go on to lose sight of the 'not simply historical' and 'they are also... a rhetorical strategy' and follow an analytic strategy which amounts to taking the further step to 'simply not historical' and 'they simply are a rhetorical strategy'.

While it is easy to agree with Bhabha about the constructedness of life, and the ambiguities and contradictions built into it by the effects of the politics under which construction takes place, it is necessary to avoid losing sight of the fact that, like all construction, the element of free play is subject to the law-like limitations of the materials we work with. These materials are given by history and place. Much is made of these when anti-universalist arguments are being propounded but they vanish from the analysis when a certain anchoredness and cultural realism is required.

We may wish to move well away from constructions of nation, culture, even personal subjects as unproblematic harmonious identities but still not agree with Bhabha's statement that: 'In erasing the harmonious totalities of culture [with a capital C], cultural difference articulates the difference between representations of social life without surmounting the space of incommensurable meanings and judgements that are produced within the process of transcultural negotiation.' (Bhabha, *Nation and Narration*, p. 312)

The term 'incommensurability' is borrowed from the post-Kuhnian debate about communication among proponents of different scientific paradigms. Perhaps we would wish to give the same answer to those who see incommensurability everywhere as was eventually given to Kuhn: somehow, people manage to overcome it. As we will see in a later chapter, MacIntyre's Aristotelian discussion provides a relatively straightforward account of this.

Bhabha says much about cultural difference that is insightful. There is always a 'loss of meaning' when we confront another culture: 'Culture difference emerges from the borderline moment of translation that Benjamin describes as the 'foreignness of languages' (Bhabha, *Nation and Narration*, p. 314).

Of course, we can argue that 'the transfer of meaning can never be total between differential systems of meaning...' (Bhabha, *Nation and Narration*, p. 314), but we need not go on to speak of this as Bhabha does on the next page in terms of '...incommensurable differences...' (Bhabha, *Nation and Narration*, p. 315).

The poignancy of misunderstanding, of never completely understanding, is not something confined to intercultural settings. It is a constant of the human condition. We can agree with Bhabha that High Modernity hubristically overlooked this or pushed it aside. The arrogance of colonial power also always seeks to do this.

But Bhabha also, ultimately, recognises the limits of incommensurability. In the closing paragraph of *Nation and Narration*, he recognises we must go beyond suspicion, by giving us Benjamin's intuition that

> ...translation, instead of making itself similar to the meaning of the original, ...must lovingly and in detail, form itself according to the manner of the meaning of the original, to make them *both* recognisable as the broken fragments of the greater language... (cited by Bhabha, *Nation and Narration*, p. 320, from Benjamin's *The Task of the Translator*).

A hermeneutics of hope *begins* here.

Niranjana points out that it is De Man's[43] interpretation of Benjamin's essay on translation, on which Bhabha relies, that has hidden from us the degree to which critical theorists like Benjamin attempted to bridge the gap between history and the free play of textuality. Benjamin tells us that while politics might proceed poetically, poetry is not politics (although it can be political).

Niranjana tells us that we must be aware, with Spivak,[44] that there is a danger in hypostatising discourses as discourse representative *of* and representing colonised cultures. The heterogeneity and ambiguity of all cultures, perhaps particularly colonised cultures, precludes such singleness of voice. But she does not appear to see that in recognising the ambiguity of cultures, the gap between member and culture, and thus between history and culture, is opened up. Whether we call this hybridity or not, what is crucial is to recognise the opportunity presented for active, i.e. authored and political, response to the situation.

The identification of the many distortions of colonial and post-colonial texts — their naturalising of '…timeless, synchronically presented, self-contained societies…' seen in both ethnography and translations — is a strength of post-structuralist critique such as Niranjana's. But the identification of distortions is only part of a viable narrative. We must also identify the positive possibility of the other. Otherwise we have no solution but a cultural version of 'ethnic cleansing'. Translation is both impossible and necessary. The presence of the other presents us with an obligation. 'One of Benjamin's most important comments about translation is that it is a *claim*' (Niranjana, p. 146).

It is true that the circumstances of the claim, the political conditions under which it is made are crucial to its fate. Writing, for instance, dislodges such claims from their context, as Derrida tells us: 'A written sign carries with it a force of breaking with its context, that is, a set of presences which organise the moment of its inscription. This force of breaking is not an accidental predicate, but the very structure of the written'.[45]

But this quality of writing is not absolute. Texts comment on the circumstances of their creation and carry the seeds of the construction of a new set of presences within themselves. This can never be a simple reconstruction; it is also an opportunity for new construction. But in this, writing differs only in degree from speech.

The fact that colonial translation is also in some sense mistranslation or disruption should not surprise. What emerges, as Niranjana ably shows, is rather like materialist historiography, in which concerns of the present organise the interpretation of the past and the best that can be hoped for, as a liberal hermeneuticist might say, is a fusion of horizons. Under different political conditions, post-colonial indigenous elites re-translate the works that colonialism appropriated (and other suppressed works). But this retranslation is also a *claim* — to a different history. As such, it is part of a dialogue. While the rationality of this dialogue may not be the old, objective, linear rationality of 'progress' within an imperially self-assured tradition, it is nevertheless rational in a more complex way.

The same capacity for betrayal/translation that colonialism exploited may be the medium of other claims, too. The relative freedom of texts from contexts has a positive as well as a negative side. Under political conditions which permit many voices to be heard, this contextual slippage becomes the ground upon which a new message may be written. Culturally absolute claims dissolve into their own ambiguity because they are broken out of their claim to absolute embeddedness in culture by the separation of text from context. While Derrideans most often point to the problems this causes for universalist claims, they seldom show an equal awareness of the difficulty it presents for relativist views. If no text is fully embedded in context (i.e. its culture), all texts are somewhat culturally detached. All texts present opportunities for going beyond existing cultures. And that is a permanent precondition not only for resistance to colonial cultural domination, but also for intercultural understanding. This may be truer of writing than of speech, but it is also truer of some speech than other speech. It depends on the relationship of the text to the context. Hybridity is only the first stage in the ontogenesis of new culture. When that ontogenesis is made the focus of our metatheoretical attention, as we shall see in subsequent chapters, it provides a new theoretical resource for a new praxis of intercultural history — intercultural history as a progressive conversation that cherishes both difference and common ground. Emawayish's questions show how such a conversation might begin.

To ask whether there is poetry and love in France is to begin a discourse which is open to a future beyond the cultural boundaries with which the question begins. Only a future self that lives in a culture which now recognises that there exists *their* poetry as well as *ours* could answer such a question.

Notes

1. F. Hegel, *Philosophy of Right*. Oxford: The Clarendon Press, 1949.
2. A. Callinicos, *Against Postmodernism: A Marxist Critique*. Cambridge: Polity Press, 1989.
3. C. Levi-Strauss, *Structural Anthropology*. New York: Doubleday, 1967.
4. J. Habermas, *The Theory of Communicative Action, Vol. 1*. London: Heinemann Educational Books, 1982, p. 276.
5. See J. Frow, 'Foucault and Derrida.' *Raritan*, 5 (1), 1985, pp. 31–42.
6. J. Habermas, *Post-Metaphysical Thinking*. Cambridge, MA: MIT Press, 1989.
7. e.g. J. Derrida, 'On an apocalyptic tone recently adopted in philosophy.' *Oxford Literary Review*.

8. P. Dews, *Logics of Disintegration: Post-structuralist Thought and the Classics of Critical Theory.* London: Verso, 1987.
9. Foucault, *Power/Knowledge.* Brighton: Harvester, 1980.
10. C. Taylor, 'Foucault on freedom and truth.' *Political Theory,* 12 (2), 1984, pp. 152–83.
11. N. Fraser, 'Michel Foucault: A "Young Conservative"?' *Ethics,* 96 (October), 1985, pp. 165–84.
12. C. Taylor, 1984, p. 156.
13. e.g. M. Foucault, *Madness and Civilization.* New York: Pantheon, 1965; *Discipline and Punish?* New York: Pantheon, 1977; and *Power/Knowledge.* Brighton: Harvester, 1980, p. 93.
14. M. Foucault, *The History of Sexuality, Vol. 3.* Published as *The Care of the Self.* New York: Pantheon, 1986.
15. *Power/Knowledge,* p. 81. See also M. Foucault, 'The political function of the intellectual.' *Radical Philosophy,* 17, 1976, (No. 4), pp. 12–14.
16. F. Baudrillard, *Forget Foucault.* London: Verso, 1985.
17. M. Foucault, *History of Sexuality, Vol. 3.* Published as *The Care of the Self.* New York: Pantheon, 1986.
18. For a discussion of H. Arendt's notion of power see J. Habermas, 'Hannah Arendt's communications concept of power.' *Social Research,* 44 (Spring 1977), pp. 3–24.
19. C. Geertz, *Works and Lives: The Anthropologist as Author.* Stanford: Stanford University Press, 1988, p. 147.
20. See J. Derrida, *Writing and Difference.* Chicago: University of Chicago Press, 1978 and *Of Grammatology.* Baltimore University, John Hopkins Press, 1976.
21. C. Norris, *Derrida.* Cambridge: Harvard University Press, 1987.
22. R. Gasché, *The Taint of the Mirror: Derrida and the Philosophy of Reflection.* Cambridge: Harvard University Press, 1986.
23. J. Derrida, 'On an apocalyptic tone recently adopted in philosophy.' *Oxford Literary Review,* 6 (2) 1984, pp. 3–37.
24. Derrida, 1984: 12 and see also J. Frow, 'Foucault and Derrida.' *Raritan,* 5 (1) 1985, pp. 31–42.
27. C. Norris 'Deconstruction, postmodernism and philosophy: Habermas on Derrida.' *Praxis International,* 8 (4), 1989, pp. 426–46.
26. Derrida, 1984, p. 12.
27. C. Norris, 1989, p. 444.
28. R. Rorty, 'Philosophy as a kind of writing.' In *Consequences of Pragmatism.* London: Harvester, 1982.
29. C. Norris, 1989, p. 445.
30. J. Derrida, *La Carte Postale de Socrate a 'Freud et au-dela'.* Paris: Aubier-Flammarion, 1980.
31. See J. Graham (ed.), *Difference in Translation.* Ithaca: Cornell University Press, 1985.
32. Callincos. *op. cit.*
33. D. Hoy, 'Splitting the difference: Habermas' critique of Derrida.' *Praxis International* 8 (4), 1989, pp. 447–64.
34. R.J. Bernstein, *The New Constellation.* Cambridge: Polity Press, 1991.
35. T. Adorno, *Aesthetic Theory.* London: Routledge and Kegan Paul, 1984.
36. R. Bernstein, *The New Constellation.* London: Polity Press, 1991 and 'The

causality of fate: Modernity and modernism in Habermas.' *Praxis International* 8 (4), 1989, pp. 407–25.

37. J. Adorno, *Negative Dialectics*. New York: Seabury Press, 1973, p. 8, ff.14.

38. R. Gaita, *Good and Evil: An Absolute Conception*. London: Macmillan, 1991.

39. B. Williams, *Ethics and the Limits of Philosophy*. Cambridge: Harvard University Press, 1985.

40. T. Niranjana, *Siting Translation*. Berkeley: University of California Press, 1992.

41. W. Benjamin, 'The task of the translator.' In H. Arendt (ed.), *Illuminations*. New York: Schocken Books, 1969.

42. H. Bhabha, *Nation and Narration*. London: Routledge and Kegan Paul, 1990. Introduction.

43. P. De Man, *The Resistance to Theory*. Minneapolis: University of Minnesota Press, 1986.

44. G. Spivak, *In Other Worlds: Essays in Cultural Politics*. New York: Methuen, 1987.

45. J. Derrida, 'Signature, event, context.' Pp. 75–176 in *Glyph*, Vol. 1. Baltimore: John Hopkins University Press, 1977.

5 The Ideal of Intercultural Learning

Habermas and Rationality

This chapter together with the next presents the core of a critical-pragmatic theory of intercultural communication. A critical-pragmatic theory is one which draws on the pragmatist approach of Dewey but adds the specific theory of communicative action of Jurgen Habermas. It is possible to synthesise the two because Habermas' theory is broadly pragmatist in character[1] and Habermas' theory of communication and meaning is a pragmatist one. Similarly, Dewey's theory is a critical theory — a theory of human learning and of the possibility of making fallible but valid human value judgements in the social realm.

It was argued in the previous chapter that a postmodernist view did not provide an adequate theory of human action and communication. It is too negative and communication is positive. Just the same, the systematic scepticism of postmodern thought provides a useful resource for theorising and it is possible to take at least some of Bernstein's or Niranjana's advice and seek to learn from it. As we will see in Chapter 7, Derrida and Foucault provide useful *methodological* resources, too.

In the introduction, I mentioned that Habermas' work has often been misunderstood. There are good reasons for this. His writing is universally considered to be dense and uncompromising. He writes for a particular audience of his philosophical peers and he writes *into* the particular debate going on among them at that time. He also writes in German, and the debates are those going on pretty largely in Germany. Most of us read him in translation and try to relate his ideas to our context. This has resulted in many quite mistaken views of his work. In addition, Habermas is a philosopher who listens to his critics and has evolved and developed his view. Translation delays led in the past to English-speaking critics responding to decades-old views. The detailed discussion which follows aims to set the record straight. However, the questions involved are complex and the reader will have to be patient with me.

Habermas and Rationality

Rationality is just the characteristic of our becoming when our learning activity is untrammelled by power, particularly the power of only one group of stakeholders in a problem situation. Intercultural rationality is just an extension of this idea. There is no methodology of rationality, in the sense that within rationality 'anything goes' methodologically. Or, to put it another way, the methodology of rationality is all apophatic. An apophatic method is negative. It proceeds by identifying and removing obstacles. The obstacles to our adaptation to circumstances are both physical and social. Physical obstacles are familiar enough. They relate to our transformation of the natural world. Social obstacles prevent our using the collective experience and wisdom in our problem solving. They are identifiable as obstacles to participation in the conversation about our flourishing. That participation is essential, because our flourishing is not merely physical flourishing, but cultural and spiritual, in the sense of our lives being given meaning and direction. With Hegel, the critical theorists recognise that lives whose meaning is given by oppressing others cannot be lives which flourish spiritually, however much of material resources they command.

Habermas' philosophical project was centred on the problem of rationality and the possibility of rationality in human affairs. A student of Theodore Adorno, a member of the Frankfurt School, his starting point was a suspicion of the development in European thought of a view of the rational which identified it with science and law-like knowledge formulations. Working within the European philosophical tradition, he tried, through immanent critique[2] to show that European modernity had lost something when it gained scientific universalism. He tried to expand the idea of rationality to include ethical, expressive and even aesthetic dimensions, and to anchor it in the particularity of the historical and communal locatedness of reasoners, while still maintaining that it was a universal human possession.

However, the area of human activity where some sort of rationality had been consistently displayed and 'progress' made over time was in the sciences and technology, so it was to science with all its fits and starts, flaws and failures, that Habermas first looked to try to understand how the conversation of human reason worked. Following Max Weber,[3] he also looked to the institution of formal legal processes as another example of human rationality at work, this time in the regulation of human affairs rather than the understanding and regulation of outer nature. Yet another area was the process of rationalisation of administration through large scale, formal organisational processes — bureaucratisation. It is worth noting that Weber by no means confined this kind of rationality to European cultures, as his study of bureaucracy in Ancient China[4] makes clear. All these forms of rationality were flawed, limited, incompletely rational, but all undeniably more orderly, predictable and explicable than prior historical processes which did similar social and cultural work. All, in their way, made human processes of large scale social coordination amenable to systematic reflection and pragmatic learning processes.

Initially, Habermas' method for studying these processes was the critique of theories of reason and knowledge. His starting point was the self-understandings of scientists and those who studied science, the view of the law of legal theorists, and Weber's view of bureaucracy. He identified contradictions, limitations and gaps in these accounts, finally locating a whole set of human processes generally left out of the picture by previous modern thinkers — the practical dimension, he called it. Just how did scientists manage the day to day business of doing science? How was the institution of the law actually made to work, however imperfectly?

Insofar as bureaucracy solved some of the problems of coordinating human activities on a very large scale, how did it do it at a nuts and bolts level? Surely, all this was done in some sort of intersubjective understanding, mediated by a continuing conversation.

Remember, Habermas like Dewey was interested in *deliberate* 'progress'. This meant that, in human affairs at least, the measure of improvement couldn't be limited to increase in technological efficiency — more energy per capita, higher speed transportation, better diet etc., because such progress couldn't explain *itself*. How was the technological progress possible as deliberate progress? Progress in human affairs also involves, as the Greeks well knew, ethical and political improvements — the elimination of injustices, better lives for people. In the case of the sciences and technology, progress occurred through the spread of freedom of opinion and investigation and economic freedom for commerce to exploit invention. The solving of practical (i.e. ethical/political) problems of this kind — as distinct from technological problems — involved different capacities and processes to those which were typically employed in solving the problems of the physical sciences. This was because ethical and political problems are problems about conduct or action, and about meanings and symbols — ownership, marriage, contracts, agreements, loyalty, betrayal, treaties, insults, status, recognition, friendship and enmity, indeed the *conduct* of science itself — are essentially matters of the bestowing and taking away (Derrida would say, the writing) of significance and of the conduct of human affairs, both material and symbolic in accordance with these significances. For instance, scientific values of truth and openness of inquiry have played an important role in science.

So for Habermas, the study of the ethical/political domain, and indeed of progress in society as well as in science was to be carried out by a different methodology to the studies *within* science. This methodology was that which is appropriate to the study of meanings and their understanding — hermeneutics. Rational practical progress inevitably means improved interpretive or hermeneutic understanding. But it also means more. As Habermas developed his ideas over time, listening closely to his critics and changing his views in the light of criticisms, he decided that his first attempt to formulate an account of rationality was flawed.

That attempt was set out in his well-known *Knowledge and Human Interests.*[5] In that book he went on from his identification of practical/hermeneutic rationality to add a third, separate kind of rationality — critical rationality — on the grounds that hermeneutics only interpreted but didn't *judge* better or worse.

Clearly, for rational progress to be made, some *critical* process of distinguishing between better and worse had to operate. But in his more recent work,[6] he has handled this issue a little differently. The critical process is not a separate different kind of reason to the hermeneutic, so much as something intrinsic to the process of understanding. This was Habermas making the linguistic turn. *In the ordinary course of understanding, we judge better or worse.* The trick is to institutionalise this capacity. This pragmatist theory of meaning — that understanding meaning necessarily involves judgement of validity — is the key to Habermas' theory of human conduct or meaning-action. Despite problems due to the cultural origins of this theory, which will be discussed in the next chapter, it provides the basis for a genuinely critical theory of intercultural communication.

However, before turning to a more detailed examination of Habermas' theory of communication, it is important to gain a clearer idea of something already mentioned above. Talk of solving practical (ethical/political) problems reminds us that communication is not normally an end in itself, although it can be. It is often a means to an end — persuasion, coordination of actions, negotiation, compromise, argument etc. The context in which intercultural communication takes place will often be one where there is a need to coordinate the action of members of different cultures, reach agreements, negotiate, and the like. Because of this, it is possible under certain circumstances, despite culturally different definitions — for the situation itself to exert its own influence on the participants, in a similar way to that in which the obduracy of the material world can exert its influence on proponents of different scientific theories who seek systematically to explore them through experience. In theorising intercultural communication it is important not to forget the concreteness of contexts and the recourse that this gives us in the task of transcending cultural limits. Too great a stress on the world defining or reality creating power of culture would theoretically close off this avenue of reconciliation. That is the realist or empirical dimension discussed in Chapter 3.

For example, when the first Europeans entered the highlands of Papua New Guinea they were perceived almost entirely through the categories of the culture.[7] It was thought that they must be the ghosts of the dead returned. But after they were seen to eat and excrete, this theory was rejected. A new category had to be developed, based on the recognition that here was a new, powerful and different kind of human being. The culture was irretrievably changed from that moment on. Through successive approximations and speculation the theory of the nature of the 'red men'(as they were called) was developed, until it shed most indigenous cultural categories altogether — a true cultural novelty. All genuine intercultural communication will involve great or small changes of this kind, in which experience and concrete circumstances will play a role *in* reality construction. Cultures are normally open to change of this kind. The closure of cultures is usually the product of special political circumstances. Politically driven cultural absolutism is the enemy of intercultural communication. Where cultures are held to be absolute there can be only cultural apartheid or cultural domination. Such absolutism has a sorry history of pogrom, massacre and genocide. We must all be open to change, to learning, even learning from cultures which are *technologically* 'inferior' to our own in some ways.

Habermas argues that rationality is universal. It may be that his concept of rationality still bears some of the marks of its European origin, but the idea of a universal reason and capacity to reason together need not be invalidated by these limitations. Habermas' idea of universal reason is nothing more than a corollary of the rejection of cultural absolutism and the acceptance that members of all cultures can learn, even from each other. Rationality is simply openness to learning. The ultimate guarantee of reason, in Habermas' view, is the expression *within* the reasoning *process* (rather than within the content or results of reason) of the existential interests and experiences of each and every individual, group, class, caste, nation or people. No set principles of logic or method, however useful they may be, is without its one-sidedness and methodological vulnerability in certain contexts. There is no guarantee of reason in methodological considerations, in falsificationism, pragmatism, realism etc. All of the *apparatus* of reason can be 'gone behind', as perennial philosophical disagreement about such questions demonstrates. The guarantee of reason is in the relationship of the reasoners, in their openness to experience and each other, especially across great differences in assumptions and methods. Accordingly, the fact that different cultures may have different methodological norms, and different sets of presuppositions about the world is not necessarily a fatal obstacle — indeed, it is an advantage.

What is at stake here is not the universalistic claims of High Modernity but a subtler, less abstract understanding of human rational capacity. This is not a Cartesian view of the 'method for rightly ordering the sciences', or the gateway to a new *foundation* for knowledge. The anchoring of reason in the learning capacity of human communities of communication also anchors it in the complexity of their cultural and historical circumstances, while still not falling into a relativism which is really simply a pessimism about human learning capacity.

Habermas saw liberal democracies (mostly European in origin) as evidence of a localised example of ethical-political progress. Indeed, Marxist critics, such as Callinicos, have criticised Habermas for being too soft on liberal democracies, and for taking too sanguine a view of them. But Habermas did not see these societies as progressive because of the actual institutions which characterised their political life, but because they had developed a set of institutions, within their cultural limitations, which permitted some degree of open or public will-formation, and thus partial democracy. Such societies were the best hope for further learning, because they were among the most open of societies to learning.

For those who, like Giddens,[8] reject the idea of progress as a chimera of High Modernity, the question must be asked: 'What then can we learn?' If we are to abandon the idea of progress, but retain, however tacitly the idea of possible regress, we might rightly be accused of simple pessimism. But if there is no possibility of progress, how can we act. We are reduced to stoicism or worse, hedonism. It is one thing to abandon High Modernity's Whig history of the world, quite another, and futile, to cease to hope. However, if we are to hope, we need some criterion of better and worse, and that is the rub.

In regard to our way of knowing the physical world it can often be the case that the obduracy of that world, its capacity to be opaque to certain accounts of it while being transparent to others, to 'reject' certain theoretically directed lines of action while bestowing its blessing on other theoretical programs by a kind of cooperation with action based on them, makes the possibility of intellectual progress more comprehensible, in a fallibilist, pragmatic way. Perhaps that is why material technology crosses cultural boundaries so easily.

But with regard to the ethical/political world the picture is very different. We do not know how to theorise in the social world in such a way as to permit the obduracy of the world to adjudicate our differences. The High Modern illusion of methodological guarantees permitted to practitioners of the physical sciences is no longer available to social scientists. In the ethical/political domain we must forego the illusion of making 'objective' ethical/political validity judgments. We must fall back on the experience of individuals and groups of individuals, the ethical/political validity of whose actions is at stake. Anything less runs the risk of substituting ideology for reason. We find both the methodological basis for valid ethical/political reasoning, and the basis of understanding in situated interaction — communicative action — the combination of ethical/political reasoning and interpretation of actions, specifically communicative actions, that is critical hermeneutics. Values are expressions of human interests, not objective or absolute law-like universals. That is, ontologically, valuing is something that humans *do*. There are two possible logical attitudes to values, you can seek to *make* them universal by somehow controlling or shaping interests — the Maoist solution — or you can engage in a process whereby a consensus is reached concerning those interests that logically can be universal, including a universal interest in *tolerance* for diversity of interest beyond the basic areas of agreement needed for living together on this planet. Whether or not it is possible to find a workable core of common interests is ultimately an empirical and historical question. In the meantime, compromises are possible.

Critical Hermeneutics

Perhaps Habermas' most distinctive contribution to hermeneutics is the argument that each time we understand an utterance we make judgement of the validity claims raised by it *as a normal part of understanding what that utterance means*. Properly understood, this contention finds extensive support in philosophical semantics, linguistic pragmatics, and common sense.[9]

From a philosophical point of view we can distinguish several kinds of meaning. Following Davidson, Habermas argues that semantic, grammatical, or dictionary-meaning is the kind of meaning that sentences still have even when we don't know what they really mean, in context. For example, you may be travelling on a train and overhear a sentence: 'It is always good luck.' Now, at one level you understand its 'meaning' — there is something (possibly an event or object or person) which is at all times and in all places 'good luck'. But without knowledge of the whole conversation, and possibly the background to it, the meaning of the utterance remains opaque. What is 'it'? What is meant by 'Good luck'? How extensive is 'always' meant to be? Perhaps the speaker is talking about finding a horseshoe or perhaps about the prosperity of fools.

Propositional meaning is normally seen as the embedded existential or referential significance of the grammatical meaning — there is an 'it' such that at all times and in all places (it will bring) 'good luck'. But as Perry[10] has pointed out, there are two kinds of propositional meaning. That of the proposition expressed *in* an utterance (type 1) and that of the proposition which is expressed *by* uttering that utterance (type 2).

The more we bring the real context of an utterance into the picture the less we are able to rely on the disembodied 'for instances' of philosophy textbooks,[11] which so often limit analysis to semantic and propositional meaning (type 1). After all, real words are spoken in real ways — smoothly, angrily, happily, slyly, sincerely. The utterance/event is not the production of an abstract object — the word — but something more complex. An utterance, in its real context, always has several layers of meaning which appear simultaneously and in a mutually conditioning manner. Even when we abstract the words, the grammatical sentences, from the *way* they were uttered, it is still necessary to deal with meaning-in-context, with the relationship of the words in question to what has been already said, what is anticipated, and with the specific socially defined *situation* in which they are uttered.

Meaning is not a single thing but a manifold. It is a theory, narrative or 'story' in which the various sources of information are taken into account — the words and sentences spoken, the way they are said, what has already been said, what it is anticipated will be said, the socially defined situation and the relevant background beliefs and attitudes of interpreters. No doubt, the feelings of speakers and hearers at the time also play a role in the 'taking into account'. In this way, meaning is something like a mathematical curve, drawn to fit a set of data points. Sometimes it proves difficult to draw such a curve and the failure to do so highlights certain data points as anomalous or 'difficult'. It is when this happens that a 'communication problem' may be said to have arisen. Conversely, as Quine[12] has pointed out, it is always possible *in principle* to draw more than one curve through a finite set of points, although as against that it may be argued that some curves become improbably Byzantine, and any application of Occam's razor would cut them out of consideration. And sometimes the only way the curve may be made to fit the apparent data is for one social category of participants to accept a story which diminishes them and their data or experience in favour of the hegemony of the experience of members of another social category — the conditions which force such acceptance, and the associated communicative practices, are called 'ideology', and the stories told, 'ideological'. But ideology can operate as easily in intercultural relations as in class relations. There we speak or racism or ethnocentrism.

The process of fitting an utterance into a story involves inference. Normally a taken-for-granted process, the inferential process can be uncovered in various ways. Sometimes changed situations bring about a breakdown of meanings which makes the process transparent. It is then we can see that our expectations and assumptions are the basis of tacit processes of inference that normally run at the speed of speech for both hearers and speakers. Normality, indeed, is the stuff of communication. When our taken-for-granted routines for meaning construction fail, communication bogs down. The flow of meaning ceases while time consuming, conscious processes of repair and re-alignment come into play. In the absence of such breakdown we don't notice the meaning making process. Deconstruction which is discussed in detail in Chapter 7 may be seen as a strategy for deliberately bringing about such breakdowns in meaning.

One of the possible sources of breakdown is mismatch between communicative form and expected content. When this occurs you tend to ask questions about what a speaker means. The assumption is that the form of the communication has been mistaken — perhaps a wrong word was used or a word was used wrongly. An instance of this would be the communication problem that arises when someone gets the names of people or things mixed up. They really mean Jack not Joe or London not Sydney. The hearer's recourse, after they experience difficulty in fitting what is said with some of the data could be to say, 'Hey! Don't you mean London?'

Problems of this kind can take many forms, but they can all be summarised in a general way as problems of contradiction between the way the resources of language are used at a particular point and the emerging story of the hearer based on previous linguistic data, the hearer's expectations, background knowledge, etc. What is at stake is the validity of the speaker's coding of an expected (it is assumed 'intended') meaning.

Habermas' view is in broad accordance with a great deal of linguistic pragmatics when he identifies four such areas of validity — areas which situated meaning-making must take into account. The capacity of a speaker to achieve acceptance at all four levels simultaneously is called communicative competence. This must be distinguished from linguistic competence. Linguistic competence is rather narrow. It is the capacity to produce grammatically well-formed utterances in a language — utterances which convey the intended semantic meaning, presumably. But communicative competence additionally involves successfully embedding these utterances:

(1) in relationship to the hearer's perceived reality;
(2) in normatively defined social relationships of speakers and hearers; and
(3) in a constructed and perceived expressive authenticity.[13]

That is, communicative competence is something we attribute to speakers when what they say (and how they say it) matches up with what we believe to be the case, is appropriate to their social relationship with us, and is consistent with the kind of person they present themselves to be. (And is coded in appropriate choice of language).

Communicative problems arise when the propositional or existential implications of what people are saying doesn't match our beliefs about reality, when they speak in a way we think inappropriate, unfair, insulting, or in some way normatively 'wrong', and when they seem insincere, affected or 'phony', or when the way they seem doesn't match our idea of their 'identity'. These problems are a product of our application, in communication, of our critical faculties, which in turn are simply a normal part of the process of making sense of the world and of stories about it. When someone speaks, we automatically interpret the existential implications of their speech. Where other aspects of meaning and context do not provide data to the contrary, these implications can be seen as indicating the believed-in reality of the speaker — his or her 'reality commitment'. When these are expressed in speech addressed to us, they are 'claims' on us. If we accept these expressions of the way reality is, we are assumed to share the same reality commitments. If we do not, we are expected to indicate this in some way. Otherwise, the speaker would quite rightly be able to object. 'Well, you didn't say anything. How was I to know you didn't agree?'

In general, communicative problems arise when the validity claims of speakers lead to difficulty 'drawing the curve', due to inconsistencies between the claims made and our other data. We may recognise that this inconsistency has occurred due to a new claim contradicting old data or we may simply be confused. The latter is common enough when the claim being advanced is a claim to some relationships between the speaker and ourselves other than the normatively appropriate one, but can also occur when existential claims set off complex forms of cognitive dissonance. Such problems can lead to anything from complete incomprehension to a general but free-floating unease. Incomprehension, by the way, is quite possible even though you fully understand the semantic or dictionary meanings of what is said, if at the same time you don't understand why it is being said, because our narratives typically involve 'protagonists', rather than being limited to some narrower or more impoverished ontology.

Judgments about validity are a normal part of understanding meanings. We do not first understand meaning and then make validity judgments, except perhaps in the narrow sense of semantic meaning. But even there, the relevant sense of validity, namely semantic validity, is a necessary part of comprehension.

For instance, when someone uses a word wrongly or uses a word you have not heard before, you may judge its validity, as a selection from the resources of language, to convey the relevant semantic meaning, assuming you have sufficient cues from the internal semantic data of the rest of the utterance to recognise the wrongness or invalidity of the usage in question. In the case of an unfamiliar word in a sentence you may look it up in a dictionary, but that looking up, given sufficient semantic cues from grammatical context, may tell you whether or not the word has been correctly chosen for its semantic role — i.e. whether its use is in accordance with its dictionary meaning or not. Similarly, a part of the meaning of the propositional implications of an utterance is the relationship between the existential validity claim made and relevant aspects of context. A proposition does not *mean* in isolation. It means as the next step in an argument, as 'meant to be' consistent or inconsistent with what has already been claimed, or has been assumed. It means in the light of the existential picture created by the addition of the new proposition to all that have gone before, in the same way as the addition of a brush stroke to a painting means in the light of the new totality that results and not simply as a brush stroke on its own. This systematic quality of validity judgments is what gives a systematic character to meaning and it is why validity judgments are a necessary part of the interpretation of meaning, not an additional element.

When the wandering pinpoint of light that was the first equatorial satellite crossed New Guinea skies the meaning of every constituent element of their culture changed because their whole way of life was now seen as relative to a new understanding of the place of their remote mountain valley in the world. So, too, each piece of incoming information either confirms or changes the existing configuration.

When it confirms what already exists, its systematic quality is more difficult to see; when there is a mismatch, the systematic quality of what is at stake becomes clearer. The example of someone speaking in breach of social norms may make this a little clearer. If someone speaks loudly in a Christian church during, say, the consecration, hearers have a number of choices. It could be inferred that the speaker is unfamiliar with churches and doesn't 'know any better', or it could be inferred that they are deliberately breaking the norm, in which case an intention to insult the pastor or the congregation (or some such) will be attributed to them. That is, the meaning of their action (speech or manner of speaking) is inferred on the basis of first judging their speech to be normatively invalid (that is, on the basis of rejecting the background claim of normative validity which all speech is assumed to make). Then a theory about that invalidity must be constructed.

But, as Habermas has argued, communicative competence is predicated upon successfully embedding an utterance in *simultaneous* relationships to reality, social relationships and expressions of one's own identity. Communicative 'problems' emerge when the claims made fail — when we do not embed our utterance in, say, the accepted view, or our hearer's view, of reality (and so on for the other dimensions of meaning). Such problems are a product of a mismatch between our assumptions about reality, our norms, our sense of self as exposed in our speech and the assumptions etc. of others. What is in conflict here is the beliefs, values and self-image of individuals. The conflict may arise from differences in background, especially cultural differences. Normally, such conflicts are not intended or deliberate. They are unintended consequences of cultural differences between interlocutors.

However when *situations* arise (or are constructed) in which one kind of validity claim is structurally at odds with other kinds of claims, a new and more serious communicative difficulty arises. This level of communication difficulty, may be distinguished from the level discussed above under the label 'problem', by the fact that the means of overcoming it are quite different from the means whereby we might overcome communication problems. When a communication *problem* arises the means of overcoming it is more communication, but communication of a reflexive kind. If our meaning/story construction process begins to break down we say: 'Wait a minute!' and enter into a process of 'sorting out' claims and relationships between claims. In a usage which departs from the norm, Habermas reserves the term 'discourse' for this special 'sorting out talk', which goes beyond or behind everyday norms and assumptions. This is difficult enough, but, in principle at least such problems of communication can be overcome by more *communication* — at least, in monocultural settings. And providing there is no obstacle to discussing differences in assumptions and beliefs, identifying them and tracking down the source of the problem, and so on. But this is not the case for the new, structural difficulties just mentioned. These 'distortions' — for so they may be labelled — cannot ordinarily be overcome by more communication of the same kind because the source of the distortion, the communication situation itself, *politically* prevents such recourse.

Communicative distortion arises when the communicative situation is such that one or more of the four basic kinds of validity claims cannot be resolved in its own right but is tangled up with or subordinated to another kind of validity claim. Most commonly, distortion arises when the claims of social relationships override existential and expressive/identity claims. Put simply, when a relationship of domination and subordination exists, it is common for the view of reality of the dominant individual (or culture) to be seen as definitive. In such situations existential validity questions are not resolved by recourse to the experience and beliefs of both speakers *and* hearers, but by the imposition of the speakers' reality on the hearer. Existential validity questions are subordinated to social relational ones. The communicative expectations of the situation are such that it is not possible to question the existential claims of the dominant party without being in breach of the interpersonal norms of the speech *situation* (as socially and politically defined). At the same time adherence to the norms means an inability to reject existential validity claims made by the dominant party. Much the same distortion can be seen at the level of identity. The subordinate interlocutor is unable to assert his or her authentic identity in situations where this would clash with interpersonal norms and the existential claims of the dominant interlocutor. This sort of situation is familiar to everyone who has ever felt 'tongue-tied' when being unfairly criticised by a superior. Thus distortion creates a new layer of communicative difficulty which cannot be tackled communicatively until the politics of the communicative relationship have been addressed. Communicative *problems* are difficulty enough. They will always be with us as long as there are differences of experience and interest. Communicative distortion adds a new, social structural layer of difficulty, due to socially defined relationships, often power relationships, creating obstacles to communicative problem solving by closing off available avenues of discursive repair of communicative failures.

In such situations, subordinate speakers who try to maintain their integrity by acting in ways they see as validly expressing a proper human relationship with the dominant communicator or allowing themselves to display a reasonably dignified and respected identity, will inevitably be perceived by an unreflective dominant communicator as bad communicators. They will either be seen as lacking in communicative competence, or as being 'stupid', 'rude', 'surly', 'insubordinate' or 'uncooperative', depending on the conceptual justification for the particular ideology of domination in use in the situation. Communicative competence is itself a matter of the 'politics of communication'.

Sometimes such politics are one-off events. They are interpersonal but not simultaneously a fact of social structure. The remedy in such situations can be to break off the relationship. However, when we are looking at intercultural distortion we are more likely to be dealing with institutionalised distortion, where participants find themselves in situations where the definition of the situation, the roles of categories of agents and the nature of the validity claims that are available for negotiation and those that are not have all been determined in advance by forces beyond the control of participants. No matter how much the colonialist may want to befriend the 'native', he must be aware of the strict taboo against 'fraternisation' or 'going native'. This is not something over which he has personal control. Only when the politics change, or under temporary conditions of isolation from the normal sanctions, can Robinson Crusoe treat Man Friday as a friend, and the process of exploring, learning and growing that 'we' think of as developing a friendship get under way. In this process, we can be involved in creating mutual understanding, not simply on our own terms, but through give and take, trial and error, given trust and a perception of goodwill. That is, we can anticipate that which is not yet — a context which is neither of our own culture nor that of the culturally other — an *intercultural context* (ICC). In this context, which is a counterfactual regulative idea that we use as a guide and as a basis for hope, we find new definitions and new roles, through intercultural learning. We may even recognise that it was Man Friday who was helping Crusoe, not the other way around.

Such learning is possible but not necessary. Again, there is a politics, both interpersonal and institutional. Like the notion of 'discourse', the communicative process of constructing an intercultural context of communication requires a politics galvanised by a will to understand and like the meta-talk of discourse, it requires certain skills. Above all, it requires an open attitude to culture, one's own and that of the culturally other, but only certain conceptions of culture permit this.

The Ideal Speech Situation

Communication situations in which interlocutors are free to investigate problems, to bring their own experience and beliefs to the resolution of validity claims, and to engage in further communication to resolve any problems which may arise in the course of solving the first lot of problems have been called Ideal Speech Situations (ISS).[14]

Habermas defines these as situations in which interlocutors must not only be free from external coercion, but must also have an inner freedom. This inner freedom is not only a negative freedom — freedom *from* psychological compulsions — but a positive freedom — freedom *to* entertain new ideas. Freedom of this kind implies an inner detachment from any absolute commitment to the assumptions and values of one's own culture of origin. Indeed, this freedom is one of the characteristics mentioned earlier under the label 'intercultural communication context' (ICC) . At a minimum, communicative understanding between members of different cultures would seem to require an awareness that one *is* a member of a culture, that it is only one culture, and that there are other cultures in which things may be seen differently *plus* the hope that this understanding is possible. This is not an unusual requirement. It is simply an extension of the requirement for effective communication between people with different backgrounds within a single culture.

But the fact is that it is not always going to be the case that members of different cultures are going to meet as putatively equal interlocutors on a train somewhere — like the legendary Irish, English, American and German businessmen who meet in a bar in Paris. Differences in culture, caricatured in the ethnic stereotypes of this kind of joke, are usually accompanied by differences in status and role. Communicative situations are not always as detached from economic and political processes as bars or train compartments. Generally speaking, communication situations are seldom, if ever, 'ideal'.

Hence, the ISS concept could be misused. If it were used as a kind of standard or measure — as a basis of evaluation or critique — it could function in a utopian way. The upshot of this kind of use is that no situation is found to measure up. The result is pessimism. As Habermas warned, the ISS was better thought of as a 'tool' to think with.[15] The concept of a communication situation free from the effects of social power or status, and from unnecessary attachment by interlocutors to their own views, and in which all parties are oriented to resolving validity claims, was a 'logical type'. It could be thought of as a situation free from obstacles to learning other than the mystery of reality itself. Learning may still be a struggle, since nature, life, reality, God's creation (call it what you will) does not yield up its secrets lightly. Understanding the world, ourselves, and the purpose of it all, will still challenge us, but at least we will not get in the way of our own learning, socially or psychologically.

The past tense has been used to talk about the ISS in the above paragraph because Habermas has since retreated from his earlier position[16] and abandoned the use of the ISS idea. However, he still retains the idea of a counterfactual dimension of communication — a communicative hope — while recognising that this takes various, sometimes non-ideal forms.

Clearly, Habermas' new approach still raises many questions. Is it methodologically legitimate to use a counterfactual tool even if no longer a rigid logical type in the analysis of real communication situations? Let us be clear about what is at stake. The problem is analogous to that thrown up by Max Weber's use of 'ideal types'. There is an added complication. Weber's ideal type is perhaps better translated 'ideational type', since there is no suggestion that it is considered to be an empirically attainable type. This rendering makes it clearer that it is not intended to represent a desirable or 'ideal' state of affairs. It is a kind of cultural type — a possible set of ideas and norms in the 'cultural logic' of a given culture or cultures. It is not used to criticise the real in the light of the ideal, but to understand the logic of the actual configurations of culture in the light of a simplified cultural 'model' (but not an empirical model). Utopias and distopias play a similar role. Habermas' counterfactual notion is also a non-empirical logical notion, but it is attributed to the logic of all communicators who begin a conversation not already understanding each other. It is argued that they would not do this if they did not hope for understanding to be achieved. That is, some sort of ideals about genuine communication are the possession of all communicators — they are not just a tool for theorists!

The use of counterfactuals in thinking is quite common.[17] It is a corollary of a sense of time and the possibility of alternatives. Some cultures possess a general sense of contingency and choice, others confine it to particular realms of their 'world'. Every time someone says the equivalent of 'if X had not happened…' they are employing a counterfactual, because the fact is that X did happen. Similarly, every time someone says 'X is not the case now, but if I do Y it will be…' they are employing the logic of counterfactual hope. Every time we seek to understand someone when we start from a position where we do not yet understand, we engage in this kind of thinking.

Is Habermas' View Idealistic and Ethnocentric?

The most cogent objections to Habermas' approach, from whatever source, centre on the way he is seen to smuggle value judgements into what is deemed to be a fallible, empirical reconstruction. His counterfactual hope is *an* ideal as well as being an ideational tool. But it is also possible to sidestep these objections, even though Habermas himself would probably object to the necessary manoeuvre. In his analysis Habermas identifies the validity questions at stake in all speech — this is the universal pragmatic dimension — and in the discussion of counterfactuals he privileges truth, rightness and truthfulness rather than their opposites. This is often seen as idealistic and ethnocentric. But it is possible to retreat from this position, without thereby going over into the opposite camp.

As I have argued elsewhere,[18] you are arguing on firmer ground when you merely recognise that each utterance and situation presents a *choice* between truth *and* falsehood etc. relative to the situational horizon. If we were to take up a postmodern insight, we could see this as the unfolding teleology of recognition of possibility as we move and our life moves through new fields of meaning. Certainly, Habermas' original objections to this move to talk of choice were a product of the arguments he had with 'positivism' in the 1960s.[19] He saw talk of choice as bringing in an irrational component, because that was how positivists dealt with it. Positivists believed that choice was about values and that because values were outside science they could not be rational. But if choice is seen in pragmatist terms it is a part of science. It is central to our human capacity to pursue our existential interests and to adapt to change.

Habermas' strategy against positivism runs the risk of the opposite error — the absolutising of choice and decision by locating it in the nature of human language itself. He argues that the fact of speech presupposes an orientation to understanding and hence to choosing truth rather than falsehood etc. However, he does not explain how action oriented to understanding becomes so oriented in the first place.

It is one thing to argue that the existence of language and speech somehow implies that the need for understanding and the coordination of human action is somehow primary and deception secondary and parasitical on truth telling. As we have seen, Davidson also advances this view. It is quite another to argue that speakers start from this in the concrete interactions into which they enter.

The alternative intention, to pursue one's own projects regardless of others is also dependent on the nature of speech communication — on its capacity for untruth, wrong and deception.

This way of putting it does not provide us with an answer to the question of how we might go about rationally valuing, but it does sidestep Habermas' critics while leaving much of his analysis intact (on the assumption we can provide other rational grounds for choosing truth, such as pragmatism provides). Robbed of Habermas' simple *fait accompli*, the rather hard road of justifying ethical analysis by other means still lies ahead. Here I can only hint at where I think that road leads. It does not lead to a separation of rationality and valuing. With Dewey and others, I would adopt an evolutionary and transactional approach to this question. The positivist notion of a 'value-free' domain would be relegated to the realm of mythology. However, it is not High Modernism (or its positivist epistemology) that is the main contemporary threat to a pragmatist solution. The postmodern view that we cannot get beyond our personal preferences is also a danger. In the wake of Rorty, and others who adopt extreme readings of post-structuralism, it is the possibility of any kind of rationality and rational learning that is to be fought for, not only the notion of rationality in valuing.

From a pragmatist viewpoint, valuing, judgement and decision is everywhere, even *in* the rational, but what is at stake is whether or not particular decisions, when acted upon solve our problems. With Dewey I would argue in favour of the rational exploration of valuing, but with Charles Sanders Peirce,[20] I would anticipate an outcome in favour of truth rather than untruth, because truth, in the long run, is of universal pragmatic value. In this view, a counterfactual vision of less constrained communication is not only a tool to permit contrast with reality, it is an anticipation of completion — that is, it is prophetic.

As a tool, it allows us to identify sources of constraint on communication. In an abstract way, these can be seen as obstacles to learning, but in any given situation a further analytical step must be taken before any particular limit on communication is declared to be wrong. Many situations create dilemmas, in which the pursuit of validity in one area, so right in the abstract, becomes wrong in the concrete. Classical dilemmas of the kind that occur when there is a conflict between telling the truth and saving lives (the Nazis are at the door, looking for the Jewish refugee you have hidden in the attic. What do you tell them? The truth or a sincere lie?) provide relatively simple examples of situations where an ideal speech situation cannot be approximated and where the form of coercion or threat inherent in the situation justifies a less than ideal attitude to validity questions ('No', you say, 'There is no one else in the house.'). Sometimes such situations are a normal and institutionalised part of a culture. Certainly, members of a culture can only imagine a communication situation being free from *those constraints on conversation recognised in the culture.*

As we have seen, Habermas declares that *all* interlocutors possess a concept of constraint free communication and *ordinarily* assume it when they are in communicative situations in which they are oriented to 'really' understanding each other. (Note: not in all situations). Conversely, he argues that all interlocutors employ this hope as a critical tool or point of comparison when they become aware of situations where people are either not trying to understand each other or are unable, due to structural features of the situation, to pursue such understanding. In short, he is arguing that the communicative values in this thinking are the values which underpin the idea of rationality itself. In Dewey's thinking, as in Habermas', this appears to flow from an understanding of rationality as *group* adaptation to change (and to overcoming the inherent problems of life on this planet, such as disease, natural disaster etc.). Individual adaptation is scarcely adaptation at all. Individual error is more likely to be checked when there is communication across difference. Only then can genuine universals emerge, whether empirical or transcendental.

At this point, a number of commentators[21] have parted company with Habermas, arguing that his conception of rationality as something grounded in ideally open speech and exploration of validity questions is really a case of a European philosopher writing his view of the ideal behaviour of philosophers into his account of universal human rationality. As such, his view is seen to be ethnocentric, or at least, Eurocentric. They argue that, while such a view may be a part of the cultural complex of European modernity, it is not necessarily a cultural universal. Of course, it may be a European concept *and* a universal. Every culture is capable of making discoveries that take the whole race into a new range of possibility, even imperialist cultures.

However, I think these commentators are mistaken, but I do see that there are Eurocentric characteristics in the way Habermas has *expressed* his insight. After all, he is trying to *rework* the categories of European thought. Immanent critique of European thought is his *starting point*. But at the least, it must be conceded that his account needs to be restructured and broadened. A separate issue, but one related to the question of the universality of counterfactual assumptions of speakers, is the issue of its adequacy as a tool for critique. I want to examine a weak, an intermediate and a strong case for the value of counterfactual hope in the study of intercultural communication.

The Case for Intercultural Hope

First, it can be argued that whatever the answer we give to the universality question, something like this hope is a necessary assumption for all who set out to communicate with members of another culture. It is an essential part of the intercultural communication context, even though that context is itself a construction of the participants. Despite the specific origins of the idea in the history of European thought, it describes the general conditions for the success of all communication between interlocutors with different backgrounds. This is the weak case.

Second, it can be argued that, in a modified form, this hope, or something like it, is the more or less conscious possession of all members of the human species, but usually in a manner specific to certain types of communication situation within a culture. Nevertheless, it can provide the basis for critique, even within monocultural settings and in cultures where 'critique' is not institutionalised. This is the intermediate case.

Third, and this is the strong case, I want to argue that while the weak and intermediate cases are clearly plausible, it is possible to go further. Every speaker of every language proceeds on the basis of a set of implicit normative assumptions about the nature of speech communication itself. While in any given instance speech may not accord with these norms, all concrete frameworks of speech assumptions are conditioned by them, negatively or positively. Following my earlier point about choice and 'decisionism', communicative hope defines the choices people face. With Dewey and Habermas I would argue that one pole of this choice defines rationality and the other the opposite, which with Foucault I could call 'Power/Knowledge' or with Marx, 'ideology'. This may be an idea characteristic of European thought, but it is far from being confined to it. Other cultural traditions recognise the opposition between power and dialogue, power/knowledge and rationality. It is also *functionally* open to intercultural extension. What is rational is a product of a potentially species-wide dialogue. Whatever the origin of the idea, we are caught up in something like the paradox of tolerance — the one thing it is safe to be intolerant about is intolerance. A concept of rationality which equates it with the democracy of the whole species-inquiry can hardly be said to be Eurocentric simply because it emanates from there.

Universal Rationality

Some of those who criticise Habermas for ethnocentrism are in fact passing over an arguably much greater and more significant European ethnocentrism of which Habermas is one of the chief opponents. As he points out in the *Theory of Communicative Action* (TCA), Vol. 1.:[22]

If we start from the non-communicative employment of knowledge in teleological action, we make a prior decision for the concept of *cognitive-instrumental* rationality that has, through empiricism, deeply marked the self-understanding of the [European, RY] modern era. It carries with it connotations of successful self-maintenance made possible by informed disposition over, and intelligent adaptation to, conditions of a contingent environment. On the other hand, if we start from the communicative employment of propositional knowledge in assertions [validity 'claims', RY], we make a prior decision for a wider concept of rationality connected with ancient conceptions of *Logos*. (TCA, Vol. 1, p. 10)

However, Habermas' reference to *Logos* here is not meant to signal a narrow cognitive understanding of the kind attacked by Derridean opponents of 'logocentrism', as we shall see. Nor does Habermas intend by putting it this way to *oppose* the communicative view to the instrumental view, rather he seeks to enclose the instrumental view within the communicative view. The word 'wider' is not lightly employed.

Arguably, it is the empirical understanding of knowledge which has dominated European High Modernity. In its apparent methodological independence of culture accompanied by the technological and economic power of modern Europe, this understanding of reason is far more likely than a discursive one to sweep aside indigenous cultures and their knowledge.

Perhaps, for this reason if for no other, those who are suspicious of the European origins of Habermas thought should give him the benefit of the doubt and be prepared to look more closely at his argument. In a discursive conception of rationality and, moreover, one in which rationality is not confined to the cognitive domain, culturally different interlocutors start off from their own cultural experience. Habermas is well aware that the modern {European} form of rationality is possible as a way of life only in a situation characterised by 'rational worldviews'.[23] He wishes to avoid simply assuming that the rationality structures specific to the modern worldview are generally valid, so he is aware that he cannot simply tacitly rely on a modern understanding of rationality as he had before writing *The Theory of Communicative Action* (p. 44). The objects of this inquiry are 'The conditions that the structure of action-orienting worldviews must satisfy if a rational conduct of life is to be possible for those who share such a worldview' (pp. 43–44). If these can be identified and shown to be necessary conditions of rationality and to be related to communicative hope, we would be well on the way to demonstrating the weak thesis outlined above. If, in addition, it could be argued that:

> The context-dependence of the criteria by which the members of different cultures at different times judge differently the validity of

expressions, does not...mean that the ideas of truth, of normative rightness, of sincerity, and of authenticity that underlie (very intuitively to be sure) the choice of criteria are context dependent to the same degree. (TCA, Vol. 1, p. 55)

We would be in a position to strengthen the argument to the degree that some idea of communication free from interference, with orientations to truth, rightness and sincerity, is possessed by all interlocutors in a manner independent of cultural differences.

Habermas provides two interlocking arguments for his views. There is an historical-evolutionary argument and there is an argument about the properties a worldview must have if it is to be able to support institutionalised and systematic learning (i.e. including critique). It seems to me that the latter argument can be extended to support institutionalised and systemic intercultural problem-solving. We have already argued in the present work that the requirements of understanding between members of different cultures requires a capacity to learn from judgements about the validity (or invalidity) of elements of one's own culture of origin. We will return to this point later.

Modernisation, Europeanisation and Learning Cultures

Habermas is in agreement with Winch that each culture has its own language and 'linguistically articulated worldview' (p. 58). He accepts Winch's criticism of Evans-Pritchard's account of Azande magical beliefs. As discussed in a previous chapter, despite his skills as an anthropologist, Evans-Pritchard still tacitly believed that the Azande conception of the world was wrong because it did not agree with his own conception of reality (as revealed by modern science). Evans-Pritchard's belief rested on the assumption that it is possible, outside the nature of scientific inquiry itself, to have a view of reality as a ground to which scientific reasoning makes appeal experimentally, as a basis or foundation for its own findings. In this he shared the foundationalism of positivism.

Winch's relativism rests on a vigorous rejection of this form of realism — foundational realism — and an equally strongly held phenomenological theory of knowledge and culture — that each culture views the world in a unique way.

But Habermas argues that worldviews may still be judged and rationally criticised, even though it makes no sense to judge them *directly* in terms of their truth or falsehood when compared to some supposed reality since they represent, if you like, primordial assumptions and basic concepts, and because there is no culturally independent tribunal against which such things can be simply judged or appraised — no reality waiting with raised gavel to adjudicate issues in a simple way. Habermas argues that all cultures possess a basic intuition about truth and a part of that intuition is always the notion that truth is a universal claim. Even if a truth is esoteric, known only to a few, or beyond the understanding of some, the notion of truth contains some notion of the *possibility* of universal assent. In this way, it is in principle possible to compare worldviews, even for the adherents of them, by a comparison of the adequacy of the set of true statements that a linguistically articulated worldview makes it possible to say. However, the possibility of, as it were, 'representative' members of different cultures carrying out such an appraisal would rest upon some contextual or environmental changes which removed the interlocutors from the closed round of daily life within each culture and exposed their systems of action relevances to new challenges.

As pointed out earlier, Davidson's discussion of the necessarily universal character of truth claims in cultures where formal argumentation is recognised employs the principle of 'charity'. In a kind of reversal of the expected argument, Davidson points out that the most charitable assumption we can make when communicating with someone different from ourselves is that they share our assumptions. This is the most charitable because, generally speaking we regard our deepest assumptions as being adequate. In any case, when we have to assume something we can only assume the things we already know.

Another version of this argument finds an absurdity in the notion that the truth of our deepest assumptions can be reasonably spoken of as 'truth for us' or 'what passes as truth'. Anthropologists sometimes speak this way to show respect for members of non-scientific cultures. But our deepest assumptions are often tacit rather than overtly theorised. We scarcely know we are making them. We do not think of them as relative to our culture, or as 'truth for us', but simply as truth or even as 'the way the world really is' and not as assumptions at all. If so, the truth for us of these truths is that they are universally true. Which leaves the anthropologist in a dilemma. If we are to be respected our 'truth' must be respected (relatively) but our truth is that our truth is universal truth.

Thus, we can add to Davidson's list the principle of epistemic 'tolerance'. When we find our original assumption is not working, Davidson tells us, we develop a 'passing theory'. This may eventually replace our original theory. But to do this we need to be tolerant. We need to learn and be ready to learn. The difference between a colonialist situation and a communicative one is that in the latter we are prepared to allow elements of the passing theory to replace some of our original assumptions. And, as Habermas tells us, this means that not only individuals, but cultures must possess some institutional recognition of difference if this tolerance is to be possible on a large scale. In effect, this means that cultures need some internal separation of realms of difference at least analogous to cultural difference. The European separation of science, the law, the arts, religion, and everyday life is the product of a historical process of a partial transcendence of cultural differences. We must not forget that 'Europe' is an example of the preservation of cultural difference *within* cultural convergence. European institutions, from nation states to the EEC, were shaped by the very problems of cooperation across cultural difference that face the whole world today. Despite Europe's imperial past it is not unreasonable to suggest that we can learn from the European experience in this respect without necessarily duplicating it. The institutional separation of values spheres is precisely a de-absolutising of them and a device for handling difference.

So Habermas recognises that the problem of intercultural rationality is not simply a cognitive problem but a problem of the adequacy of an articulated worldview as a part of a way of life (TCA, p. 59).[24] In the contemporary world, though, the way of life we must take into account is a future global one. Cultures must be sufficiently tolerant of difference to permit openness to this future and in practice that means they must institutionally separate spheres of meaning within their own society, so that areas of difference can be free from political, religious or ethnic constraints. The notions of freedom of speech and inquiry in European culture when coupled with legal/political establishment of an organisational base for these activities, in the press and the university, represent just such an institutionalised separation of meaning-action. Let us look at an example of this.

As Winch points out, the contradictions between Zande beliefs about magic and events in Zande life are recognised by the Azande, but only when the foreign anthropologist brings his culturally different demands for consistency into the Zande context through the practice of persistent, systematic questioning of Zande informants, something that didn't normally arise in that way of life (until now, that is). Zande life did not separate specifically logical and critical questioning (inquiry) from the ordinary business of making sense of the world.

Winch[25] argues that the European who would see the European worldview as superior, because it is less tolerant of contradiction than the

Zande view, is being ethnocentric because the demand for consistency is itself a cultural product:

> it is the European, obsessed with pressing Zande thought where it would not naturally go — to a contradiction — who is guilty of a misunderstanding, not the Azande. The European is in fact committing a category mistake.' (Winch, p. 21)

If by this Winch means that the European observer is simply failing to recognise that the Zande impose less exacting standards of rationality than European cultures and therefore should not impute to them his own interest in resolving inconsistencies, it would not be a very forceful objection. But Winch seems to be inveighing against a stronger argument. That argument, as presented by Robin Horton,[26] is that some worldviews hinder cognitive — instrumental (i.e. scientific) learning processes. Such worldviews, Horton argues, prevent learning and bind the consciousness of participants to a 'mythical–magical' view of reality in which the possibility of scientific knowledge is closed off by taboos on questioning 'sacred' understandings of the world.

Habermas is in agreement with Winch in finding this argument to be a projection of a one-sided misunderstanding of European rationality and the application to Zande views of a one-sided criterion of judgment. Worldviews which value things other than instrumental achievements can scarcely be judged in terms of their possible closedness or openness to instrumental rationality alone. But it can be pointed out that the reason for this is, in part, because such views do not permit the cultural differentiation of spheres of meaning — into the separated scientific/factual, moral, and aesthetic domains of European thinking — and the relatively independent progress of each which, in the European context, has given rise to the accelerated (and independent) development of science and technology, legal institutions, and the arts.

It is certainly a Eurocentric error to take the dominant scientistic misunderstanding of science in European High Modernity as *the* standard for the judgment of worldviews or to fail to recognise that the separation of the three institutional structures and value spheres has imposed cultural costs as well as conferring benefits. The separation of the sacred from the pursuit of knowledge has resulted in a pervasive disenchantment of life. This has its benefits — in freedom from superstition — but it also has its costs — in the loss of wonder. But the question at issue is whether or not there is a separate and incommensurable concept of rationality for each and every culture. While Habermas recognises that much of the discussion of non-modern cultures has involved an '...uncritical self-interpretation of the modern world that is fixated on knowing and mastering nature',[27] he argues that there *is* a common and universal understanding of the rational. What differs from culture to culture is the relationship between the rational and the rest of life and the degree of differentiation of the various spheres of rationality. If there is a cultural mistake in all of this, other than the one-sided standards referred to above, it lies in expecting our European desire for systematic learning to be replicated in all cultures and in a failure to appreciate the obstacles to systematic learning in our own culture, let alone others.

Contrary to the earliest European accounts of 'pre-logical' savages, members of all cultures are capable of recognising logical contradictions and of learning that theories or accounts of the world fail to work under certain circumstances. A failure to learn (in the sphere of the cognitive adequacy of accounts of the world) can be brought about in many ways. A reluctance to entertain particular accounts because of their content, a reluctance to question the accounts of those in authority, or to break with one's own past identity — all these things can prevent learning in European cultures, too. What is at stake is the closeness of the web of institutional linkages between the political sphere (authority), the personal sphere (degree of individuation and expressive freedom) and the cognitive or epistemic sphere (knowledge), and the forms of learning these linkages discourage or encourage. What is at stake is the freedom to entertain new ideas in a context free of constraint from authority and power. Presumably Habermas would agree that the Azande, given changes in their way of life brought about by circumstance, would learn, through logic and observation, and so make epistemic changes, in much the same way as any human beings would learn.

The Azande's view of the world represents a limit case. The relationship of the individual to Zande society is one which places heavy emphasis on conformity to socially defined reality, and ritual action forms. Azande society does not burden the individual with the task of personal adaptation and learning beyond that necessary for socialisation. The processes of communicatively achieved learning are confined to quite particular and limited spheres in Zande life. Under the impact of the modern world and technological change, the way of life changes. Traditional modes of production are no longer possible, traditional institutions no longer supportable. The scope of limited spheres of discursively reached agreement about behaviour in the face of contingency — on where to hunt, where to graze the cattle, or who is or is not a witch — is insufficient for the new circumstances. Previously mythically organised domains of thought must be opened up to discussion.

While we may lack contemporary witnesses of this process among the Azande, we do have witnesses of similar processes among a number of New Guinea societies. There, under the impact of colonisation and the technological invasion, a process of problem-solving of a roughly rational kind did occur.[28] Hitherto unquestioned spheres of life were made the subject of discursive reconstitution. Even basic myths of social origin were re-worded to take account of the new phenomena. Learning took place. The white invaders were now seen to have better communication with the ancestors and better knowledge of their secrets of how to produce food, goods etc. than the indigenous people themselves. Old myths had to be reworked to include this decentring of the previous privileged position of the local people. What was previously an unquestioned account of the origins of the world and everything in it became a disputed 'theory', with factions arguing over different accounts, and a continuous process of social disputation about accounts of reality that has continued to the present day. (This is sometimes discussed under the label 'cargo cults'). The result is a movement towards an uncoupling of value spheres.

Thus, societies may be compared on a continuum of institutionally permitted learning. All societies permit some areas of discursive problem-solving (learning) but only modern societies permit it in every conceivable sphere. (Even though only a few members of such societies actually engage in it in any given sphere).

The historical process of individual and cultural decentration may have occurred unevenly (with a particular concentration in some occupational groups in Europe in the comparatively recent past) and the differentiation and institutional separation of the spheres of rationality may be a very recent (and temporary?) phenomenon. Certainly, the cultural colonisation that occurred in the very recent historical phase of European global expansion gave rise to an ignorant and ethnocentric imposition of Eurocentric self-understandings on the rest of the world. But it also gave rise to Anthropology. At first colonialist and Eurocentric, Anthropology is, in principle, the study of all humankind. It is natural enough that it reflected the culture of its practitioners and the political purposes of those who funded it. But what has to be explained by those who would dismiss it utterly, is that it did this very imperfectly. It was often a voice speaking on behalf of colonised peoples. As previously excluded voices obtain a hearing within the potentially universal discourse, anthropology itself becomes the site for a dialogue about our common human future. Criticism of past anthropology should not stand in the way of a recognition of the universal character of human rationality: the cultural difference between Europe and the rest of the world did not lie in the superior rationality of Europe's individual citizens. Nor did the *cultural* difference between Europe and the rest of the world lie in the difference between rationality and irrationality. It lay in a series of changes (differentiations) which opened up every sphere of European culture to the *possibility* of rational pragmatic problem-solving through discursive resolution of validity claims, and in a social institution-alisation of these rationality spheres, in universities, law courts and bureaucracies, which permitted a sudden acceleration of their develop-ment, giving Europe a temporary technological and organisational edge — the very edge that made large scale colonisation possible.

The crucial point is that the separation of scientific (and cultural) inquiry, aesthetic expression, legal/administrative state activity, the personal sphere and the public sphere, however imperfect and however mytholo-gised within the political debate in societies of European origin, has allowed and demanded de-coupling of the control of conduct and expression from the demands of group survival and cultural purity. The bringing of more and more areas of life under the purview of inquiry permits these to be uncoupled from the dimension of life where difference is seen to be a threat to the cosmic positioning of the whole society. We no longer have to kill people who are different because they might interfere with the weather. The irony, though, is that this uncoupling can have its costs. Life is demythologised and thereby disenchanted. The power of homogenous cultures — cultures that are homogenous in the sense of keeping cosmic, personal etc. together — has been usurped by the legal/administrative value sphere, which threatens an internal colonisa-tion of the others. We will explore this problem further in the next chapter.

The conditions a cultural tradition must satisfy for the separation of values to occur are roughly that it must:

(1) differentiate between question of truth, power, and personal feelings;
(2) permit reflection on its own dogmatisms in each of the three domains and also reflection on the connections between these domains;
(3) permit such processes of reflection to be socially institutionalised (in communities of inquiry); and
(4) permit a separation of instrumental from other forms of action and the emergence of instrumental institutional action complexes (such as bureaucracies and universities or research institutes).

It is these things that have created the context in which thinkers like Foucault and Derrida could emerge in the first place.

The European developmental model represents only one path to a degree of institutionalised tolerance of difference. Other, non-European societies have also achieved a degree of tolerance of difference, largely in situations of trade, by carefully creating zones where a hybrid set of rules applied. However, at the least, this theory accounts for the otherwise surprising fact that it is in the cultures responsible for the most recent imperialisms that cultural tolerance, however imperfect, is most fully developed and most widely and openly discussed and agitated for.

But it should be noted that I am not arguing that societies which do not display these developments are incapable of rational learning or that they are in any way inferior. However, they may be mal-adaptive at a time when global problem solving is crucial. They are functionally able to do some things our modern societies cannot do and are functionally unable or less able to do other things. However, I am arguing that such societies tend to have these learning processes confined to *more limited* areas; areas where such learning is permitted by the integrated nature of the culture. What separates the modern from the non-modern is not the presence or absence of rational learning but the difference in the scope permitted to such processes and their degree of institutionalisation and differentiation and hence, freedom from the control by ritual (and other) processes. Foucault's analyses, even if they exaggerate the degree of epistemic uniformity in modern society, should give us pause if we wanted to claim more than this.

Separation of this kind may be distinguished from a second kind of cultural separation that occurs *among* modern societies — societies which share the differentiation of cultural spheres but which do not share either detailed agreement within each sphere or definitions concerning the relationships between spheres. We will come back to these two kinds of cultural separation below.

Universal Pragmatic Features of Rationality

Normally, interlocutors in a society where institutionally permitted discursive problem-solving is confined to a few narrow spheres perceive attempts to expand these domains as a distortion of communication. Counter-factual communicative hope is the hope of escape from culturally recognised constraints on speech. As a counter-factual concept possessed by all interlocutors, it is open-ended, but it cannot be open-ended in ways the culture cannot recognise. Where institutionally integrated elements of the sacred, of status and power, and of fundamental conceptions of the world constrain the culturally recognised sphere for discursive consideration of validity claims, it is too much to expect that members of the culture concerned will possess a conception of freedom from communicative constraint that cuts across this cultural construction of discursive locations. Communicative hope is a conception of freedom from *culturally recognised* forms of communicative constraint but, in turn, these forms of recognised constraint are constituted by the culture's prior identification of contexts of situation as being situations appropriate for solving problems through speaking. Within such context — village meetings, litigation, disputes etc. — untrue speaking, lack of straight speaking, deception, lying and the like are all recognised as possible sources of communicative distortion and there is a presumption of the possibility of their absence.[29] The reason why there are speaking situations where hope is not presumed by speakers is because there are situations where the communicative task is not seen as one in which the presence or absence of culturally recognised constraints on valid speaking are at all relevant e.g. ritual situations. Such situations exist in all societies, it is just that in some societies they are more common than in others. Foucault has argued that despite the institutionalisation of inquiry by professionals, modern society has maintained a nexus between on the one hand these domains and on the other the power structure of society. So the high degree of separation that Habermas would claim is disputed.

However, and this is crucial for the strong thesis — situations where problem solving is not involved are systematically recognised as differing from those in which speech is more unconstrained in terms of a conceptual framework which tacitly incorporates communicative hope.

Speakers in all cultures make validity judgements as a normal part of understanding meaning. These judgements are manifold, not single or separate, but are part of an overall situated 'story' about meaning that speakers and hearers construct. It is normally the standards of the culture that provide the assumptions, norms etc. against which validity is judged. Only when the 'story' construction breaks down does talk (reflexively) turn to attempts to repair or reconstruct meaning. Such recourse does not usually turn immediately into a full-fledged exploration of differences in assumptions, norms etc. — differences in culture — but may go through a series of more routine stages before the nature of the communication problem is recognised to lie at a deeper level. The kind of recourse that is available is related to the culturally defined situation type. In some situations recourse to discursive explorations of differences in the background of communicators is only a remote possibility because the situation is defined in such a way that communicative breakdown is automatically attributed to factors other than differences in background e.g. witchcraft, ill-will, demonic possession, oracular speaking.

However, even within a culture, situation definitions are sometimes disputed or unclear. All mature communicators have some experience of this uncertainty and presumably develop skills for probing differences of definition and for discursively negotiating an alignment of situation definitions. Under some circumstances, these skills may be called on in intercultural communication.

It is useful to distinguish between intercultural communication contexts where the interlocutors come from cultures widely separated on the modern–mythical dimension and contexts where culturally different members of modern societies are communicating with each other. For instance, the first context might be illustrated by an American agricultural scientist communicating with a member of the Herero hunter-gatherer society in Southern Africa; the second context might be illustrated by communication within the UN building between Russian and British diplomats.

In the first example, the likelihood of a mismatch between situation definitions is quite high. This would result in a mismatch of communicative expectations of the kind that might occur when the agricultural scientist tries to employ discursive argument to convince a Herero cultivator to act in a certain way in a domain of action regarded as sacred and ritual-governed in Herero culture. Under these circumstances it seems unlikely that coherent communicative interaction could occur at all. A monologue by the scientist is the likely communicative form. In the second example, one might expect problems to arise from detailed differences in beliefs or attitudes which show up *within* a relatively coherent communicative interaction in which general communicative expectations are shared e.g. that communicators would both advance arguments, ask questions etc.

Which is *not* to say that these generalisation will always apply. It is a matter of the specific situation definitions and whether or not their communicative expectations and speaker roles match up, and, of course, of the insight and ingenuity of speakers. We might expect mismatches to be more common when the cultures concerned differ *structurally*, that is, in terms of the relative differentiation of separate cultural spheres of the modern type.

As suggested above, communicative difficulties might be located on a pair of dimensions which cross-cut each other. Where situation definitions, views about the expected course of the speaking and views about the speaking roles of categories of participants are all broadly shared, but where different assumptions of fact, beliefs about normative detail or personal attitudes exist, one might expect minor communication difficulties — let us call these mis-communications.[30]

As stated earlier, there exist a range of readily available communicative remedies for these communicative ills, in further communication which clarifies, checks, corrects, aligns etc. However, on a second, cross-cutting dimension, basic features of a situation definition may not be shared, and interlocutors may differ very broadly on the definition of the task, the expected course of action and the speaking roles of categories of participants — possibly even about the categorisation of participants or the kind of categories relevant for participants in these situations. This presents a more severe communication *problem*. However, it is still possible to resolve differences of situational definitions communicatively. When one person does not appear to behave in a manner appropriate to the sacred it is possible to attribute this to ignorance rather than a blasphemous intent. In small children, we all have experience of social members whose conduct is ignorant rather than malicious. A special category of 'like a child' can be constructed for the cultural stranger.

Neither of these dimensions of difficulty deserve the label of 'distortion', because both kinds of problem may be discursively resolved. It is where the nature of the relationship between interlocutors is both the source of the mismatch of definitions *and* an obstacle to discursive exploration of communication difficulties that a genuine 'distortion' may be said to occur. The commonest form taken by such relationships is that which is found wherever differences in power align themselves with differences in cultural membership.

Conversations with other Cultures

Winch's remarks on the wisdom of learning from other cultures are approvingly quoted by Habermas.[31] He finds value, too, in Horton's recognition that in other cultures Europeans may be able to find '...*Things lost* at home. An intensely poetic quality in everyday life and thought, and a vivid enjoyment of the passing moment...',[32] all of which are characteristics of cultures where the values spheres are more clearly intertwined rather than separated. Habermas is open to what we might learn from conversations with other cultures, including what we might learn about our own through the experience.

For Habermas, Horton's remarks are an example of an incipiently self-critical understanding in Western thought, a recognition of its one-sided privileging of an instrumental conception of reason and its failure to acknowledge the breadth of reason — its aesthetic/feeling and moral/practical dimensions . My partial backing away from Habermas' opposition to decisionism broadens this understanding of the nature of rationality a little, reintroducing some of the lost mystery.

However, the poetic quality of traditional societies of which Horton speaks is not the mystery to which I refer. This mystery is a result of a discursive process of rediscovery and reintegration of the kind which faces European thought rather than the continuing existence in the modern era of cultures in which these dimensions have never been separated from each other. In the latter case, this unity gives such cultures their integrity and wholeness — but it also limits their capacity for collective learning and restricts their adaptability in the face of the ravages of technological, environmental and geo-political change. We postmoderns are faced with the task of re-integration, but this would be a tragic development if it somehow robbed us of what we have gained through modernity.

For Habermas recognises that, while the separation of the spheres of culturally recognised rationally is one of the things that makes the independent and rapid development of such spheres possible, it is also the source of many integrative problems for the individual and for society at large. It is the focus of a 'loss of meaning' as well as of a disenchantment. Moreover, he recognises that the separation of value spheres is far from complete, as we will see in the next chapter. But his solution does not involve an abandonment of reason or any simple equation of power with knowledge.

The individual forms of rationality, each with its own limits to be sure, nowhere *within themselves* contain a basis for critical judgements and rational progress of a whole way of life or, for that matter, an individual biography. That is, life presents problems that call upon more than the form of rationality and which go beyond rationality to questions of the meaning of life itself — to those overarching goals and meanings which we might call 'spiritual' in the broad sense of the word. For instance, a capacity for improvements in instrumental reason and technical applications of this reason contains no guidance for the development of, say, appropriate, non-threatening technologies. Similarly, the development of our expressive powers provides no guidance for a life of the artist (or the art of life).

Dewey once remarked that the spiritual represented the higher integration of values and knowledge towards which evolutionary pragmatic thought moved.[33] It is something like a broader and more balanced version of the concept of truth. In an evolutionary understanding of 'truth', it can never be described as attained, because the present stage is always incomplete, fallible and actually in error, if only we knew where. Truth is a direction — it is a normative term which bespeaks an awareness, however liminal, of a completeness to which we move and in which we hope. This is how I would prefer to think of rationality — the anticipation of an interculturally shared completion of reason. This is certainly an eschatological vision, but then, a little inspection of the commonplaces of daily life reveals that the ordinary is also the extraordinary.

In the past, European societies have tended to resolve the question of balance in favour of a one-sided development of instrumental forms of reason. We have called this High Modernity. In addition, the myth of the separation of knowledge from power became a part of Europe's cultural self-image. In the unguided development of science and technology, in the overdevelopment of the role of the State in the practical sphere, and in the commodification of art, the balance that has been struck by Western culture is a lop-sided one. That at least, was the burden of Habermas' critique in his earliest work.

We can learn something from non-modern societies about the value of different kinds of balance, without necessarily sharing their cosmologies. We can also learn from non-Western *modern* societies, such as Japan, where a different balance has been struck among nevertheless differentiated cultural spheres.

Habermas' conception of the universality of rationality and its discursive assumptions may still have a speculative character, but it is not quite so obvious as some critics would have us think that it is merely ethnocentric and just another attempt to impose European cultural ideas on others.

If some sort of understanding of communicative hope is indeed a common human possession, the business of intercultural communication may be easier than it would otherwise be. In any case, if it doesn't already exist something like it would have to be invented if we are to communicate successfully across cultural barriers. Habermas' concepts of conversational action as reciprocal, respectful, yet critical conversation across difference offers a possible path forward. But more needs to be said about just how this conversational concept differs from other talk of conversation in Rorty or Foucault and how it deals with problems of action, agency, reproduction and emancipation — in short, how it deals with *politics*.

Notes

1. Shalin, D. 'Critical theory and the pragmatist challenge'. *American Journal of Sociology* 98 (2), 1992, pp. 237–79; and Jons, H. 'An underestimated alternative: America and the limits of critical theory'. *Symbolic Interaction*, 15 (3), 1992, pp. 261–75.
2. Immanent critique is the extension of internal critique of a tradition of thought by confronting it with the material (and cultural) conditions of its own production. It is not externalist critique — that would simply criticise one cultural tradition in terms of another.
3. M. Weber, *The Theory of Social and Economic Organisation*, and J. Habermas, *The Theory of Communicative Action*, Vol. 1. London: Heinemann Educational Books, 1982 (TCA, Vol. 1).
4. M. Weber, *Ancient China*. New York: The Free Press, 1952.

5. J. Habermas, *Knowledge and Human Interests*. London: Heinemann Educational Books, 1972.
6. J. Habermas, TCA, Vol. 1. and more recent works such as G. Cochrane, *Big Men and Cargo Cults*. Oxford: The Clarendon Press, 1970. See also I. Jarvie, 'Explaining cargo cults', Chap. 5 in *Revolution in Anthropology*. London: Routledge and Kegan Paul, 1964.
7. P. Lawrence, *Road Belong Cargo*. Melbourne: University of Melbourne Press, 1964.
8. A. Giddens, *The Consequences of Modernity*. Cambridge: Polity Press, 1990.
9. For a discussion see my *Critical Theory and Classroom Talk*. Clevedon: Multilingual Matters, 1992. Chaps 4 and 5.
10. J. Perry, 'Cognitive significance and new theories of reference'. *NOUS*, 22 (1), 1988, pp. 1–19.
11. See M. Walzer, 'A critique of philosophical conversation.' *The Philosophical Forum*, 21 (1–2), 1989–90, pp. 182–203.
12. W. Quine, *From a Logical Point of View*. Cambridge: Harvard University Press, 1980.
13. J. Habermas, *Communication and the Evolution of Society*. London: Heinemann Educational Books, 1979.
14. J. Habermas. *op. cit.*
15. J. Habermas, 'Reply to my critics' in J. Thompson and J. Held (eds) *Habermas: Critical Debates*. London: Macmillan, 1982.
16. Habermas. *op. cit.*
17. Counterfactual explanation appears to be a part of everyday talk as well as the hypothetical discussions of historians: 'If Rome had not fallen…'; 'If I had put more sugar in the cake…'
18. R. Young, *A Critical Theory of Education*. New York: Teachers College Press, 1990, Chap. 9.
19. J. Habermas, *On the Logic of the Social Sciences*. Cambridge, MA: MIT Press, 1988.
20. See J. Habermas, K. and H. I., Chaps 5 and 6.
21. I will offer no citation here, as this kind of criticism has become a commonplace.
22. TCA, Vol. 1.
23. TCA, Vol. 1. p. 43.
24. TCA, Vol. 1. p. 59.
25. P. Winch, 'Understanding a primitive society.' Pp. 8–49 in P. Winch, *Ethics and Action*. London: Routledge and Kegan Paul, 1972.
26. R. Horton, 'African traditional thought and Western science'. *Africa*, 37 (1 and 2), 1967, pp. 50–71, 155–87.
27. TCA, Vol. 1. p. 66.
28. See Note 7.
29. C. Frake, 'Struck by speech'. Pp. 279–273 in J. Spradley (ed.) *Culture and Cognition*. San Francisco: Chandler, 1972.
30. I am indebted to Dr Christine Fox for this concept. C. Fox, 'A critical analysis of intercultural communication,' University of Sydney PhD Thesis 1988. I would also like to acknowledge the value for the analysis presented in this book of the many conversations I had with Chris Fox over the years.
31. TCA, Vol. 1. p. 65.
32. *loc. cit.*
33. Dewey's notion of the spiritual was that the word should decode as the end towards which we worked, even as we revised it in the light of experience.

6 The Politics of Intercultural Communication

The nature of cultural politics is not the nature of politics as it has been represented in most political theory. That is because most political theory has been developed in monocultural contexts. And, since the linguistic turn, it is clear that politics is not about power so much as definitions of reality. And definitions of reality are about difference — differences between people as members of culturally-defined groups. The excessive cultural individualism of European societies has led to a theory of politics being about individual power, either in the theory of elites or in class theory, which is a theory about categories (classes) of individuals similarly placed economically. But cultural membership is deeper than class membership. An economically upwardly mobile cultural group retains its cultural characteristics whereas an upwardly mobile working class member typically does not.

A politics of culture is a politics of definition, and definitions are both part of a culture and a mediated product of communicative processes. Oppressive definitions must be maintained or those oppressed by them will throw them off. The maintenance of such definitions requires a huge expenditure of cultural energy in the maintenance of the engines which manufacture the definitions — the communicative practices of society. These practices are the domain of communicative professionals — the definers. This is the category Foucault calls 'pastoral' professionals — teachers, journalists, social workers, managers, software writers, therapists, social scientists and the like. The battles of cultural politics will be fought among them — they will also be fought by them. This chapter describes the terrain and the logistics for such battles. In the final two chapters (7 and 8) the strategy and tactics of battle are set out.

What is Politics?

It is also said that politics is about power. But that describes only one kind of politics. Politics is also about hope, equity and solidarity. In a linguistically-constituted human world, politics is about equity and solidarity in world-disclosing and world creating. When we speak of choice, it is a meta-choice between hope and the kind of despair that feeds on the belief that the only possible world is one ruled by self-interest and power. It makes sense in such a world to decide to be the top dog rather than the underdog, but only because it is a world without hope.

And just as Foucault has expanded our understanding of the fact that power is not simply a matter of individuals or groups being top dog, but is also about cultural-institutional *systems* of power, so, Hannah Arendt[1] has shown that there is a countervailing power — the power of human solidarity. There are relationships of mutuality as well as relationships of pastoral authority, and institutional concomitants of mutuality, such as voluntary associations and social movements.

It would be tempting to say that whatever politics is being pursued it will be the historical and cultural context that determines their success or failure, tempting, but not adequate, because the context is partly *constituted* by the meaning-action of particular groups, coalitions, parties and individuals. These social formations are formations of intersubjectivity. That is, their members have group awareness, functional interactions within the group, common group boundaries and membership criteria, and, forms of meaning-action specific to the group, perhaps in the form of rituals. The kind of politics being pursued is just a form of this meaning-action. Meaning-action is about intersubjective constitution of the world humans inhabit and only secondarily about access to material resources. The politics of a group is about the meanings the members will inhabit and the meanings other groups will inhabit, with special attention to the meanings that are inscribed in the group members by others. The politics pursued by a group may be the politics of an emerging profession making a bid for a legal monopoly of knowledge/power in some field of pastoral intervention and influence, or it may be about overcoming obstacles to the meaning-action necessary to the flourishing of the group's members as respected and dignified participants in a wider political-economic system.

At any historical moment, the political landscape is just a configuration of the particular kinds of politics pursued by a set of groups operating within the framework of more inclusive institutional and organisational contexts and practices. Ultimately, it is a global politics and it is about sharing and survival.

So we can reparse notions like 'nation' as the *kind* of boundaries recognised by a set of groups, generally constituting a group of a national kind which at some level, and not always without contestation, may be seen to be pursuing *inter*national politics as a group. Nation is not equal to 'ethnic group', so the unity of multi-ethnic nations is often problematic. However, this does not always mean that internal contestation is mirrored in contestation of foreign policy. It is quite possible for a multi-ethnic nation to pursue internal multiculturalism while holding more or less unanimously to external policies that imply the suppression of cultural difference.

The complexity of the analysis of the interaction of kinds of political strategy, types of social formation (groups, organisations, parties, individuals), social institutions (as clusters of roles, practices and beliefs) and culture (languages, technical skills) is such that effective analysis of the politics of communication is best done around specific historical situations and opportunities. But greater accuracy is only one of the reasons for distinguishing between what one can say about the analysis of communication in general and actual analyses. The probability of an analysis reflecting the interests of the variety of groups involved in a situation is increased if members of the groups concerned carry out the analyses, and the likelihood of creating new cultural meanings which permit at least compromise of interests is increased if the members of diverse groups carry out the analysis in dialogue with each other.

While postmodern readings of the character of the political celebrate particularity and recognise the weight of institutional sedimentation of past practices, and duly point to the systemic character of power rather than the group-dominance process within the system, they have little to say about the power of solidarity. An effective politics of solidarity is not only an effective politics of cultural group lobbies it is a politics of equity across difference, and of the promotion of diverse kinds of flourishing. Separate ethnic lobbies cannot succeed if they are against each other and they are just this if they are not in some sense *for* someone else. Foucault and Derrida are virtually silent on this matter and some readers of them espouse political strategies which would actually diminish equity. However, newer readings of postmodernism attempt a synthesis with other traditions such as pragmatism or critical theory and, like the interpretation in this book, attempt a middle road. Ways in which the problem of equity and diversity might be addressed are discussed in the first half of this chapter. It is argued below that, among other things, Habermas' ideas offer a perspective that can supplement postmodern thinking.

In the second half of the chapter, some of Habermas' ideas are explored and the general character of a post-metaphysical (rather than postmodern) politics is outlined.

Internal Colonisation

One of the main problems for much contemporary discussion of intercultural relations is that it is carried out with both eyes firmly fixed on the rear-view mirror. But if, in counterfactual hope, we could gaze into the future we might be surprised to see that the colonial era has disappeared from view, no matter how many examples of colonialism and neo-colonialism we can still see around us today. In this admittedly improbable future, a new constellation of politically decisive forces is at work, creating a new set of distortions in intercultural relations, even as the smoke is barely a haze in the sky over the old battlefields and only desultory skirmishes and alarums of the old battles continue to break out. In this crystal ball, the main threat to colonised and minority cultures comes no longer from metropolitan and majority cultures, or from the dominance of modern over traditional cultures, but from the internal colonisation everywhere of the lifeworld in all its culturally specific forms.[2] The virus of rational-instrumental administration and the commodification of private life and voluntary association is culturally trans-specific, seemingly able to infect all societies. This much, at least, we can learn from Foucault.

It is not accidental that Habermas chooses the term 'colonisation' to refer to the process whereby systemic forces invade areas of the lifeworld displacing discursive possibilities. This could be the only form of neo-colonialism with a future.

But in the present rather than the future, many political struggles still centre on the relations of cultural groups and social classes, or on the gender relationship. People deeply involved in the risks and sacrifices of these struggles might understandably resent someone who comes along to tell them they are fighting the wrong battle. Fortunately, that is not what I am doing. Rather, I am saying that an additional enemy has arrived on the old battlefield, complicating things. In many ways this enemy is willing to form alliances of convenience with your old adversaries, but as often as not, for this new enemy, your exclusive concentration on the old enemy is a useful diversion, and a valuable form of attrition.

I invite readers to suspend judgement long enough to consider an alternative perspective on the politics of intercultural relations — that which is implicit in Habermas' analysis of the differences between 'modern' and 'traditional' cultures. His attempted identification of universal pragmatic features of communicatively achieved learning, and his account of the problems and distortions of late modernity (along with his critique of both High Modernity and postmodernism), provide an alternative basis for analysing a cluster of intercultural problems, including those involved in a theory of intercultural communication and understanding. In this analysis, it is plain enough, many viewpoints which are commonly found in discussions of intercultural relations will be criticised and reconstructed. However, Habermas does not himself directly tackle the problems of intercultural relations, minority groups, racism or multiculturalism. His theory of cultural modernity, traditional society and cultural learning processes was developed with a view to the diagnosis of internal learning problems within European modernity. The social movements, pathologies and cultural disturbances of late modern societies, often regarded as evidence of a 'postmodern condition', are seen by Habermas as by-products of the colonisation of the lifeworld, or as responses to it. The implications of these ideas for intercultural studies have not been well developed and are consequently little known.

Misunderstanding of Habermas' main line of analysis are common enough, let alone condemnations of his theory on the basis of fragments, asides, and sometimes poorly phrased theoretical suggestions concerning culture, gender etc. Condemnation of what Habermas has written on the basis of what he has not written are extremely common. No distinction appears to be made between identifying an area of incompleteness in a theory and issues of the validity of what *has* been theorised. The failure of theory to achieve completeness doesn't necessarily invalidate the theory as a part-theory, nor does it demonstrate the incapacity of the theory for the necessary expansion. Even relatively perspicuous critics, such as Nancy Fraser,[3] are sometimes guilty of condemning Habermas' theory for the absence of a totality to which it laid no claim in the first place — in her case, for the absence of a theory of gender.

Habermas has no developed theory of intercultural relations — although he makes a few asides which indicate the directions his thinking might possibly take. No doubt this absence can be explained in part by the culturally homogenous German milieu in which Habermas himself works. Habermas is well aware of the sinister historical causes of this contemporary homogeneity. But this absence shouldn't be taken to mean either dearth of interest, or disdain. Habermas has shown great empathy and concern for intercultural understanding in some of his occasional writings, for instance.[4] However, as we have seen, he *has* a theory of traditional and modern societies, and of the institutional/structural internal differentiation of society necessary to certain sorts of deliberate, institutionalised learning processes found in modern societies, of the reasons for these particular learning processes being far less available in (but not absent from) traditional societies, and also of the losses and problems which accompany the processes of differentiation he describes — a set of losses and problems that might be summarily labelled the problems of 'instrumental reason' (providing we do not jump to the conclusion that the use of the word 'reason' here means that the analysis itself will fail to take account of the embodied, sensuous, and particular).

By an extension of Habermas' arguments, in the long run the colonisation to be most feared is the 'hidden' colonisation, which instrumental reason (the characteristic reason of High Modernity) carries out as it becomes in one form or another the leading edge of the globalisation process. The process of colonisation of regional cultures is not exhausted by analyses along the fashionable dimensions of north–south and first–third. The cultures of the societies of the first, northern world are being colonised by this process, too, even as they are themselves still close to their global high tide mark in the old, political, colonisation process. We must simultaneously fight and win two sets of battles — the old battles between oppressor and oppressed groups, classes and categories, which, contrary to my earlier image of the aftermath of battle, are still very much battles to be fought, and the new battle for a global culture of a sustainable, just and learning world society in which cultural difference is maintained. That is one of the problems with history — turning points are seldom clear and old institutions and practices often continue alongside the new.[5]

The New Politics and its Agents

As Charles Taylor pointed out, whether he would have wished to or not, Foucault offered an analysis of the concrete processes of managed discourse in which instrumental reason manifested itself in the governmentalisation of human relationships and social life. Whatever the limitations of Foucault's analysis, we are indebted to him for a gift he did not intend to give us — a sharper edge to the critical power of our humanism, because Foucault has shown us how we have moved culturally from the old political power relations to the 'rational' relations of pastoral power.

> Seen in this way, Foucault offers the Frankfurt School [of which Habermas is the heir, RY] an account of the interconnection between the domination of nature and the domination of man [sic]... (Taylor, p. 160)[6]

But these are precisely the themes with which the present book began —

we are one world, space ship earth, one ecology, one polity, one commonwealth.

In the analysis of the gains and losses of modernity, in the role in colonisation processes of systemic extra-cultural forces of modern society, and in the cultural role of the many contemporary forms of instrumental reason in the management of these forces, we can begin to see the outline of an alternative relation of cultures and their members.

While all cultures are internally differentiated (even the most homogenous being sharply divided into 'gender cultures'), the relationship between members and 'their culture' in (many) modern societies is qualitatively different from anything that has gone before. Many modern societies are multicultural societies and their members typically relate to their own ethnic culture (and to others) in ways not typical of other historically prior societies or contemporary non-modern societies. True, the relationship of members of a dominant culture(where there is one) to their own and other cultures within the society is different from the relationship of members of non-dominant minorities to their own, other minority cultures and to the dominant culture. But all of these relationships are typically different from those obtaining in the non-modern world.

The history of the analysis of mass culture is the place where the emergence of the new relationship is most evident. There, the fragmentation of discourses and the detachment of fantasy (virtual reality) from systemic processes of power and money is most clearly seen. What is not often realised is that the commodification of mythical resources, through the commercialisation of entertainment, while influenced by the cultural segmentation of multicultural society, as often as not transcends it. Large areas of cultural life (music, film, television) are increasingly detached from the tradition-influenced cultural resources of ethnic provenance and the cultural hinterland of systemic processes of the market and bureaucracy is also only loosely connected with culturally specific lifeworld resources, anchored in ethnic traditions. The international extension of this process is sometimes seen as a form of cultural coca-colonisation but there is more to it than that. Admittedly, the economics of mass media production and patterns of dissemination involve the spread of American culture, but much of that which is involved transcends any particular culture of origin and defies cultural typing. The influence of rock music and youth culture is almost universal. The paradoxical commercialisation of the music of African American youth protest should warn against simplistic analyses.

The communicative politics of intercultural relations are subject to many problems and distortions. The way in which relationships of power, such as colonial power, structurally precluded recourse to indigenously integral validity judgements has already been mentioned (Chap. 1). The burden of the argument of this chapter is that this dimension of communicative distortion is employed in the service of a process of governmentalisation which is as much a threat to minority cultures as majority cultures in their anxiety and ignorance ever were.

In Chapter 4, while the approaches of the post-structuralists were heavily criticised, in Foucault's case care was taken to circumscribe this criticism in a particular way. Foucault's analysis of pastoral power and governmentalisation was recognised (despite Foucault himself) as a possible candidate for a sociology of the role of instrumental reason. That is, it is possible to take a great deal of Foucault's description of *how* constellations of institutional structures, people and discourses work (dispositifs), but put the analysis to humanistic uses. What is at stake is the way the pastoral institutional structures of modern penology, psychology and sexual therapy etc. may be both a source of domination, when controlled by the State and a source of freedom when democratically influenced by communities at a local or decentralised level.

True we may only partly accept Foucault's analysis because it is too totalising and from a strictly empiricist point of view, Foucault may be suspected of massaging the data when he finds such homogeneity in, say, penological thinking in France. So much counter-hegemonic thought, and so many differences of opinion about healthy human sexuality, mental health, etc. are glossed over in Foucault's 'history of suspicion' that it becomes suspicious history. We may also, rightly I believe, suspect a view of history which is the exact reverse of the Whig view. Ambiguity, plurality, and a constant current of opposition and critique, of vary degrees of radicalness are easily demonstrated (if not, where did Nietzsche and Foucault himself spring from?). We may rightly suspect Foucault of that same Utopian pessimism as was evident in those Marxists whose criticism of capitalism was so virulent that they entirely lost sight of Marx's view that it was an historically progressive form of society. Just the same, the processes of the development and interlocking of discursive 'regimes' or dispositifs that Foucault describes, and the way in which claims to rational benevolence are also claims in some sense to power, is valuable and illuminating, as is clear from the use to which such critical ideas have been put by others.

In terms of the present analysis, alongside the analysis of the distortion of the constative and expressive validity of dialogue due to the fixing of the normative (power) dimension we must place the characteristic mode through which pastoral power is exerted. The power of colonial master–servant relations was power operating at the interpersonal level but derived from the class relations of categories of people (gentleman, common man, master, servant, white, black, Christian, Jew). In contrast, the power of governmentalisation is the power of the manipulated market. Missing to a degree from Foucault's analysis is the clear identification of the necessary cultural intermediation of the effective exercise of this power, and the intellectual and ideological basis of its legitimacy (its acceptance as rational and benevolent). While Foucault dealt with knowledge, sexuality, and the resocialisation processes of modern systems of 'justice', he did not deal in the same depth with other central aspects of rational power. For this, we must look to an analysis of neo-conservative thought, and to rationalist economics, public choice theory, and specific manipulative managerial practices and theories, and to related professional ideologies of manipulation, often concentrated in the public sector of the economy. These have displayed transcultural efficacy. They work without recourse to social categories such as race, although they may harmonise with them for reasons of convenience.

Pastoral power is the power of strategic action (manipulation) under the guise of professional communicative action. The basis is systematic professional deception (and self-deception) rather than overt socially categorical power. The academic home of anti-humane sources of power is the behavioural and managerial sciences and economics, as much as modern psychology and criminology. But this is also the place where we should look for hope in a certain sort of academic domestic violence, as we will see below. In short, the ideological basis of pastoral power is the High Modern theorising of professional practice, not the critical modernity which has always opposed this kind of domination. Professionals, who are the agents of this power, can also be the main critics of it.

Habermas on Modernisation and Colonisation

To understand the new colonisation process it is necessary to understand the development and emergence of new kinds of social organisation and new kinds of social processes as a part of the emergence of the modern world. We are not talking here about the usual historical self-image of Western societies — the by now classical narrative of the development of cosmopolis — but an account of change that is as much negative as positive and of the world-historical emergence of a set of processes which is spreading or has spread worldwide. These processes are as inimical to Western culture (in a certain sense of culture to be explained below) as they are to other cultures. The fact that multinational capitalism, the international system (UN, GATT, ILO etc.), the international banking system and clearing systems and so on emerged from European societies (including transplanted ones, like USA), while it may give them a particularly European cultural form, does not make them, from a world-historical point of view, European — they have demonstrated their independence of any and every culture, and their capacity to be imposed on all cultures.

Habermas begins his analysis of this process from a reconstruction of Weber's analysis of European modernisation. In Habermas' view, Weber's analysis concentrated too one-sidedly on the process of change towards the employment of goal-oriented or purposive rational methods in more and more areas of life — the development of the 'iron cage' of purposive or 'instrumental' reason. Weber correctly recognised that the embodiment of these methodologies of problem-solving in institutionalised social structures required the attainment by groups of members of society of postconventional or principled moral reasoning of a strategic kind. However, while he recognised both the enabling power and the dangers of this strategic reason, he did not recognise that the rationality of action could be understood more broadly and that alternative means of rationally reconstructing the traditional world and its patterns were available to modernisers. The strategic means–ends calculus which, admittedly, dominated a great deal of institutional development in the modernising period, particularly in processes of bureaucracy, was not the only non-traditional form which society could adopt. Weber failed to distinguish between instrumental or strategic reason and the forms of reason *internally* characteristic of the sciences' own method of procedure despite his own injunctions to scientists to honour non-strategic values of truth and ethical conduct.

As Habermas tells us

> I have attempted to meet this [deficiency], analytically and in terms of the history of social theory, by elucidating such concepts as 'action oriented to mutual understanding', 'symbolically structured life-world', and 'communicative rationality'. (TCA, Vol. II, p. 303)

In addition to his notion of reason, Weber's analysis was also limited by the inadequacies of his concept of action. For Weber, purposive-rational action (strategic action) and its associated institutional sub-systems (e.g. the bureaucracy) was simply an action-orientation in conflict with consensually-achieved concurrence of worldviews and social life at large. Like Hayek much later, Weber saw the matter of ends and values as essentially an area of anarchy, unable, in principle, to be the subject of rational agreement. Thus he saw the action-orientations associated with value-achievement as being in simple opposition, in various personal circumstances, with the purposive-rational action orientation — tradition versus rational organisation. As discussed earlier, when Popper endorsed a similar view during the 'methodenstreit' (in the 1960s) this position was labelled 'evaluative decisionism' — about values or ends one could not reason, one could only make a decision.[7]

But Habermas argues that what is at stake here are two different levels of social organisation:

> The rationalisation of contexts of communicative action and the emergence of subsystems of purposive rational economic and administrative action are processes that have to be sharply distinguished analytically... [they are also] ...principles of social integration. (TCA, Vol. II, p. 303)

This produces a two-level conception of the process of European modernisation, in which the system level processes of the market (and its strategic management insofar as economic knowledge etc. permits this) and the legal-bureaucratic regulation of life (insofar as this is effective and administrative theory and planning etc. is workable), are seen to have gained increasing autonomy from the lifeworld level (cultural) processes of socialisation and the creation of meaningfulness, motivation and personal identity. This autonomy is associated with Weber's famous diagnosis of the loss of freedom and meaning, because it is an autonomy *against* the lifeworld and traditional values. But the processes of strategic management and manipulation of system level processes, guided by economics and rational management theory, are contrasted by Habermas with *both* the process of taken for granted lifeworld reproduction *and* the process of reconstructing the lifeworld through democratic communicative action (in both the public and the private sphere). The simplest example of this contrast is that between the collegial process of decision-making among a group of peers (academics in a faculty, teachers in a school) and bureaucratic systems of control over such groups, of the kind introduced in Thatcher's Britain or Keating's Australia. So the iron cage of rationality and the market falls around everyday life and the well-springs of cultural meaning but there is a way out *through* modernity and beyond. That way is to a self-conscious reconstruction of culture through communicative value consensus. Bureaucracies administering 'multicultural' policies cannot do this for us. They will be guided only by reasons of state; their ethics, as Ian Hunter[8] tells us are the ethics of *realpolitik*. Only in the democratic public domain can a poly-ethnic society work out an agreement on just what cultural values will be shared by all citizens of a nation and what modifications each culture will have to undergo to allow this common core of values. In this way, a democratic poly-ethnic state can become a bi-cultural nation, with each cultural group sharing the democratic core beliefs as well as possessing its own democratically modified culture. This process of intercultural learning requires democratic processes to take up the cause of professional autonomy — something quite difficult so long as professionals fail to act responsibly themselves. In the case of ex-colonial elites, this process of building a 'national identity' is often perceived as the restoration of a lost or destroyed culture, but that is a nativist myth. The past cannot be reconstructed and original cultural innocence recaptured once it has fled. The result is too often an internal replication of the former colonial system of domination.

Habermas' colonisation thesis derives from Weber's prophetic insight that there may come about a loss of freedom through the extension of (strategic) rationalisation resulting in a

> ...shell of bondage which man will...be forced to inhabit someday, as powerless as the fellahs of ancient Egypt...if a technically superior administration were to be the ultimate and sole value in the ordering of their affairs...a rational [strategic] bureaucratic administration with the corresponding welfare benefits. (Weber quoted by Habermas in TCA, Vol. II, p. 302).

The welfare bureaucracy Weber feared has come into being, although in a lesser degree than 'ultimate'. Ironically, it was brought into being largely by the political gains of the working class political parties, and the development of tax-funded schools, hospitals, aged care, unemployment benefits and the like, as a form of either 'limited social justice' or 'containment of the class struggle' (take your pick). Now, with modern methods of surveillance, and computer dossiers on our every credit card transaction, it has acquired the technology to totalise itself, and, as Ian Hunter has argued, has acquired a certain autonomy and hegemony as a process of governmentalisation of life.

Habermas' argument here also concurs with Foucault's — the new system of rational (i.e. 'knowledge-based') welfare is a system of control. But, unlike Foucault and Weber, Habermas sets the lifeworld and its resources and the possibility of a public, non-strategic or non-manipulative democratic rationality over against this governmentalisation and its processes of pastoral power. In this evaluation of the rational possibilities of the democratic political process, Habermas is more optimistic than

Weber (and Foucault). He is also more culturally open, since lifeworlds are cultural worlds.

The colonisation process is said to occur in a number of ways. But it is important to recognise that *at one level of analysis* the system level processes of money and power can be said to be *extra-cultural*. As we saw in Chapter 2, the anthropological conception of culture — the way of life of a people — tends to run into some difficulties because it glosses over quite fundamental differences in the processes and phenomena included in 'a culture' and includes everything, no matter how different in kind between one level of analysis and another . This point will emerge more clearly below.

The social subsystems differentiated out in the process of European modernisation as the organised institutions of the money system, stock market etc. and the bureaucracies (public and private) have made the coordination and integration of the affairs of very large populations possible (e.g. the EEC). While hitherto great empires, such as those of Rome or China, had existed, they were often very loose confederations of semi-autonomous, tribute-paying regions, grouped around a central power, rather than in any sense, centrally-planned economic or political systems, nor had their management processes been rationalised in the systematic, hierarchical and principled employment of strategically rational technical processes. (The nearest was probably Ancient China, cf.: Weber).

But this process of rationalisation enacts a price, epitomised by the effects on the life of welfare recipients:

> [This process] sets in when the destruction of traditional forms of life can no longer be offset by [the benefits conferred on society as a whole]. The functional ties of money and power media become noticeable only to the degree that elements of a private way of life and a cultural-political form of life [the public sphere] get split off from the symbolic structures of the lifeworld through the monetary redefinition of goals, relations and services, life-spaces and life-times, and through the bureaucratisation of decisions, duties, rights, responsibilities and dependencies. (TCA, Vol. II, p. 322)

In addition, in modern societies, the effects of membership of formal organisations on the individuals who make their working lives in them no longer involves the personal development and ethical challenges of a calling or vocation, or if it appears to do so, does so only in the service of the creation of the kind of subjectivities required by the State.

While governmental organisations depend on their members bringing with them attitudes and values which are the product of the lifeworld (honesty, friendliness), and those inculcated by the pastoral institutions of schooling, they also demand of their members a distancing from that world (despite the persistence within the unofficial relationships of the office of the lifeworld itself). In general, the members of such organisations must create a gulf between their private convictions and the dispositions they must display when acting officially as members. Organisations render themselves immune from the private goals and dispositions of members, as far as possible demanding obedience to organisational norms and goals.

In a sense, then, organisations detach or partially detach themselves from culture.

> Modern forms also need to be independent of legitimating worldviews, in general from cultural traditions that could previously be used only through interpretively continuing and developing them. Organisations use ideological neutrality to escape the force of traditions that would otherwise restrict the scope and the sovereign exercise of that competence to shape their own programs. Just as persons are, as members, stripped of personality structures and neutralised into bearers of certain performances, so too, cultural traditions, as ideologies, are robbed of their binding power and converted into raw material for purposes of ideology planning...for their own legitimation needs.... (TCA, Vol. II, pp. 308–9)

The existence of this detachment from culture, or rather from the level of culture of the lifeworld, and from the reflected upon theoretical world of public, democratic deliberation, which is a shared but not taken for granted cultural resource (found in all societies), indicates that either:

(1) When we speak of modern cultures we are, relative to traditional societies, speaking of systems or processes with another layer or level and with accompanying interlevel complexities, of which lifeworld colonisation is one.

or

(2) When we apply the concept of culture to both modern and non-modern societies we should recognise that the cultural sphere of society does not exhaust all its dimensions and that there are extra cultural processes at work in all societies (but which are more fully differentiated only in modern societies).

In a sense, the system level media of social control with the accompanying institutional processes (e.g. banking and finance systems, bureaucracy) are now loosed in the world at a global level. They have colonised large areas of cultural life in modern societies and they continue to invade more, just as they have spread globally and do the same everywhere, at the level of national and increasingly international systems.

In many respects, the citizen of a modern society is in the same relation to the unexamined values of his or her (cultural) lifeworld as the members of a non-modern society to their culture. Only the degree to which the public sphere has developed in the modern case, and the reflection of the systemic and formal organisational level in the lifeworld, differentiate the two experiences (apart from culturally different content of the lifeworlds in question). The relatively higher prevalence of formal educational processes and their accompanying thought processes are an example of the organised process of transformation of citizens from an enculturated situation into one in which they are able to participate in the extra-cultural levels of sociation required by transcultural organising institutions and processes. More and more citizens of modern society are becoming cosmopolitan. But the degree of culturally autonomy which modern steering systems require is a two edged sword. It cuts against the lifeworld and immersion in traditional culture, but it enables mature learning processes beyond one's culture of origin and between different cultures — always providing situations in which such learning can take place can be found. This possibility points to a kind of intercultural version of the public sphere — an arena for rational-discursive reconstitution of problematic areas of the lifeworld. It is in this domain that we can find the values of our common citizenship of nations, even as, internationally, we *express* our citizenship of the world. The domination of citizens by governments everywhere inhibits this learning and threatens the genuine preservation of interculturally adapted cultures.

Thus, it is not the process of the institutional separation of the spheres of formal education and the family, of large scale organisation and the small, local social group, or of scientific inquiry from everyday practical problem-solving that is responsible for the pathologies which accompany colonisation. Nor is the loss of meaning and freedom Weber speaks of a product of the lack of meaning-giving power of secularised worldviews or of the complexity of a society which has grown beyond the integrative power of the individual. Something more specific is at work. In other words, it is not modernity as such that is at fault but a one-sided development of modernity, aided and abetted by the 'inhumanities' — public choice theory, rationalist economics, neo-liberalism, managerialism and behavioural science. These deny or displace the public sphere, which is the cultural and social space in which democratic reasoning processes can occur. Ideally, the communicative media of press and television are also the media of communication in this sphere, but they function only fitfully in this way today.

They deny or displace traditional cultural values, particularly minority ones and more and more directly threaten the lifeworld. An example will make this loss of meaning clear, and it will also show us some of the implications of instrumental reason untempered by humanism of any kind. The story is told in Washington of a leaked memo of an official of the World Bank. In this memo, which the official concerned claimed was meant to be ironic, the question of the economic benefits of exporting pollution to the third world is canvassed. Many of these countries have clean air and water. This is a commodity. It can be sold by permitting polluting industries to be established. From an economic point of view such air and water is inefficient. It becomes economically efficient when it, too, carries its share of pollution. The same can be said of the mortality and morbidity associated with pollution. Since per capita incomes in the third world are low, the 'negative externalities' of sickness and death caused by pollution are cheaper, because loss of income when someone dies in a low income country is less than in high income countries. So, locating such industries there increases world gross product, i.e. it is economically efficient according to a theory of economics which is largely about rational maximisation of wealth (things that can be bought and sold). As I write these lines, the Chicago futures exchange has set up trade in pollution rights. Irony has a way of becoming reality in the postmodern condition.

Rationality, Colonisation and Pastoral Power

Foucault's attack on the kind of 'truth' that underpins the power of the 'rational' helping professions and provides for them a positive 'knowledge-base', relativises all truth to a regime of power. But truth and the process whereby we discover and corroborate it is far from an agreed and uncontested zone in contemporary intellectual life. It may be valid to argue that much institutionalised professional practice is underpinned by a conception of truth and method which is not only open to abuse but also facilitates, even requires, the use of pastoral power, but to see this as essentially uncontested ground, opposed only locally and marginally, is to do violence to the reality. There are critical professionals as well as acquiescent ones. Foucault may be on firmer ground when he talks of 'bio power', the more primary socialisation process (or 'normalisation' process) which begins in infancy and involves very basic shaping of the body and identity. That would appear to be a ubiquitous accompaniment of social life. However, even there, Foucault does not adequately handle the argument that it is necessary to distinguish between 'necessary repression' and 'surplus repression', to use Marcuse's terminology. Again, this form and level of power has not been innocent of critics prior to Foucault (e.g. Mackie, 1979)[9] and at the professional level, there has been a vigorous and widespread campaign of critical rejection and diagnosis which has in many ways anticipated both levels of Foucault's critique and gone beyond it. This critique can easily be traced back to the 19th century and earlier.

At the heart of pastoral power is a process in which a truncated conception of rationality supports an 'expert' culture, and a paternalistic self-image among experts supports a manipulative form of professional practice in the service of government power. In various areas of practically-oriented theory, whether in economics, management, or the applications of behavioural science, the essential structure is the same — an epistemology which supports a control-oriented, monological and instrumental understanding of knowledge, a fragmentation and specialisation of this knowledge which, coupled with educational systems, makes this knowledge available only to a few, and an ideology of practice which justifies the technical 'application' of this knowledge to the professionally-defined 'needs' of clients for the sake of preserving the state. Arguably, Adorno's analysis of instrumental reason or Habermas' early critique of control oriented reason can tell us something worthwhile about this process, even if Foucault's cultural and institutional analysis of the governmentalisation of life through the system of discourse and practices in modern penology, education, social work, or research provided a new level of penetration of it.

A separate critique of each sphere of thought and practice would be necessary if the various forms of the power/knowledge connection were to be adequately explored — that is, we would need a genealogical anthropology of the way rationalist economic theory underpins the practices of a class of economic bureaucrats and redefines the limits of the political sphere by building an essentially apolitical, trans-cultural economic subject into the theory from the beginning, a similar analysis for public choice theory, managerial theory and so on. In each sphere we would have to come to terms with the way

> In an unjust state of life, the importance and pliability of the masses grow[s] with the quantitative increase in the commodities allowed them. (Adorno/Horkheimer, *Dialectic of Enlightenment*, 1979, p. xiv)[10]

Limitations of space (and no doubt the competence of the author) preclude any substantive treatment of these themes here. However, critique is well under way elsewhere. The present argument must focus on the communicative implications of the mode of power called 'pastoral', and its expression at the institutional level of governmentalisation. We are talking about the kind of distortions that can occur when experts deal with lay clients and about the policy process whereby governments steer and systematise this. These distortions increasingly rival the more direct distortions of traditional political and cultural power and are characteristic of the experience of more and more of the powerless and oppressed of the world.

Habermas has identified the central distortion of strategic reason as the distortion of concealed strategic action. In his analysis of types of action and interaction, Habermas identifies strategic action as ego-centred calculation directed at finding the best means to ego's ends. This analysis extends to actions calculated to benefit a group. We are familiar with action (and interaction) of this kind in competitive games. It is Weber's purposive-rational action pursued egocentrically or ethnocentrically rather than universally. At the collective level of the state, ego-entrism gives way to absolutising the survival and growth of the state. (Habermas does not discuss the possibility of the collective pursuit of the interests of a particular class or culture-group or the broader ideological processes of concealment that may be associated with collective deception, but it would appear that the analysis could be applied to intercultural relations and action systems as well as to interaction between individuals).

By itself this process does not always lead to distorted communication. Distortion arises only when the strategic character of action is concealed beneath a communicative mask. However, distortion of this kind is common enough, perhaps even definitive of social relations in much of the modern world: the person in business, pursuing a sales objective, but pretending to be concerned about the client's interests; the boss who consults employees more for the purpose of making them feel consulted than with an intention of actually taking their views into account; the politician who makes lots of 'sincere' speeches, carefully crafted by media minders on the basis of polls, with no intention of implementing the stated or implied policies; spouses who show the necessary affection in order to get their way sexually; the development consultant who pays lip-service to local culture but has arrived in a third-world country determined to implement a pre-decided development scheme; the teacher who seeks student opinion but does not value it or allow it any *logical role* in the lesson's structure of reasoning; the list goes on...

These are ancient and familiar deceptions, and you might well ask what is specifically modern about them. It is this, that modern societies have professionalised and institutionalised such deceptions, so that they have become definitive of much modern expert or professional practice. Reasons of state have become disguised as ethical concerns. The State, seeking to mobilise more of the reserve of human capital for reasons of survival, speaks the language of equity and the equality of minorities and women.

The problem from a communicative point of view, or, rather, from the point of view of a communicative conception of rationality, is that it is not possible to respond to a concealed validity claim (unless you guess what the other person is trying to do). The concealment of an intention closes off the normal communicative and mutual access to validity judgements, whether this concealment is through untruth, the improper adoption of a speaking role, the appearance of a sincerity not actually present, or, and perhaps more importantly, the concealment which results from an institutionalised structure of controlled communication and restricted information flow. The apparatus of the governmental state is such a structure — a systematic concealment of the decisions of the state from genuine democratic scrutiny and validity judgement.

This concealment introduces a communicative distortion, which, eventually, results in disillusionment and distrust, because all such concealment eventually will out — when the other person goes away and acts in a manner contrary to the expectations they have aroused, or a policy development consultation results in an oppressive policy.

It is not simply a communication problem, a mere difficulty in making validity judgements, repairable by a temporary conversational repair sequence, or realignment of speaker perceptions. It is a fundamental defect in relationships and in the public process. Even done with benevolent intent, it constitutes an act of treating another person or group either directly or by institutional default as less than an interlocutor, as less than beings capable of making and having a right to make, validity judgements. Bureaucracy typically treats the public this way. Two examples may make this point clearer.

What we object to when a used car salesperson adopts a friendly tone and talks of 'helping' us, using our given name, is not that we cannot see all this pseudo-friendship is a sales ploy, but that it makes it all the more conversationally difficult to ask pointed questions about the age of the automobile and the state of its engine. We suspect that all the show of friendship can coexist with an intention of drawing our attention away from the defects of the car.

What we often object to when the boss engages in a process of calling the workers in one by one for consultation is not that our ideas aren't always translated into policy but that we are unsure whether our ideas were taken seriously and we usually get no feedback about just how many of our colleagues may have agreed with what we said. That is, we are unsure the extent to which something concealed is going on and the process of consultation is genuine. The systematic misuse of opinion polling and surveys by government are also an example of this. Instead of setting up opportunities for members of cultural minorities to have a direct voice, they are effectively gagged in all but controlled channels of voice.

The problem here is quite distinct from the 'old' political problem of communicating with the colonial administrator who overtly proclaimed his superiority. Those who may issue commands do not generally see a need to manipulate, pseudo-consult and the like. Only as nation-based colonial power fades does the often transnational institutional power of professional control and market management, with its technologies of control and motivation, begin to grow in importance.

So money and power are indifferent to keeping faith communicatively. They are uninterested in sincerity, only the persuasive effectiveness of appearing to be sincere, even if this currency is fast liquefying and running into the sands of cynicism. The strategic form of communicative distortion is the epitome of distortions of colonisation of the lifeworld in all cultures, because the choice of being communicatively sincere is reduced to just another strategy, to be replaced by strategic concealment if it is deemed that that would be more effective. In this way, the study of rhetoric is reduced to the study of persuasion. Truth is lost sight of — and pragmatic truth is about the genuine voice of peoples.

What is at stake here is the politics of the political situation or context. There is no substitute for political action *by cultural movements at the level of context* because genuine communication is not possible unless certain contextual requirements are met. Whether we are talking about the public sphere, or interpersonal interaction, the reconstitution of the disturbed areas of the lifeworld cannot take place unless the requirements for discursive reason are approximated. What, up to now in this chapter, we have considered negatively, under the rubric of modernisation, the separation of institutionalised instrumental reason, the colonisation of the lifeworld, and forms of distorted communication, we must now consider positively, in terms of the conditions for constituting a sphere of mutual understanding, even across the chasm of cultural difference and in the teeth of governmentalising processes indifferent to the preservation of the unique genius of each culture. The politics of anticolonialism (internal or internal) cannot work if they are simply an anti-politics, they must also be a pro-politics. We have seen what we must be against, let us now turn to what we must be for, and how we must be for it. Only then is politics as strategy possible, albeit, in a democratic politics, openly strategic.

The Political Conditions of Intercultural Learning

Intercultural learning is one of the products of the *extended* or global public domain — a democratic or public good which accrues to individuals initially, and eventually to groups of individuals as members of cultures. This process is essentially the same whether it occurs within a multicultural society or between cultural groups which are also national political groups (and increasingly, with the decline of absolute national sovereignty, there is less and less difference between the two).

It is necessary to recognise the crucial role of intellectuals (all those who give real thought to issue) in this process. The primary concern of intellectuals is the spiritual situation of their age — overarching meanings, goals and values for both persons and communities and the actual condition of our attainment or non-attainment of these. As Charles Taylor tells us, the purpose of theory is to make our practices 'clairvoyant' in respect of our goals, including those practices whereby we articulate them. In *totalising* perspectives the politics of intellectuals becomes a dogmatic politics of dialectically-required antithesis, rather than a morally charged politics of marginal voices and readiness to learn from others. Such perspectives are called 'totalising' because they see the totality of social life as being conditioned by one set of influences (e.g. the 'economy or national efficiency') and they generally see these influences as being beyond rational control and so unavailable for direct political action (e.g. the market, capitalism).

This definition of the role of intellectuals, and of theory, seeks to avoid the prevailing, and fashionably avante-garde cultural and political atomism (and antihumanism) and reinstates an understanding of the learning process of individuals and groups and of the role of theory (and intellectuals) in this learning. Intercultural learning fits into this framework as a form of learning which, at its structural level, functions in the same way as dialogue among individual interlocutors in any learning community (e.g. physicists), and is valued for the reasons already advanced by intellectuals such as Dewey or Habermas.

In this metatheorising of intercultural learning, I am seeking to reinstate a vision of shared knowledge and the general good, but to reinstate this at the level of interculturally shared spirituality and the species good (which includes in some sense the good of other species). I am also seeking to insulate this learning from the dangers of a dogmatic collectivism where cultures square off against each other with no intention of learning from each other. It is a metatheory which seeks to address the spiritual situation of our age. It is thus intended to be a historically situated *diagnostic* study, which takes as its field of study both the conditions of life at a given time and place as well as, reflexively, the emerging theorising of this life. As such, it is a theory of the lifeworld, its breakdown, its colonisation, and the alternative, communicative processes through which it may be reconstituted interculturally through the creation of an intercultural public space. Sociology, cultural studies, education and related disciplines emerged with the development of the modern world and progressively, especially under 'postmodern' conditions address the modern world's self-conscious character.

As Charles Taylor says, 'there has never been an age so theory-drenched as ours', but the presence of these theories is *constitutive* of modernity since the theoretical self-consciousness of our institutions is a corollary of their cultural differentiation. The implication of this for intercultural learning may become clearer if we examine for a moment the institution in modern societies which is quintessentially associated with their theoretically self-conscious character — education.

An atomistic understanding of public goods, including schools and colleges, is one in which the social and political process is conceived of as an order of reality constituted by the aggregate effect of individual action, with no provision for any role for consciousness to provide a non-totalising means of going beyond mere aggregation. The primary theoretical reflection of this view of society is a liberal political theory and an associated market theory of social choice. In this view, the public domain can only be a manipulated sphere of massaged political images, reduced to an arm of public administration. It is coupled with the market, which Hayek tells us is an apparatus for optimising decisions where irreducible value pluralism rather than rational legitimation processes exist. In other words, if all is commodity, then we turn to advertising to make markets for products and we do this in *all* spheres of life, including those in which we define the value of life and life values. The result is that rational, democratic expression of difference in life-values including cultural difference is reduced to who has the most marketing power. We not only lose rational persuasion to the market but we also lose the particular vision of the world groups of people have developed in their way of life — their culture.

In this view, society is just a pattern of interaction of individual agents seeking to satisfy their desires. Some readings of Foucault and Derrida reflect this same social atomism. In this view, society can only be judged in terms of the efficiency with which it satisfies 'consumers' as individuals or by its overall level of distributive demand-satisfaction. It is, if you like, the opposite error to that of totalisation of society according to the life-values of only one group and it is also opposite in its effects. The marketisation and thus individualisation of culture is the destruction of culture and its resources, because culture can only be sustained by a way of life — its individualisation and reduction to a market preference removes it from the source of sustenance.

For instance, schooling, in such a view, is a consumption process with a small investment component. The purpose of much of the curriculum, beyond the elementary school, is to meet consumer demand, not public need, and pedagogy is judged as a secondary good in terms of client satisfaction with the efficiency of the certification process. Schooling becomes thereby just another business. The connection of schooling with culture and of public schooling with democratic citizenship is broken.

However, the idea of education is a quintessentially modern idea. It *replaced* older ideas of personal cultivation, or marginalised them, and it is not compatible with the newer, more philistine ideas of personal consumption of instruction which neo-conservative educators of the economic rationalist kind appear to favour, but neither is it compatible with a lifestyle radicalism confined to issues of cultural marginalisation. The idea of education is based on the notion of a *shared good*. Unlike common goods, which are goods many individuals may unawares seek in common, shared goods must be commonly appreciated and are constitutive of individuals *qua* members of a commonwealth or republic. The context of education is the good life, not just questions of justice, despite their great importance. So an educational politics based on the participation of all marginalised groups in the existing market society is a poor politics — educationally — because the market does not address *shared* problems, such as the global problems with which this book began. What is needed is a conception of the shared good sufficient to sustain common citizenship and which extends to the good *we all derive* from the presence in our society, beyond the needs of citizenship, of culturally diverse groups.

Rousseau's concept of the 'general will' requires that citizens not ask themselves what is in the interests of each but what is the appropriate content of the general will. Kant's notion of the 'categorical imperative' by which the moral domain is defined by just those rules which an agent can understand to be of such a character that they could justly bind all equally, also picks out a domain of shared goods. Clearly, though, these and other attempts at characterising shared goods have run into difficulties of various kinds, foremost among which have been problems for individual liberties and cultural differences. Education is about the resolution of these difficulties. In the case of education of children it is about the introduction of them *into* the search for an understanding of the possibility of a shared life which while not constitutive of the oppression of individuals or minorities, is not simply a life defined by the negation of oppression, but a life defined positively, in terms of possible goods, including the good of individual and cultural diversity. For example, we can negate oppression of women by getting rid of the 'glass ceiling' and so on. Women could then participate quite equally in the current system of oppression! Or we could acknowledge differences while pursuing common justice for women.

In this view, the discipline of education centres around the problematic of learning and adaptation itself. It is a problematic of problematics. But it is also a particular kind of problematic, the problematic of the individual in the public domain. The values that motivate educative learning are just those of republican communities, which at this stage of their evolution, have come to understand that they face globally shared problems of common good, common peace, commonwealth and the preservation of their common environment, and at the same time a deep-seated threat to human diversity. The communities have begun, this century, to create the beginnings of a multicultural republic of the whole species, but both its capacity for common ground and for the preservation of diversity are under threat.

Intercultural understanding is implicated in the whole range of human striving and the whole range of human relationships, but when we talk of public goods as species goods, we are tilting the intercultural playing field in favour of a particular role for theory and for intellectuals. Critical theory, at least in Habermas' version, has a built in value-tilt of this kind. This statement implies a preference for a democratic form of empowerment, for a critique of ideology which locates the institutional and communicative obstacles to empowering communication, and a preference for a developmental logic which leads towards progressive decentring of the ego (and the culture of origin), while not washing away all difference.

The road ahead lies neither in the exaltation of separate cultures as total, complete and worthy of entire preservation, nor in the triumph of one culture over others. Ironically, the rescue of oppressed cultures can only be carried out by a process of dialogue in which both they and oppressor cultures in their pure forms are given up. Multiculturalism, within the boundaries of a single political entity (e.g. a nation), cannot be a process of preservation of separate cultures. It *can* be a process whereby each culture is respected and protected in its dialogue with all others, as it, and they change, and a (better) interculture emerges. The politics of multiculturalism then becomes a politics of deconstructing discourses for their tilt towards one culture or another, and a politics of communication and its culturally asymmetrical political structures and practices. Clearly this must lead to a politics in which intellectuals must play a role. But it is not a politics driven by intellectual dogmatism or the pretence to science — the role of intellectuals and professionals in this politics is something I will return to in the closing chapter.

In the critical process, cultural differences are de-absolutised, but are not necessarily reduced to a set of quaint customs. What is necessary to such a process is the development of bi-cultural and tri-cultural people, respect for difference, and intercultural understanding. Ironically, for this to occur, it is necessary for 'traditional' societies to become, in some degree, modern, not in the sense of High Modernity, but in the sense of a de-absolutising of both culture and instrumental reason — a tolerant, humane and pluralistic *critical* reason. Becoming modern, is not the same thing, by any means, as becoming European, as the Japanese example shows. Becoming critically modern in a non-European way would seem possible for Japan, but there are few signs of it as yet. For change of this kind there will need to be a more numerous and vocal class of Japanese intellectuals among other things.

Make no mistake, what I am arguing is contentious. An example will clarify what is at stake. In some cultures, the status of women is problematic by comparison with that of men. There is a clear subordination of women and a denial to them of basic rights, such as the right to drive a car or travel. In a dialogue between cultures there can be no question of such a culture claiming the privilege of freedom from criticism on this point. Equally, within North America, there can be no question of simultaneously achieving equality for women and preservation in all respects of minority cultures that do not accord women equal rights. Conversely, some of the very cultures where the status of women is problematic can teach the dominant culture of North America something about caring for the elderly and respecting the rights of children. No culture has a monopoly of virtue, but, equally, no culture can be immune from critique. Difficulties emerge for this process of mutual learning when critics from another culture do not understand what it is they think they are criticising, or where one culture is so dominant that the learning is expected to be all one way. Intellectuals from dominant culture backgrounds, like myself, need to practice consid-erable restraint in this process of critique (but not necessarily in the process of meta-critique) because it is possible to drown out the voices of the oppressed even when speaking *in their name*. Indeed, Habermas defines a key term 'mündigkeit' or emancipation, as precisely the capacity to speak in one's own name.

If we follow Habermas' categories, intellectuals may be said to have three roles. The first role of intellectuals is meta-theoretical critique — the theory of how we may make our future selves and do it in some way that gives us a better than even chance of making better selves. Philosophy and social theory provide some of the tools for this. I hope this book is in some degree an example of that.

The second intellectual role is ideology critique. This must draw on sociology and history for resources, but it must be carried out by those with a direct stake in the problem situation, because critique is socially and biographically constitutive, not simply cognitive. Intellectuals may propose critical analyses, but they cannot validate them in socially-formative meaning-action. The voices of marginalised and oppressed peoples must have a major role in this. Deconstructive studies and cultural criticism are useful tools for this work, but some critique of social structures and institutions is essential too. However, unless this critique is allied to the politics of social movements it will be ineffective.

A third role is critical communicative studies, the most important mode of which is critical empirical pragmatics (CEP). This can be a kind of ideology critique, but it differs from cultural and structural critique because it focuses on the process of meaning-action itself. It is the detailed study of practices to show their effects on cultures and individuals.

If we set aside for a moment that the work of theorising is also a form of practice, then the practice of intercultural action consists of politically effective change of institutions based on detailed critique of reality creating practices within them. These are what is dealt with in the next two chapters of the book.

Notes

1. H. Arendt, *The Human Condition*. Chicago, University of Chicago Press, 1971.
2. J. Habermas, *The Theory of Communicative Action*, Vol. 2. Cambridge: Polity Press, 1986.
3. e.g. N. Fraser, 'Michel Foucault: A 'Young Conservative'.' *Ethics*, 96 (October), 1985, pp. 165–84.
4. Habermas, 'On the German-Jewish heritage'. *Telos*, 44 (Summer), 1980, pp. 127–31.
5. See W. Feinberg, 'Interpretation and the postmodern condition'. *Philosophy of Education*, 1993, pp. 14–18.

6. C. Taylor, 'Foucault on freedom and truth'. *Political Theory*, 12 (2), 1984, pp. 152–83.
7. See K. Popper, *Objective Knowledge*. London: Routledge, 1971.
8. I. Hunter, *Re-Thinking the School*. Sydney: Allen and Unwin, 1994.
9. F. Mackie, in R. Young *et al*. (eds), *Issues and Critique in Australian Educational Policy*., Geelong: Deakin University, 1982.
10. T. Adorno, *Dialectic of Enlightenment*, with Max Horkheimer. New York: Herder and Herder, 1972.

7 Critical Cultural Action: Pragmatics, Genealogy and Deconstruction

Critical Research for Cultural Reconstruction

The last two chapters of this book are about 'Critical Multicultural Practice' but it might be objected that they aren't very practical. They provide no technology or step by step set of guidelines for action. There are two reasons for this. First, no such technology of action exists. Action is creative; it is an art. Second, action is something that can only be creatively designed and carried out by *participants* in a situation. No external recipe is possible.

It might be useful to have included a section on successful lobby groups and social movements — women's groups, the gay rights movement, civil rights activism and so on. There is a wide range of strategies and tactics that have met with success, but there are also instances where the same tactics or strategies have failed. No book can be a substitute for people in situations deciding what risks they are willing to take and how much time and effort they are willing to devote to a non-private cause. Habermas discusses this issue in *Theory and Practice*. For more tactical guidance, readers are referred to recent books describing the successes (and failures) of social movements.

This section is guidance for practice at the level of guiding the analyses that practice and social movements require — to indicate the *direction* action should take, to uncover ideological practices, to develop alternative, theoretically-grounded definitions of reality. That is, guidance for cultural action. For effective, local political decisions, it is necessary to understand ideology at several levels — the levels of the social system, particular social institutions, communicative interaction in institutionalised situations, and at the level of the ideological texts which encode the 'metaphysics' of ideology. The last of these levels is the one usually thought of when people speak of ideologies — sets of beliefs and associated categories and expressions.

Critical communicative studies are empirical studies of communicative structures and practices. They are critical because they seek to identify ideological practices and to connect critical empirical research in face to face situations with the further institutionalisation of democratic political practices. They do this by identifying instances of communicative distortion and by pointing to the institutional and cultural roots of these. They are a resource for politics but do not of themselves constitute a politics. Nevertheless, they have to be conducted with political acumen because they must mesh with wider political strategies. Ultimately, like ideology critique of which they are a part, they must be validated in the experience of participants.

Critical communicative studies have two main dimensions — the first is the study of institutionalised communicative structures, including those which differentially distribute social roles and social situations among categories of people such as 'races', classes, linguistic groups, ethnic groups, and gender groups. The second is the study of communicative practices in these situations, including both those which influence the formation of written texts and those which structure spoken texts.

In the institutional dimension, a key focus must be the extension of the colonisation process, whereby money and power are reintegrating the modern global society by subordinating not only cultural lifeworlds but also hitherto separate value spheres of aesthetic action and institutionalised inquiry. Increasingly, the commercialisation of art and forms of public expression, and the development of 'cultural' policy by governments, is having an impact on the wide array of expressive and performing arts. A new form of 'capitalist realism' is emerging, matching 'socialist realism' in its morbidity. The growing internationalisation of education presents great opportunities for growth in international understanding, but these are being squandered as the marketisation process grips educational programs more tightly. The imposition of state and international governmental economic priorities on school curricula and university research programs, coupled with greater integration of research with military and commercial goals is drastically limiting the openness of inquiry, particularly in countries with constitutional power over universities. In turn, this process further increases the steering power of the bureaucratic apparatus and the force of the market. Foucault's pessimism may be excessive when applied too widely, but it appears less unrealistic when applied to the academy. As we will see, his discussion of the nature of the apparatuses and processes of control provide useful guidance for the study of colonisation.

In the study of communicative practices, Derrida, read as a philosopher, can offer useful insights into the *results* of inscription, as coercive apparatuses of state control of culture and expression violently write meaning into the ontogenesis of bodies of various kinds. Deconstructive critique uncovers the traces of this meaning formation, particularly in written texts.

However, it is Habermas who offers us most illumination of face to face communication practices, since Habermas theorises process and action rather than structure. It is fair to say that there is a sense in which Foucault and Derrida, often called post-structuralists, can still be seen as structuralist.

One place where you would expect critical analysis be well-developed is in the study of cross-cultural communication. However, the state of the art in intercultural education and training is less than satisfactory. The typical level of analysis, the methodology and the forms of learning and critique commonly found, all fall short of the level of adequacy necessary for solving our global problems. This chapter begins with a brief look at the present state of 'cross-cultural' training. Much of the work in this field displays all the faults of behavioural approaches to this field discussed in Chapter 3: individualist analysis, literalistic or conservative hermeneutics, inability to deal with change or political action for cultural change, an implicitly stereotyping methodology, lack of a developed social-structural and institutional level of analysis, failure to cope with cultural and personal ambiguity and a view of interlocutors as lacking in both critical distance from their own culture and culture-changing agency.

Discussion then moves on to Habermas' analysis. The limits of this analysis are identified. Generally speaking, Habermas' approach is too abstract for empirical use (which he himself acknowledges), is lacking in a cultural critique, has a developed discussion of only a few of the kinds of distortion in communication, and fails to develop an institutional critique beyond the rather abstract level reached in Volume 2 of *Toward a Theory of Communicative Action*.[1] I will argue that Derrida's approach handles empirical cultural critique at the level of critique of cultural forms and codes better than Habermas' somewhat ad hoc approach, but is not incompatible, in my reading, with Habermas' process oriented analysis of ontological structuration (as Derrida himself would appear to agree)[2] and that Foucault's theoretical ideas, suitably shorn of their absolutism and pessimism, allow us to identify a range of structural and institutionalised communicative distortions. Building on Habermas' general theory, I will outline a form of critical hermeneutics of communicative interaction which is useful at the interpersonal level. Finally, I will argue that communicative hope offers us a useful tool of criticism that the other theorists lack, providing normative guidance for the positive development of communicative cooperation.

'Cross-Cultural' Training Manuals

In Chapter 3 we looked briefly at behavioural analyses of intercultural communication. The focus there was on the theorising of culture and meaning. Now we pick up the thread again with the same work which was criticised in that chapter, Y.Y. Kim's study[3] of cultural adaptation. It was argued earlier that a focus on what was effectively a behavioural psychological analysis created a narrowing of perspective. The same narrowing is carried through to the definition of communicative competence. This is defined solely in terms of adapting *to* the host culture (p. 49). All critique of the host culture is described as a disorder and as an evidence of failure and as 'defensive reactions' (p. 55) and all stress as 'the internal resistance of the human organism against its own cultural evolution' (p. 55). As Kim puts it:

> The successful adaptation of strangers is realised only when their internal communication systems (i.e. self-talk and identity, RY) sufficiently overlap with those of the natives. ...For the natives, such internal communication capacity has been acquired from so early in life and has been so completely internalised into their personal (i.e. internal, RY) communication system, that, by and large, it operates automatically and unconsciously. (Kim, p. 61)

'Automatically and unconsciously'. At one level this is descriptively accurate, 'by and large', but are human agents incapable of *any reflection*? A curious symmetry between the analyses of textualists and Kim continues to emerge. In the first, the dominance of the text is so complete that it defines all that is meaningful — regardless of the mechanisms (unstated) whereby the individual possesses, absorbs, is absorbed by or 'memberships' in the culture. In the second, the individual just *is* the communication capacity (values, beliefs, assumptions, grammar, vocabulary, rules for speaking, approved identities etc.).

There is no trace here of an awareness of ambiguity and contradiction, of the ideological character of aspects of culture (e.g. gender identities) and resistance to it. In addition, there appears to be no awareness of the research literature on bilingualism and of the possible ways in which growing up in multicultural society might offer insights for the immigrant situation (to which Kim's theory is limited by stipulation). The relationship between cultural ambiguity and cultural criticism is not explored.

When host society 'variables' are factored into Kim's model they are a given. The 'receptivity' of the host society is a fixed quantity as is the level of 'conformity pressure'. Of course, it must be fixed if there is no possibility of a politics which would bring about changes in the receptivity of the host society, through education, racial discrimination programmes etc.

The assumption which creates this distortion is expressed by Kim at one point in these words:

> The dominant culture of the host society controls the life activities of individual immigrants and sojourners, which necessitates an adaptation of individuals, not vice versa. (Kim, p. 37)

Presumably textualists would agree with Kim and say that the cultural text defines what is meaningful and if immigrants wish to be seen to be meaningful they must operate within that text.

While this may be descriptively true if expressed far less absolutely, it misses one crucial point. When individuals can engage in a politics of ethnic recognition and assertion, they may have a much greater sense of power and control, and be more able to make any necessary adaptation than those who are unable to do so. Culture to both children and immigrants may be largely experienced as a given, but it is changeably, flexibly given and the application of the descriptions available in it to any given instance of 'rule following' is negotiable.

So much for the contradictions in this kind of behavioural theory. The problems identified are characteristic of all empiricist approaches to these questions. Broadly, empiricism is characteristic of traditional theories. At best, such theories describe how society is at the present time but because they lack an adequate explanation of the present state of affairs, they also lack any vision of difference or change, particularly of any politics of change. Traditional social theories connect with traditional and moderate hermeneutic theories, because they rest on a view of communication which fails to foreground its active ontogenetic character — the way change is built-in whenever we communicate.

There are also absences in this kind of theory. Absent is any sense of the many situations where the process of adaptation is less one-sided. While there is some casual recognition of the processes of world wide change there is little of this vision built into the theory and so there is no long term value in the theory as a *general* theory of intercultural communication. The 'global village' will not be created by immigrants everywhere adapting to host societies but only by 'host societies' also adapting to immigrants and both immigrants and hosts moving to a more sophisticated awareness of intercultural problems. The stipulative limitation of the theory to the adaptation of individuals to the host society is not simply a limit of the usefulness of the theory in different situations, it is a limitation on the usefulness of the theory in just the situations it is supposed to apply to — specifically, that of the USA today — both by reason of its internal contradictions, and by reason of its inappropriateness for the demographic politics of states like California which will soon be evenly balanced between 'white-anglo' Americans and 'newcomers'. Who will then do the adapting?

Absent, too, is any attempt to come to grips with the central theoretical problem of intercultural communication — that of how it is possible for members of different cultures to understand each other *without* one culture surrendering its integrity to the other, an outcome implicit in Kim's focus on the adaptation of the individual immigrant to the host culture by acquiring the assumptions, identity, rules for speaking etc. of the host culture, even to the level of internalisation. Only some theory which outlines, in the place of adaptation, a notion of mutual adaptation and critique, and of inter-evolution, can meet this requirement, but such a theory can only rest on a theory of culture which sees it as open to the two way processes of structuration.

As an attempt to provide a framework for the study of intercultural communication that is 'objective' and 'free from ideology' Kim's study is a signal failure. Its failure seems to flow as much from its methodological individualism and simple positivism as from the limitation of its focus to one-way adaptation processes.

I think I have said enough to show that Kim's theory has failed the empirical test of adequacy to the *whole* situation is supposed to deal with. But it should not be surprising that Kim's theory has failed empirically, even though the empirical area is the area in which this kind of theorising would claim its greatest strength. The flaw lies in the traditional hermeneutic theory which behavioural theory has tacitly to rely on in its attempt to make sense of communication. This theory is, admittedly, not the same as the more familiar traditional hermeneutics. That relies on notions of empathy, or on accounts of the objectivity of public meaning. Kim's work displays the behavioural equivalent.

But most cross-cultural training manuals appear to do much the same.

There is little point in dealing with most manuals in the same detail as I have dealt with Kim's book. Many of them have a certain usefulness, if their readers are monocultural provincials. It is useful to learn that things you may have taken for granted, such as greetings, bodily comportment, customs and the small rituals of everyday life are different in different cultures. But surely there can be scarcely anyone who watches television or attends the movies who hasn't learned this already? The problems of most manuals run deeper.

It is common to encounter a rules-based view of culture. The cultural rules are often depicted somewhat absolutely. This results in a reduction of the process of communication to a question of who will learn and use whose rules. There is no ambiguity or ambivalence. No room for the negotiation of hybrid sets of rules. And the problems of communication are typically reduced to problems of miscommunication and little or no reference is made to the distorting effects of the politics of relations between cultures. There is rarely any reference to empirical research on what people typically do when confronted with the need to communicate with someone from a different culture. Research of this kind, on interlanguage, stranger talk, intercultural talk strategy, lingua franca, bilingualism etc. is valuable because it shows that people draw on the widest range of resources when confronted by the intercultural communication situation.

However, the more research-based manuals do make some effort to discuss research of this kind.[4] They provide useful discussions of how communicators simplify, repeat themselves, wait, use more gestures than usual and increase the redundancy of their messages etc. But the list of strategies is typically incomplete. There is seldom any reference to the strategy of talking *about* the difficulty in communication or to the problems posed by very different levels of *linguistic* competence in the language in use.

But perhaps the most pervasive error is the social abstraction of most treatments. The context and the communicative task is seldom taken into account. All communicators are assumed to be business people in a conference or negotiation, or, often enough, there is not even a putative context of any kind. No attention is paid to differences in the language of communication (Is it theirs, ours or a third language?), differences in the politics of communication (Are we meeting as equals? Does one party feel superior?), in the task (Is it negotiation, planning, exchange of information, artistic sharing etc.?), or to differences in the institutionalised arrangements surrounding the communication (Is it an international organisation with established protocols or a casual encounter among fellow tourists?). Finally, while there is an acknowledgment of cultural differences — usually defined in terms of concepts or worldviews, little assistance is given to coping with this. The net effect of these shortcomings is that the would-be intercultural communicator learns a short list of somewhat misleading 'rules' for doing things like presenting business cards with both hands in Japan, or allowing the oldest person to speak first in some African countries. These rules sometimes fail, because they cannot cover all situations, but they have some usefulness.

The problem is that the list of rules we would have to learn to be culturally successful is so long that it could not effectively be contained in such manuals. And what is involved in 'following a rule', as we saw in Chapter 2, is not so simple. Of course, these difficulties are not as significant if we are talking about a communicator who is fluent in a second language. Learning a language to the level of fluency, especially by modern methods, is also learning a culture. Situations where the communication is in the language of the politically, institutionally or culturally dominant (or would-be dominant) party are more significant sources of difficulty and distortion. Strangely enough, situations of this kind are often implicit in the discussions in cross-cultural training manuals.

The possibility that the culturally other may be a sophisticated, cosmopolitan communicator is seldom entertained. The possibility that the culturally other may be a critic of their own traditional culture is seldom entertained. Instead, we are presented with a stereotype, even while we are being warned against stereotypes. Along with illustrations and examples, and even, for the beginner, catalogues of useful rules of thumb, we need tools for deeper critique and awareness. Habermas' depiction of ontogenetic conversation, in which interlocutors make ontological claims and commitments, in institutionally structured exchanges, which are sometimes distorted in various deep ways provides a better model for understanding what goes on in intercultural communication. Conflict resolution models approximate this process and the pedagogy through which people learn conflict resolution skills is more appropriate than that which most manuals currently employ.[5] Learning intercultural communication would proceed better if it proceeded through relatively complex and carefully constructed simulations of culturally embedded institutional talk contexts, and focused not on rules but on strategies and critique.

Habermas' critical pragmatics can allow critical analysis of talk. Foucault's institutional critique can be extended from the monocultural settings of his own genealogical anthropology (French prisons etc.) to the identification of the dispositifs of the United Nations General Assembly, the international scientific conference, the US–Japanese business and trade relationship and so on, and particular situated communications can be located within these wider institutionalised relationships. And the ontological commitments — the metaphysics — of interlocutors can be understood by deconstructive readings of the coding of reality presented in their texts.

Intercultural Oppression and Critical Analysis

Not all intercultural talk is genuinely communicative. As we saw in Chapter 1, communication in a fuller sense is somewhat different from manipulating others through talk. It is possible to represent this difference in somewhat the same way as Dewey conceptualised it, by contrasting mechanical and normal communication:

> ...within even the most social group there are many relations which are not as yet social. A large number of human relations in any social group are still upon the mechanical plane. Individuals use one another so as to get desired results...

but

> By normal communication is meant that in which there is joint interest, a common interest, so that one is eager to give and the other to take... (*Democracy and Education*, p. 217)[6]

What is at stake, then, is the difference between what Habermas has called strategic action and communicative action or 'normal' communication. A certain degree of understanding is necessary even for mechanical communication, but the understanding required is limited to agreement on the semantic meaning of the words. It does not extend to agreement about the relationship between the speakers, or to any revelation of inner states between them. That is, the ontogenetic agency of some is subordinated to that of others. In place of agreement about relationships in which particular words are spoken, there is some form of power, to which the response is not genuine agreement but temporary submission. In place of an opening up of the inner world of the self to the other, there is a denial of access to the personal dimension in the relationship. The concomitant of power is impersonality or rather the depersonalisation of the oppressed person.

Habermas deals with this issue by speaking about the connection between 'understanding' and 'reaching an understanding'. He argues that there are connections between understanding the kind of validity claims being made and actual judgements of validity. These judgements take the form of a recognition of the equality of the other because they take the form of an intersubjective agreement to accept the validity of a particular norm or way of seeing the world as reality.[7] Critics have called this a confusion between different kinds of analysis but I would prefer to say that it is the critics whose analysis is shallow.

In a single utterance, a speaker makes claims about the factual truth of the existential claims of the utterance, the normative appropriateness of both the relationship of the communicators, and of uttering the kind of existential claims made in that relationship. Speakers also make claims about their own inner feelings about all of this, in a given socially defined situation. Only in judgements about these claims, in the context of the situation, can hearers understand the many dimensions of meaning, including the dictionary or semantic meaning of the words uttered, and make an account of them. This account is built up through a recognition of the standing of the relevant claims in the context of lifeworld assumptions, and against the store of accepted claims that has already been built up in this and previous interactions (accepted claims = store of commitments). The account will 'take account' of contradictions of new claims with the old, of contradictions between now explicitly advanced claims and lifeworld background claims, of normative departures, and of personal/ expressive consistency or inconsistency, and the like. That is, judgments of prima facie validity are a necessary part of the building up of the overall account which is the 'meaning' of the utterance. Actions have meaning precisely as valid or invalid according to social expectations — else how would we ever surprise, insult, challenge, invest or reveal. The description of all this is complex, but in everyday life we perform the miracle of interpretation all the time, usually without much conscious thought.

We can learn from the Fang is that an utterance which doesn't fit lifeworld expectations *complicates* things. In such circumstances we have trouble giving our meaning-account. The narrative unity of our construction of meaning is disturbed and we must take more time and pay explicit attention to the problem thus created if we are still to be successful in constructing a coherent meaning-account.

Several options become available. We can reconstruct what was actually said, saying to ourselves (or to the speaker): 'You mean X, don't you?' (when Y was said).

If we say this to ourselves, we then go on in the dialogue to speak as if the necessary correction (the correction which would enable us again to construct a coherent account) had already been made. Button[8] calls this an 'embedded' correction. But 'corrections' can occur in the non-cognitive domains, too. Someone can speak inappropriately or insultingly, but we can ignore the insult or choose to interpret it as a jest. Similarly, a person can act 'out of character' and display, say, an uncharacteristic anger. We can make allowances for this and control the emotional tone of our response so that the tension doesn't rise.

If we make corrections 'out loud', they become 'exposed' corrections. But an exposed correction has the property of making the existence of the inferred error 'topical', at least momentarily. The speaker has to take conscious cognisance of the 'error'. This opens up the possibility of the speaker *denying* that it is an error, denying that the error identified is the real error, or otherwise beginning a public process of problem definition.

While many exposed errors may be dealt with by relatively routine corrections or elaborations of stores of commitments, some cannot be so easily handled. Lifeworld resources are seen to have broken down and some portion of the hitherto taken-for-granted background is 'made theoretic'[9] — subjected to explicit attention — and a process of reworking or coping with this is begun. Again, this is seldom thoroughly critical or profound and means of ad hoc repair of previous assumptions can usually be found so that lifeworld disturbances are minimised.

If we embed our corrections we do not foreground our differences. If we expose them we choose to make a point of our differences. When speakers all come from a common cultural background this often means that we are entering into a process of disputation. In intercultural situations this would most often be unproductive. In such situations we must learn to expose differences without rancour, and tolerate living with difference.

The situation of intercultural communication represents an extreme of lifeworld problematisation, since it becomes clear, for at least one of the parties to such communication, that beliefs which could once have been taken-for-granted can no longer be. In politically symmetrical intercultural communication, all interlocutors are in this situation. In order to understand, and reach understanding, they must enter into a process of negotiation of a new, shared definition of situation, roles, associated norms, and of the expression of self. Earlier, I called this the creation of an intercultural communicative context or ICC. In short, we cannot easily embed our corrections in intercultural communication. We must foreground them in order to make problems explicit. This mutual recognition of problems and the differences underlying them is the ICC.

Intercultural communication produces a pressure for reconsideration of interlocutors' own cultural background knowledge. Under conditions of relative political symmetry, and situational necessity for communicative success (as in the classical problem of culturally different castaways providing food and shelter on a desert island), the 'external' pressure of the problem situation pushes interlocutors into trying to construct common ground and this, in turn, has its own effect on previously absolute (rather than relativised) cultural assumptions. But what is this except critique? The de-abolutising or decentring of the old, its reconsideration in negotiation with others, appraisal of its limits, of what is good and not good in it, and the creative development of the new. This is learning — not mere information acquisition — but educative development. Intercultural communication fulfils, almost automatically, the necessary conditions for critical communication — learning through dialogue.

But in many intercultural situations there is precisely no symmetry and this is the result of an institutionalised difference in the power of speakers. Under such conditions the communicative problem becomes more difficult — so difficult that it cannot be solved by more communication.

In any intercultural situation there are communicative difficulties because of different assumptions, sources of address, politeness, appropriate ways of speaking and the like. For instance, when some Navajo people meet a stranger, the appropriate behaviour is silence. You do not speak to strangers until you get to know them. It is not appropriate to try to hurry this process by introducing strangers to another person. To non-Navajo this is difficult to interpret and is sometimes interpreted as hostility or sullenness. But this is not an insuperable difficulty. It can be communicated about by third parties. You can read about it in cultural manuals. Eventually, the silence is broken.

However, if there were an institutionalised difference — a permanent social structural difference — the silence would never be broken. The King remains a king and the commoner remains a commoner and they can never be on easy speaking terms — at least, not in an absolute monarchy whose dignity is guarded by a vigilant court. Something like this operated in colonial situations. Only under the extreme conditions of war could John Bull recognise that Gunga Din was 'a better man than me' (Rudyard Kipling).

When communication about communicative problems or difficulties is institutionally blocked by roles where power difference is central to relationships, communicative difficulties become *ideological distortions*.

Distortions can occur in more limited ways, too. Whenever someone trades on the appearance of sincerity while concealing their true purpose, such as they might when pretending friendship in order to sell a used car, win promotion, or a benefit, they are distorting the communicative relationship because it is not possible to respond to their real purpose which is concealed. An undistorted communicative relationship is one where each understanding the other is the goal. Difficulties and problems may occur, but further communication can overcome them. Distortion of the communicative relationship occurs when further communication is blocked. This sometimes happens when people have neuroses. It happens to a degree in many situations, but it becomes a political rather than a personal matter when it happens as the product of a social institution.[10]

What Makes an Analysis Critical?

But what specifically is 'critical' analysis? Is it simply that communicators are making validity judgements? That may be necessary but it is not sufficient. An additional dimension is necessary. Validity questions are normally resolved by reference to existing institutional structures and past interpretations of the applicability of norms. For a critical result it is necessary for something new to emerge — something that addresses the problem against the historical background in a way which leads to a new or altered situation. 'Critical' designates no more than the making of 'relatively' *unfettered* validity judgements through judgements of the truth, rightness and sincerity of other people's actions and through being able to act truthfully, rightly and sincerely oneself. Or it refers to the identification of obstacles to this. Here 'relatively unfettered' does not refer to any ideal or perfect speech situation but to a notion of critique relative to the historical learning level of a society and/or to the level of maturity of an individual. Unfettered adaptation to changing circumstances is necessary for efficient adaptation of cultures. This is an adaptive, pragmatic model of validity, not a logical one. Communicative hope is only a philosophical tool with which we contrast the existing learning level of a society or individual and so also, identify the 'zone of proximal development' with respect to it (to use a Vygotskian concept here).

Critique that goes beyond existing learning is 'relatively' unfettered by the horizon of assumptions and relationships characteristic of it. In this sense, three constructs are required — an account of existing communication and its constraints, a vision of a possible but less constrained state of affairs, and an ideal model of speech without constraints, implicit and logically implicated in the first two. Of course, we still require criteria of 'going beyond' and 'learning level', and Habermas derives these from a view of history which is itself based on the degree to which mutual understanding in communication that is constitutive of social reality is socially institutionalised in democratic institutions and open inquiry. 'Democracy', in the form of the representative governments of countries like the US, UK or Australia, or 'half democracy' as Adorno calls it, represents the existing learning level of society and is defined in terms of the degree to which it institutionalises open communicative participation by various groups, including cultural minorities, in ontogenesis.

What Derrida has underlined with his critique of the notion of the presence of meaning is that all utterances oriented to understanding break free of the existing horizon because they point in their hope to future meanings. There is a kind of teleology in this view of learning levels and it is possible to point to a kind of convergence between Habermas and Derrida here. Derrida employs a notion of immanent teleology[11] — a kind of ontological unfolding. We cannot predict this on a principled basis, nor is it a lawlike unfolding; it is contingent. Like learning, it is not a necessary, but a possible process. But like learning, we can guide the process as it emerges. Dewey's teleology is of a similar kind. Cultures on our planet must unfold their potential for intercultural tolerance.

In the empirical analyses of actual speech it quickly becomes evident that two limitations of the formal analysis of meaning and validity claims must be overcome. First, actual speech tends to be governed by speaker assumptions or presuppositions about the inner and outer worlds, and validity testing under real conditions is often confined to checking that the truth stated is the 'accepted' truth, that the normative standing of actions (such as imperative speech acts) is socially sanctioned, and that the degree or kind of revelation about inner states is of the socially approved kind. That is, actual speech situations are not 'ideal', they are located in the cultural and institutional background of an actual, historical society. Speech situations are often situations where there is a struggle for reproduction of meaning rather than change. Validity judgements in reproductive speech tend to be constrained to 'matching' judgements. They may detect mismatches with existing norms or beliefs, but do not usually go beyond this. This means that successful ideology is almost invisible.

The second limitation of formal pragmatics is that the meanings of actual utterances, and their illocutionary force, cannot be understood atomistically. Single utterances (or speech acts) are usually part of more complex patterns of speech interaction. Utterances themselves are often complex, oblique, ironic or fragmentary, indexical and obscure. Formal theory is too neat to be any more than a useful simplification for theory-building purposes. It is necessary to analyse language with the more flexible tools of empirical linguistics — while still permitting identification of the validity questions which are at stake. It must also be recognised that each and every utterance raises *each* type of validity claim simultaneously.

But to return to the ontological question. Each type of validity claim raises claims about a different 'world'. Truth claims raise claims about *what is in* the objective, external world (and how it works); rightness claims raise claims about the normative rightness of relationships (and actions towards others) in the social, external world; sincerity claims raise claims about the revelation of or concealment of the inner world. These claims are claims about what is the case, but here we must recognise a general anthropological condition previously referred to — human plasticity or 'programmability'.

To an extent, reality is socially created. Even the external objective world is, in a great degree, lived in according to our perceptions of it rather than according to its 'real' character. Assuming that those who make claims, as well as those upon whom they are made, accept the claims about what is true, right or authentic, they thereby constitute or reconstitute the reality they inhabit, particularly, in social, cultural and personal realities. The ontological claims of utterances, if accepted, become ontogenetic — they make 'the world' we live in and they make us (or, at least, our social identities). Given our constant enmeshment in movement, growing old, coping changing and learning, there is no escape from ontogenesis and its positional politics. A political and institutional one-sidedness in cultural-ontogenesis is racism (or at least ethnocentrism).

As discussed in the previous chapter, in a totalising approach to social theory, the causal primacy given to the structural level by some theorists (e.g. the class structure) reduces the dynamics of this process of world-building to a mere reflection, 'superstructure' or derivation, depriving it of any but secondary ontogenetic force. The perceived politics of this process become limited to a politics of unmasking, but only when structural contradictions have reached the stage where he dialectical mixture of structural forces makes it historically possible to act. In this view, there can be no hurrying the dialectic of change only a conservative politics of delay and opposition to this. All this is familiar enough from certain sorts of Marxist theory. We are also familiar with the charge of 'idealism' levelled against those who espouse holistic views of society and the political process. The 'idealism' in question appears to consist in permitting a role for thinking agents in a politics of structuration which is always historically available. I am happy to plead guilty to this idealism.

In contrast to totalising views, holistic analysis focuses on the conditions under which interaction can be something other than a repeater station for the causal forces of structure. In this way, holistic analysis concentrates on the historical struggle between agency and structure and the role of democratic learning processes in lifting agency beyond the local and peripheral to the centre of the societal process via the public domain. Thus holism is not structuralist, although acknowledging the role of structure. A corollary of this is that, never having been structuralist, it need not proclaim itself 'post'-structuralist to make critical points. Cultural agency is the assertion of members of a culture of their right to a distinct cultural identity.

In this view, idealism is not the characteristic of views that thinking agents, understanding structure, can change it through political processes, possibly consensual ones, but of views that ideas are products of structure that have historical force independently of the agents and their situated claims. However, a holistic critical view does not imply that ideas have the kind of autonomy from the individual attributed to them by those who so freely throw the word 'idealism' around, nor does it imply that ideas have an internal evolutionary logic independent of social structural influences. Indeed, the textualism criticised in this book is a form of idealism.

An empirical pragmatics that is also critical must cope with the full, culturally located, linguistically complex process of reality creation by agents, at the same time as recognising just how validity judgements are situationally conditioned and limited so that social actors are often unable to express their identity in unstigmatised ways and meet their existential needs — the basic needs for an identity and a role characterised by integrity, dignity and authenticity. It is the use of communicative hope as a critical tool which permits CEP to go beyond mere description of speech as a caused product of a totalised regime of power to an account in which emancipation is an emergent possibility. In short, it is a view in which politics is a struggle against totality.

Critical Empirical Linguistics: A Practical Tool for Analysing Interaction

The formal and acontextual description of Habermas' speech act theory can be replaced by an action-oriented linguistics, which provides a framework for the empirical analysis of situated speech (and writing) as a form of socially recognised action. It is an analysis which cuts two ways:

(1) from the standpoint of the linguist it allows the observed structures of speech to be explained (and to an extent predicted) on the basis of a knowledge of culture, situation definition (including social task or purpose) and roles of participants/including specific role components related to the task in hand);

(2) but from the standpoint of the social analyst, observed speech structures provide evidence from which accounts of social structure can be adduced (and it provides a means of testing social theories).

While systemic linguistics began within linguistics, and focused primarily on understanding speech and writing as products of socially created (i.e. interactional) semiosis or meaning-making, it has developed rapidly in recent years to the extent that it can now very readily play a social analytic role. Systemics falls into the general category of linguistic pragmatics. Initially, many linguists tended to see pragmatics as being outside linguistics proper. Linguistics proper was seen as concerned only with language as a system of signs and rules for combining them correctly. More recently, the way in which speaking and writing act back on language has been understood more clearly — now pragmatics is firmly on the linguistic agenda. At the same time, as discussed earlier, there has been a 'linguistic turn' in social analysis. Initially, few social analysts conceived of social analysis in linguistic terms. The detailed structure of daily life lay outside social analysis proper. But the influence of phenomenology on social thought, and developments in sociolinguistics, ethnomethodology and, most recently, post-structuralist thought, has led to a growing understanding of the way social structuration occurs in a double process. Social reality is now seen to be socially constructed through semiosis. Now language is firmly on the sociological agenda. The concerns of linguists have led them from grammar and lexicon, to speech structure, to social semiosis and finally to the analysis of rationality, ideology and culture. Social analysis began with these concerns, but lacked a clear model of their actual, concrete realisation. Today, the two concerns meet in the Theory of Communicative Action.

As I argued in *Critical Theory and Classroom Talk*,[12] the systemic linguistics of Halliday and Hasan provides a very close fit with Habermas' action typology, with the additional advantage that it can provide the conceptual and methodological basis for the *empirical* pragmatics that Habermas called for but did not himself develop. But no doubt other social-action oriented linguistic descriptions would be equally useful. The problem with systemics, until recently, was that it was more descriptive than critical. Only recently has this deficiency been addressed. Since the above-mentioned book, in which I outlined a critique of systemics, Hasan has recognised a convergence with Habermas' and acknowledged that in some circumstances communicators themselves are oriented to making claims and to making validity judgements in respect of them.

> Habermas links his notion of 'validity claims' to the kind of speech act that is performed in uttering what I have called the claim...my approach is quite close to this... (Hasan, p. 50)[13]

Systemics is an action-oriented pragmatics. Utterances are construed as meaningful deeds of a special kind whose meanings are interpretively created by hearers by reference both to the words (lexicon) and structures of words (grammar), to the social situation, and to the more general background knowledge of the culture. This is precisely Habermas' view.

In systemics, speech and writing relate to context of social situation (and cultural background) in several ways. There is said to be a 'field' relation, a 'tenor' relation and a 'mode' relation of all meanings or messages.

The field relation is realised through the referential or existential/logical functions of language — roughly, what is believed to be the case; the tenor relation is realised through the interpersonal or relational functions of language (social relationships believed to be appropriate), and the mode relation is realised through the poetic or textual functions of language (the kind of talk that is called for).

Habermas also identifies this range of simultaneous functions in each message, but distinguishes between two ontologically different aspects of the interpersonal function, the normative and the expressive. In terms of the ontological picture outlined earlier, a statement (say) may refer to things in the outer world (e.g. all philosophers are liars), both in asserting that some things exist and have certain characteristics and also in its logical form. But the statement was said in an interpersonal context, to an audience, and so, in its concrete utterance it has an (implicit) relation to the social world. To state something *to someone* is usually as much an interpersonal function as commanding them or warning them, although unlike commanding or warning, its surface form does not display this function. This is the normative dimension of the interpersonal function. Presumably, too, it was said in a certain way, with indications or expressions, perhaps non-verbal, of anger or commitment. This is the expressive dimension of the interpersonal function. Finally, it is said by using the resources of language in a certain way, within an appropriate 'style' of language. This is the textual function.

However, systemics goes beyond Habermas' somewhat atomic and abstract language act analysis to look at regular *structures* of talk and empirical variation of them, as well as more elliptical and less well-formed utterances than the formal, complete language acts that Habermas discusses. In this, it meets the requirements an empirical pragmatics which Habermas himself outlined.

For instance, in a school classroom the situation of a 'lesson' is part of an institutionalised set of roles, practices, norms and beliefs — 'schooling'. Particular categories of actors have distinct roles and their role relationships are governed by beliefs about who is knowledgeable, norms of authority, and detailed expectations about rights and obligations of teachers and learners. There is also the specific subject matter and practices of the planned lesson. (The teacher has the 'right' to plan lessons in conventional schooling.)

The role players will 'cooperatively' unfold the lesson as they play out their expected parts. Teachers will ask most questions, introduce and guide the discussion and generally control who will speak and when. Students will answer questions, ask a few (but of a different kind to the teacher) and more (or less) suffer the teacher's guidance can control. A common talk structure will be:

Teacher Monologue	(lecture)
Teacher Instruction	('carry out some activity')
Student Question	(about the activity)
Teacher Question	(about the subject matter)
Student Answer	(to the teacher's question)
Teacher Question	_____
Student Answer	_____
etc.	_____
etc.	_____
Teacher Monologue	(summing up)
Teacher Instruction	(homework; 'leave quickly')

The field will include background beliefs about the institution of schooling, seldom referred to but assumed, and more explicit knowledge claims in the lesson itself. The tenor will be expressed by the relatively formal, authority centred mode of teacher talk and the relatively formal, submissive mode of student talk. The mode will be the way language is used in classroom talk, slightly bookish, formal and oriented to general conclusions.

This is all familiar enough, but when this pattern is mistaken for a genuine dialogue and the educators concerned see themselves as encouraging students to express their own views etc., it becomes ideological.

Let me give another example of how institutionalised distortion might work. The social situation is a doctor's surgery during a consultation. The doctor's talk is relatively formal with a high level of social distance. The task, from the doctor's point of view is to persuade the patient to agree to a piece of surgery which causes some risk. The patient is afraid, and uncertain. They are seeking to find out what is going to happen to them, but they feel inhibited because they do not understand the technical issues.

Doctor: I'm going to refer you to Dr X. He's a very good surgeon and has a good record of success.

Patient: Can't I just...can you give me a prescription or something?

Doctor: It's past that, I'm afraid (writing referral note to surgeon).

Patient: This thing, you know...that's growing there...can't someone just kill it with radiation...?

Doctor: Dr X is the expert. I'm sure she'll consider all possible lines of treatment. You'll be in the best of hands.

The doctor's talk is all about professional standing and achievement. She is defining the issue as one of expertise and the implicit claim is that the patient should entrust himself to that expertise. The patient's talk is about the disease, its nature and the technical possibilities. It is talk oriented to the possibility of making an informed choice and it demonstrates the absence on the part of the patient of knowledge of the full range of options and their pros and cons. The implicit claim is a claim to be informed and that claim is never acknowledged. The only reference to it is a reference to alternatives being considered by *another expert*: (I'm sure she'll consider…)

From the standpoint of critical theory, this is a situation of distortion. The claim is being made by the doctor, through the whole structure of claims, that the process of medical treatment is not only an acceptance of expertise but the surrender of judgement about acceptable risks. But medical expertise is confined to the data available about success rates and complications or side effects of each treatment. The doctor is no better off than the patient in making judgements about which risks the patient regards as acceptable and which not. What would you rather lose, your sight or your hearing? Perhaps a musician might give a different answer to a painter. The distortion here is revealed in the inability of the patient to by-pass the doctor's definition of the role relationship, and by the institutional support for that relationship in the medical/health institutions of society.

Now replay this doctor/patient scene in an intercultural setting. Perhaps the operation concerned is 'female circumcision' and the patient, an immigrant, is arguing with the doctor to get her to perform this procedure on her daughter. The doctor in turn is seeking to prevent the operation from being done by adopting the same emphasis on expertise and the need to trust to professional judgement about what is desirable as we saw in the above example:

Patient: I want you to do the operation for my daughter.
Doctor: There are always side-effects. It is a risky procedure and she may later regret it.
Patient: But she will not be regarded as a proper woman if…
Doctor: Its not really appropriate here.
Patient: But it will be a problem for her to get married.
Doctor: You must trust my advice. By the time she grows up this will be regarded as something belonging to the past.

In this example there is more engagement of the doctor with the patient's argument. There has been something of a reversal but it is not a role reversal, just a different social task. Here the patient is trying to persuade the doctor to a course she is reluctant to follow not vice versa. The expert/lay role relationship is intact. Now it is not just the value judgements of the patient that doctor seeks to usurp, but the culture and its future valuations. The distortion is now more entrenched because membership of the dominant culture has joined institutionalised professional role superiority to block lines of communication.

The point about critical analysis of this kind is not that it is highly technical or difficult. At a fairly general level, as the above examples illustrate, it is easy enough to do. Using a more technical systemic analysis it is possible to do it at greater and greater levels of detail and precision.

For instance, 'You must trust my advice' is a command. Its overt validity claim is one of authority. It makes implicit claims to expertise and to a role relationship in which it is appropriate to issue such commands. The term 'advice' codes the command in false colours in the same way as parents issuing orders to children may say 'honey, would you like to…'. The field, tenor and mode metafunctions are not exhausted by these brief analytical remarks, but you get the idea. When distortions are so entrenched that attempts to reject or expose them attract sanctions, we can speak of structurally embedded distortion or ideology in the grand sense. Further reading can be found in the works of Kress.[14]

From Interpersonal to Structural Distortion

What remains to be added to the above systemic analysis is a means of analysing and evaluating critique in terms of truth, justice and authenticity — in terms of whether it is such that is capable of leading to further 'growth of knowledge, social development' or, personal growth in maturity and integrity. Habermas asserts that it is not only philosophers who are able to compare the developments in a situation with some criteria of cooperative social or moral 'progress' but that speakers themselves, insofar as they are oriented to really understanding each other through more speaking, are oriented to these things, too. That is, that the addition of this critical dimension to the linguistic analysis is not an imposition of outsider value judgements but a recognition of the ever present possibility of such judgements *in the talk*. The concept of communicative hope is the tool with which this analysis is constructed by the critical linguist but it is also the possession of every speaker. That is why the critical analyses of intellectuals are, ultimately, only validated by participants who find that they make sense in *their* situations.[15]

This counterfactual tool can be seen as a logical extension of the awareness of the possibility that speech can conceal or reveal, an awareness which exists in all cultures. It is an awareness that in some situations (i.e. situations where participants are really trying to understand each other, possibly in order to discursively solve problems) participants can raise questions concerning the truth, rightness and sincerity of each other's speech. The possibility of greater or lesser truth, rightness and sincerity is raised. The idea of constraints on true, right and sincere speaking is present or the idea of reasons of a hidden, strategic kind for untrue, normatively incorrect or insincere speaking is present. The notion of a situation free of constraint or covert speaking strategy is implicit — it is a logical extreme type, implicit in an open-ended dimension of more or less truthful etc. speaking. All cultures recognise this in at least some spheres of social life. All situations in a culture are potentially subject to comparisons with situations of a more open kind. All cultures contain some recognition of this openness. In many cultures this awareness is explicitly recognised, codified and named. And the cultures which have a clear awareness of these issues are by no means confined to technologically developed or literate cultures. For instance, in the Yakan culture of Borneo there are names for each kind of communication, from casual conversation through a series of steps such as serious decision making to sworn testimony controlled by strict 'rules of evidence', such as we find in American law courts.[16]

However, it should be clear that it is not being asserted that all speech situations in a culture are situations where issues of valid speaking are equally recognised to be at stake. Nor is it being asserted, even in such situations, that the specific list of constraints on speech recognised by Habermas are recognised by all other cultures. But each culture recognises some constraints on speaking. The possibility of lying is not something available in some cultures and not in others, although each culture has its own theory of lying and its significance. Similarly, the possibility of strategic speaking is recognised. It is, indeed, difficult to imagine any culture which engages in extensive commerce, trade or barter, not recognising that speaking in the context of selling merchandise may be different from speaking in other situations.

Intercultural situations clearly could be identified as situations where issues of validity are at stake, under appropriate political circumstances. Where a problem is seen as shared, and the need for a solution is also seen to be mutual, the very idea of discursively solving the problem may anticipate the possibility of a move away from existing assumptions and practices, at least where the problem concerned is not seen as routine or where it is not readily solved by a minor extension of an existing procedure or practice. Structurally relevant problems, if I may call them that, are problems which cannot be solved within the existing cultural scheme. Attempts to solve them force interlocutors into the 'zone of proximal (intercultural) development'.[17] Solutions result in a changed learning level.

(We will explore just what this means in the final chapter.) Clearly, though, members of both cultures must recognise the situation as one which constraints on speech must be overcome and in which their interlocutors may feel the impact of constraints *which they themselves are not aware of.*

But as discussed earlier in this chapter, the analysis of distorted speech, which flows directly from the use of the notion of communicative hope, must be connected to the structural, institutional level of social analysis. Habermas identifies three kinds of distortions, although he deals at length with only two neither of which is strictly social structural. First, neurotic distortion which results in speech pathology. Second, strategic distortions, where one party to an interaction is pursuing a concealed strategic intention *through* pretending to speak communicatively. This involves deception at all levels of validity. Third, Habermas mentions a range of types of distortion which can arise when the situational demands in one area of validity prevent participants from reacting to validity claims in another area. The main example of this is relationships of domination in which a subordinate participant is unable to express her true beliefs or genuine feelings because to do so would run counter to the norms of interpersonal relationships in play in the situation and so attract sanctions from the person in power. However, we can identify a fourth level, involving institutionalisation of communicative distortion by the translation of these interpersonal constraints to the social structural level. At this level, ownership and/or control of the mass media, organisational or bureaucratic control of communication channels, agenda, and even something as simple as control of photocopying, institutionalises the repression of communicative participation. But this brings us to systems of power, and the work of Foucault.

Genealogies

Foucault developed genealogical history as a method for showing how a discourse (or cluster of institutions and texts) of power was brought into being. The same approach may be applied to multicultural settings.

Perhaps the best place to begin if we want to understand the value of Foucault's thinking is with the notion of 'dispositif', or, as it is sometimes translated, 'deployment'.[18] The notion of dispositif is one which bridges theory and practice. In his earlier work on the history of ideas, Foucault had attempted an 'archaeology'. The purpose of this was to uncover the hidden history of ideas. Foucault later moved toward a broader notion of method when he moved from archaeology to 'genealogy'. In earlier work, the ideas uncovered by archaeology, and the discourse in which they were expressed, was set against the non-discursive aspects of society in a fairly crude way. But in the notion of dispositif, we are presented with a more holistic understanding of discourses as integrated parts of a whole social ensemble.

The closest that any other philosopher or sociologist has come to this notion is probably Thomas Kuhn's notion of a paradigm.[19] Properly understood, scientific paradigms were not simply theories or sets of ideas, they were an ensemble of individuals, sites, theories, particular puzzles, methods, techniques, equipment and the like. In short, the whole concrete, actual apparatus of a particular line of scientific work as well as the discourse that gave it meaning.

Deployments of social and cultural resources work in a similar way.[20.] They are first brought forth as a set of interlocking inventions and innovations. The development of modern penal systems can serve as an example. The architecture of prisons, the practices of surveillance by warders, the use of numbers and uniforms, and all the apparatus of penology were a process of gradual assembly of interlocking technologies, roles and texts over a period of time. Development is piecemeal and interrelated, requiring adaptation and adjustment, and a certain practical adhocery. This phase Foucault calls 'functional overdetermination'. It is a stage when the institutional complex in question 'settles in' through an interlocking of its parts and levels. There is a second phase which occurs as the unintended consequences and inadequacies of the socio-cultural invention manifest themselves. This leads to waves of 'reform' and adjustment which Foucault calls 'strategic filling'. In prisons, this is exemplified by the move from Alcatraz-like institutions to more 'humane', psychological/psychiatric settings.

Again, similarities with Kuhnian paradigms can be seen. A scientific paradigm goes through a constructive stage with adjustment, puzzle solving and filling out. Some of this is technical, and reliant on technological innovation in laboratory equipment, instruments etc. Some organisational, and related to the building up of a human base for the paradigm — in the form of research programs, institutes and careers. And some ideational, in the form of elaboration of auxiliary theory and theoretical detailing of the consequences of the core theory of the paradigm.

Now, the whole point of Kuhn's insights is that the progress of science is not a rational, deductive affair, confined to the realm of ideas, but a human, institutionalised process. Over time, the paradigm accumulates problems and areas of difficulty. Perhaps it vies with a rival paradigm in disputed border territory. In any case, anomalies and unintended consequences arise.

Foucault's point about the modernist project of prison reform is that its key ideas — that prisoners will be reformed by changing their attitudes and ideas — are expressed in an organisational structure and set of legal, administrative and carceral practices which create new forms of oppression, arguably as cruel as the old (as anyone who has watched a prison movie will recognise).

This insight is generalised to the whole apparatus of surveillance and control that is modern society — from prison wardens to parole officers, from teachers and social workers to bureaucrats in general. Foucault calls the process of control 'normalisation' and sees it as a process which creates the specific subjectivity, feelings, bodies and conduct that modern societies and their organisations require. To the extent that the organisations and apparatuses of the state are involved in this process, it is possible to speak of the 'governmentalisation' of people's subjectivity.[21]

The first step in Foucault's method is the identification of the object or discursive field. In intercultural relations, any institutional-organisational complex having to do with cultural difference would be a likely candidate for analysis. 'Multiculturalism' in Australia, Canada, or in the US, 'minority policy', could constitute a discursive field. Now, the issue here is not whether multiculturalism is a good idea or not, but whether the institutional complex of ideas and practice, taken as a whole, is characterised by forms of power/knowledge which ought to be an object of critique.

Multiculturalism would be described ethnographically. Who is involved? What ways of speaking can be identified? What legal and organisational expression of the ideas can be found? What culturally recognised groups are involved? How are traditions formed and transmitted, both of ideas (i.e. ways of speaking) and practices? In this way, the factual dimension of the dispositif is uncovered.

Then, according to Foucault, several analytical rules are followed. The first, is that all difference between knowledge and power is bracketed. No area of knowledge claims are taken at face value. Foucault calls this the rule of immanence. The second rule is the rule of continual variation. We are dealing with an institutional complex which is in change and motion. Its existence depends on its adaptation. It cannot be expected to stand in a fixed relation to other institutions. The third rule is called the rule of double conditioning. The ideology is as much conditioned by the continual tactical adaptation made necessary by social change, the vagaries of politics, unintended consequences etc., as the tactics are an expression of the ideology. Finally, Foucault warns that discourses are tactically polyvalent. It is not the case that all discourses that seem to struggle against power actually do so. Discourses are ecologically conditioned and their precise effects are a product of their positioning in a wider, unstable social and cultural process.

In the study of a complex discourse such as that of multiculturism, it would be necessary to bracket well-meaning claims about culture, equity and democracy. These notions, and the claims to moral or cognitive correctness associated with them — claims we may personally advance in another context — must be made suspect. We would then go on to track the variation in the institutional complex as it adapted over time and from site to site. The study of variation would allow us to demonstrate the extent to which local adaptation permitted tactical necessity to so condition the multicultural idea that, in the name of orderly administration (i.e. power), something was born that is contrary to the motivations with which multiculturist policy began. In these local and specific circumstances, particular discursive rhetorics may be seen to function in specific ways, often ways contrary to our intentions or in positive and negative ways simultaneously.

So the actual deployment — the discursive fact — of multiculturalist policy might be seen to bring about consequences other than those ideologised by its spokespersons. That is, the net effect of a multicultural policy may, in fact, be cultural assimilation behind the facade of preservation and difference.

As a tool of criticism, this genealogical method, which is only a set of methodological hints, rather than strict rules, can uncover covert, structural processes of cultural oppression. It can work at the seam between rhetoric and reality. The critical role in this is the role of what Foucault calls the 'specific intellectual'. Specific intellectuals are intellectual workers who are located within the dispositif. We will discuss this role further in the final chapter. However, for the moment, the important point is the way this kind of critique might fit in with Habermas' communicative critique.

Habermas' communicative critique, developed as a critical empirical pragmatics, provides tools for critique at the level of communicative encounters in socially and culturally defined 'situations'. But Habermas provides only a very general system level discussion of the way 'situations' might be distributed and organised across whole societies or the way members of culturally recognised categories, such as minorities, races, genders, or classes, might be distributed across roles and situations.

Habermas' system level analysis of the legitimation crisis of late capitalist societies[22] and the colonisation of the lifeworld is of value, and can contribute to the analysis of the relationship among social institutions at the system integration level, but it provides little basis for analysing institutions internally. This is where Foucault's method comes in (and the specific intellectual whose location is internal to an institutional complex), Foucault's method studies the construction of 'complexes of situations', or institutions, while Habermas' communicative approach allows analysis at the level of individual situations themselves (in addition to the system level). In other words, Foucault fills in the missing middle-level theory. While neither author has provided extensive discussion of cultural difference, they have provided all the tools for this discussion. For Foucault, the power/knowledge nexus is culturally specific. The power is that of a race and the knowledge that of the culture of that race. Habermas' understanding of cultural difference has already been explored. The essential issue is interpersonal distortion of the intercultural conversation, caused by the institutional constraints on discourse that Foucault's work helps us to understand. Derrida allows us to understand how the metaphysic of a culture is encoded in documents and people.

Derrida's methodology complements Habermas'. Habermas analyses speech or writing *roles*, Foucault institutionalised distributions of these, while Derrida's contribution is a different one again. In analysing texts, Derrida allows us to understand the discursive 'codes'[23] through which particular ideas are connected with practice at the site at which a text is uttered. That is, he helps us to understand the worlds that ontogenesis would bring into being.

Deconstructions

Deconstruction complements Habermas' critical empirical pragmatics rather than displacing it, because the systemic linguistics with which it connects employs a linguistic method of analysis while deconstruction 'exceeds' or 'explodes' the linguistic level of analysis (to use Derrida's terms). However, it is not the communicative level of systemic linguistics that Derrida puts 'under erasure', but the level of analysis of language as 'code' — the process whereby a selection is made from the structural whole of the totality of available linguistic elements that reciprocally define each other.

The term 'linguistic' is often used ambiguously. At the structural level, a 'language' is a system of differences, whereas the communicative process whereby texts are produced, often in mutual interchange is sometimes distinguished from linguistics proper by the label 'pragmatics'. It is linguistics in this restricted structuralist sense that Derrida rejects.

Derrida's main starting point is Saussure. However, while transcending Saussure, Derrida may be said to preserve some of the errors of his structuralism. We will need to identify one of these errors in order to be clear about how Derrida's deconstructive approach fits in which what has been discussed in previous chapters of this book.

The error concerned is a certain sort of atomism or lack of holism, coupled with a semiotic understanding of meaning rather than a pragmatist one. Saussure[24] speaks of language as '...a system of distinct signs corresponding to distinct ideas' (p. 10). However, by 'distinct' he did not mean that each sign possessed its own meaning independent of the others. Meaning could never reside in one term. It resided in the relationship of differences among signs. That is, the meaning of a sign is defined by the set of differences it enters into with other signs in the total set of signs of the linguistic sign system.

However, in Davidson's terms, the meaning referred to here is only first level meaning — dictionary or semantic meaning — not second level meaning of the utterance of the relevant sign string in context. While simple atomism is rejected, in which each sign fully possesses its own present meaning, a systemic atomism remains. In this form of atomism, meaning is still present at the atomic or sign-system level as the set of contrasts of atoms. In a more holistic or macroscopic view, indeed, a view that borrows something of Foucault's notion of the embedding of ideas in practices, meaning, in its fullest sense, is a narrative, theory, or episteme which is provoked by the semantic meaning of an uttered sign string in a context but which goes beyond that meaning. This error must be kept in mind, since it helps us to recognise the limits of deconstruction, and thus to see deconstruction as complementing communicative analysis and genealogy. Essentially, Foucault and Habermas have the same hermeneutics. But what critical empirical pragmatics on the model of systemic linguistics lacks is a critique of ideology at the level of the coding of speech — the selective system that draws upon the resources of language to produce utterances of a particular form. Deconstruction provides this.

The basic technique of deconstruction may be explained in a number of ways, but perhaps the most useful for our present purposes is the explanation developed by Ronald Schleifer,[25] which is based on the logic of phonetics. The following is a summary of Schleifer's argument.

Phonology is a systemic analysis of a system of differences, rather than a pragmatics. The study of actual speech variation is phonetics not phonology. Phonology studies the system of differences that convey semantic meaning — not all variation in sound is relevant for meaning difference, even though phonetics may identify and describe it.

For instance, there is a phonetic difference in English between the aspirated 't' as in 'ton' as opposed to the unaspirated 't' in 'stun', but this difference never functions to convey different meanings, as it is not a *phonological* difference.

But the distinctive differences associated with meaning difference never occur independently but only in combination. A cluster of such differences makes up a phoneme or unit of meaning related sound. So, while English may have many phonemes, they can be made up of a smaller number of distinctive differences — voiced versus unvoiced, aspirated versus unaspirated, and so on. In English 'd' as in 'duck' is voiced it involves the vocal chords whereas 't' as in 'tick' is unvoiced. The absence of a distinctive feature, voicing, can be as significant as its presence.

The crucial test of a phoneme is that its presence or absence does not merely add additional information, it transforms the meaning. For instance, consider the difference between 'it is a roe' and 'it is a road' where the 'd' phoneme is added.

However, there are places in language where phonemic differences are neutralised. Consider the difference between voiced and unvoiced in the pair of phrases 'it's due' and 'it's stew'. The difference is neutralised. (In a certain sort of American pronunciation they sound 'the same'.) This neutralised phoneme has been called an 'archiphoneme' — the set of properties that two otherwise distinctive phonemes have in common.

Archiphonemes are usually unmarked. That is, where a difference is created between a pair of phonemes that is not neutralised, it is created by some process which *marks* one phoneme relative to another. In the case we are examining, it could be marked by adding voice to the existing sound 't'. This same process occurs at the semantic level too.

For instance, old is opposed to young. They form a pair (and are part of a wider system of closely related signs). When we say 'He is old', we give the semantic meaning of old as opposed to young full value. When we say 'He is four years old' we neutralise 'old'. To say 'He is as old as Paul' conveys less information than 'He is as young as Paul' because 'old' is neutralised in the first sentence and so no longer conveys the contrastive information derived from its place in a system of semantic relationships with other terms.

Now Derrida points out in one of the places he discusses deconstruction that his purpose is to overturn classical binary oppositions. He wants, though, to avoid both simply *neutralising* the binary opposition of metaphysics and simply *residing* within the closed fields of these oppositions, thereby confirming it.[26] Deconstruction doesn't simply neutralise marked/unmarked pairings, such as young/old, but displaces them or explodes them so that their embodying of the metaphysic is clear.

Schleifer is worth quoting at length here:

> Let me make this clear in the semantic opposition between 'speech' and 'writing', to *say* as opposed to *to write*. In this opposition, 'to say' is the unmarked term: the sentence 'Derrida says so and so' indiscriminately can mean that he 'says' so in an oral interview (such as *Positions*) and in a written text (such as *Margins*); the neutralised sense of 'to say' is/to assert/. On the other hand, 'writing' is the marked term: the sentence 'Derrida writes so and so' can only mean in a text or book. In English 'to say' (in the sense of 'to assert') neutralises the opposition between saying (speech) and writing. Deconstruction, then, would 'overturn' this opposition, this hierarchy, and assert that speech, in fact, is a species of writing, that writing is the originatory term of which speech is the special case: language itself, Derrida asserts in *Grammatology*, is 'a species *of* writing' (52). Such an overturning or reversal, however, simply resides in the closed field of this opposition; it reinscribes the old hierarchy in a negative form. In order to *displace* this hierarchy, deconstruction presents a *deconstructive* term in the position of the neutralising term in such a way that it resists and disorganises the hierarchy. It accomplishes this by *positioning* the marked term as if it were unmarked. In the opposition between speech and writing, Derrida coins the term *arche-writing* not only to conceive of speech as a species of writing, but to displace our 'received' sense of language. In this term he seems to echo Trubetzkoy's term of *archiphoneme*.
>
> This is not, as we say, simply a matter of 'semantics', simply the trivial case of different words for the same meanings. Rather, such a deconstructive term reorients us in relation to the seemingly 'natural' and 'self-evident' meanings that inhabit our language. This disruptive reorientation is perhaps more audible in the use of the pronoun *she* in contexts that call for the neutralised general term *he*. For instance, in the 'Translator's Preface' to *Grammatology*, Spivak notes that 'as she deconstructs, all protestations to the contrary, the critic necessarily assumes that she at least, and for the time being, means what she says' (1, xxvii). In such contexts we cannot but *hear* the attempt at, and the failure of, neutralisation, the denial and negation of neutralisation, in the same way we cannot help but note the oddity of referring to

someone as 'ninety years young'. *She* conveys more information than simply 'a critic', the general critic, the critic as person: we are presented with a 'female critic', and that greater information makes the 'third term' impossible, 'irreducibly nonsimple' (*Margins* 13). The deconstructive term *she* conveys what Derrida calls the violence inscribed in the seemingly 'natural' and 'self-evident' use of *he* to mean 'person', or *man* to mean 'humanity', or *old* to mean 'possessing any age at all'. The deconstructive term is neither marked nor unmarked, and thus it can resist constitution as a 'third term': it is neither second nor third.

(Schleifer, p. 308–9)

When we analyse what systemics calls the textual function of language we can apply deconstruction to the key terms of a text to uncover its hidden violence.

Concluding Remarks

So deconstruction permits us to uncover and demonstrate the role of the coding system in language as it is manifest in specific texts, which in turn, as Habermas shows us, are constitutive of our reality. Derrida speaks of the 'inscribing' or writing of texts into our bodies so that our identities are formed, but he does not tell us how this inscription takes place. Habermas does. Our metaphysics becomes our identity in the constitutive process of communicative meaning-action. To be critically effective we need a social-system level critique of the institutional integration of society as a whole, an institutional level critique of the dispositifs of an order of culture/power (in the modern case, knowledge/power since knowledge is the central idea of modern culture), a pragmatic critique of the interactive process whereby meaning, through claims and commitments is inscribed in people, and a coding level of critique which shows how the metaphysical or reality disclosing character of language is marshalled to provide the metaphysic which we attempt to inscribe or resist having inscribed in us.

Habermas' analysis of the institutional separation of value spheres and the consequent colonisation of the lifeworld provides, together with his argument in *Legitimation Crisis*, the beginnings of a social-system critique. Foucault's genealogical method, suitably adapted, can provide an *intra-institutional* critique, Habermas again, coupled with systemic linguistics' communicative analysis, can provide a critical empirical analysis of pragmatic interpretation through analysis of the interactive practices that inscribe culture through what Davidson calls second order meanings, and, finally, Derrida's deconstructive method can help us to identify and explode the metaphysical codes in the semantic meaning of texts.

Of course, all of this seems dauntingly intellectual and only super-critics, it would seem could be competent to do all this — or ought intellectuals play a more modest, specific role? This and related questions will be addressed in the final chapter.

Notes

1. *TCA*, Vols 1 and 2.
2. Norris also makes this point: C. Norris, 'Deconstruction, postmodernism and philosophy: Habermas on Derrida'. Pp. 167–92 in D. Wood (ed.), *Derrida: A Critical Reader'. Oxford: Blackwell, 1992.
3. Y. Kim, *Communication and Cross-Cultural Adaptation*. Clevedon: Multilingual Matters, 1988 and Y. Kim (ed.) *Interethnic Communication*. London: Sage, 1986.
4. e.g. C. Faerch and G. Kasper (eds) *Strategies in Interlanguage Communication*. London: Longman, 1983.
5. Conflict resolution approaches to intercultural training escape many of the criticisms I am making, although they tend towards an individualistic analysis rather than a structural one.
6. J. Dewey, *Democracy and Education*. New York: The Free Press, 1944, p. 217.
7. Habermas in TCA, Vol. 1.
8. G. Button and J. Lee, *Talk and Social Organisation*. Clevedon: Multilingual Matters, 1987.
9. This is Schutz's phenomenological term. See A. Schutz, *Collected Papers, Vol. 1*. The Hague: Martinus Nijhof, 1973.
10. Of course, the personal/political dimension is not the same as the private/public dimension, nor is there any point on it where there is not some influence of the opposite pole of the continuum. I reject arguments which would dissolve these distinctions altogether.
11. C. Johnson, *System and Writing in the Philosophy of Jacques Derrida*. Cambridge: Cambridge University Press, 1993.
12. R. Young, *Habermas and Halliday*. 1982 n.p. and *Critical Theory and Classroom Talk*. Clevedon: Multilingual Matters, 1992.
13. R. Hasan, *Rationality and Everyday Talk: From Process to System*. 1991, p. 50 (mss).
14. See G. Kress and R. Hodge, *Language and Ideology* (revised). London: Routledge and Kegan Paul, 1993.
15. But see J. Martin, 'Politicising ecology: The politics of baby seals and kangaroos' in T. Threadgold (ed.), *Ideology–Semiotics–Language*. Sydney: The Pathfinder Press, 1986.
16. C. Frake, 'Struck by speech'. Pp. 271–93 in J. Spradley (ed.), *Culture and Cognition*. San Francisco: Chandler, 1972.
17. The 'zone of proximal development' is the area in which it is possible for an individual to learn if they are supported and helped by others (roughly).
18. M. Foucault, *Power/Knowledge*. London: Harvester, 1980.
19. See T. Kuhn, *The Structure of Scientific Revolutions*. London: Routledge and Kegan Paul, 1968.
20. See J. Bernauer (ed.) *The Final Foucault*. Cambridge: MIT Press, 1988.
21. I. Hunter, 'Personality as a vocation: The political rationality of the Humanities'. *Economy and Society*, 19 (4), 1990, pp. 391–430.
22. J. Habermas, *Legitimation Crisis*. London: Heinemann Educational Books, 1975.

23. The systemics concept of 'register' — roughly the set of words brought into play in a context — can provide a useful first descriptive step for a deconstructive analysis.

24. F. Saussure, *Course in General Linguistics*. Paris: Editions Payot, 1972.

25. R. Schleifer, 'Deconstructive and linguistic analysis'. *College English*, 49 (4), 1987, pp. 381–94.

26. J. Derrida, *Positions*. London: Althone Press, 1972.

8 Conclusion: A New Postmodern Professionalism

A critical-pragmatic theory of intercultural communication is a theory in which communication is said to have occurred when participants reach a just, pragmatic concord. This is not a perfect solution to problems of justice, merely a historical step forward. It is just relative to the historical horizon — pragmatically just. In the same way, the level of communicative understanding achieved is not some perfect mind-reading, but merely a pragmatically-effective understanding.

In this view, it is necessary to recognise that such concord is achieved for the time being in concrete situations. The validity of any agreement is always conditional and revisable, but if we cease to speak of validity we can have no criteria for knowing which of a range of alternative possibilities we might choose. Too great an emphasis on cultural difference, in the postmodern manner, would deprive us of the possibility of a middle ground where cultures can learn from each other *enough* to live peaceably together, on one planet, or within one political nation.

Culture must not be absolutised or we run the risk of losing our humanity to it. Members of all cultures have some possibility of autonomy in respect of them and it is this that makes it possible for them to see the possibility of intercultural spaces.

Habermas' often misunderstood account of culture shows us that one of the key historical developments that makes cultural learning possible at an *institutionalised* level is the relative insulation of various parts of culture from each other. This insulation was recently given clear recognition in the enactment of Racial Vilification legislation in Australia and elsewhere. In this type of legislation incitement to racial hatred is codified as a specific crime, but freedom of speech in research, the courts, and parliaments is specifically recognised, thus recognising the separation of the various cultural spheres.

Perhaps legislation of this kind could serve, too, as an example of colonisation of the lifeworld. Certainly, it is an expression of the cultural politics of definition, which is a politics of communication in all the specific contexts of social life.

The practical conduct of intercultural action will occur at many levels and in many contexts, but intellectuals, whether of the 'grander' type or the more local, professional type, will play a significant role in it. That role may be guided by specific empirical-critical analyses of social structures, institutions and associated roles, and ideological texts and systems of meaning. The practical work of intellectuals also occurs within the context of organised political action. If that action is to lead to just, intercultural relationships, appropriate balancing of the need for common ground with the need to recognise difference must be found.

Why Critique Must be Intercultural

In today's world, effective critique is necessarily intercultural. In the previous chapters it was agreed that intercultural discourse was necessarily critical because you inevitably placed your own culture in a critical framework when you opened yourself to learning from another culture. In this chapter, I want to make a stronger point: that intercultural learning is necessary for critique. The internal resources of a culture, its capacity for self-critical learning are limited — too limited, perhaps, for effective criticism unless we are willing to learn from other cultures.

If we remember the critical pragmatism with which we began, this is not such a surprising conclusion, because critique is no more than the mediating moment in rational learning. It consists of the process of appraisal or judgement whereby we enter into a dialectic between our existing frameworks of sense-making and the circumstances which force us continually to adapt them. But the circumstances which we face today are pre-eminently global in character. We are no longer isolate. The crucial problems are general problems for the whole human species, not local problems. The various frameworks with which we face these problems are our disparate cultures — and they must adapt, first to each other, and then to the world context of our shared problems. This is one of the reasons why we should value diversity. As we have seen, in this process of adaptation, intellectuals have three roles. The role of critical communicative studies has already been discussed. This role is, in fact, common to the other two. Whatever intellectuals do, they must address the linguistic process whereby we make our reality. But there are two distinct ways in which this can be done — as general intellectuals and as specific, local intellectuals.

That is as intellectuals whose critique is conveyed in writing to a general audience even if this critique is a report from the battlefront of local and specific problems, and as intellectuals whose critique is conveyed — lived — mainly in interaction with others in a local context. Of course, for most of us, the several roles will be combined in some way, although our emphasis may be in one or the other direction. In the same way, our communicative critique may be done for a general audience, in the form of written analyses (or orally delivered conference papers etc.) in which case it can only be provisional, or it may be an analytical adjunct to a local politics.

The task of critique may be carried out at a variety of levels and in a variety of ways, but it will always involve the analysis of communicative power/ontogenesis and it will always have an intercultural dimension. It will always involve the critique of the power distortion of our collective participation in ontogenesis because this distortion is the device through which culture is formed in ways which oppress. Whether or not this oppression is internal to a polity and involves categorisation of people by gender, sexuality or some other criteria (such as ethnicity in a multicultural society), or external to a polity, thus usually involving international cultural difference, the communicative distortion involves the same exclusion of voices from ontogenesis, and the same focus on the building up of central groups on the basis of culturally-defined 'positional' goods — 'intelligence', good manners, values, skin colour, purity/pollution etc.

So effective critique is necessarily intercultural — in today's world. It is no longer possible to conduct critique for one culture (or one nation). While critique within a culture may have once been possible — when cultures tended to stand alone — the critique that was so realised was only half critique. While the existing culture was relativised, it was only half relativised. Learning was only change *within* a broader set of deep cultural assumptions and so learning was channelled and limited by the limits, ambiguities and contradictions of a single culture. Now, however, we are no longer able to see the world or our problems monoculturally. Only a strategy of denial, which leads to a kind of collective neurosis, can permit the knowledge of the other to be rigidly excluded from our conscious awareness of our learning. But denial is never completely efficacious. We proceed in our monocultural dialogues with a constant looking over our shoulder. The monocultural dialogue is tacitly shaped by the absence of the known yet mysterious 'other'.

In addition, if we adopt Dewey's definition of learning — as the solving of genuine problems in the biographical development of individuals and the social development of the species — it becomes clear that most of the problems we face today are problems in which the culturally other is implicated. How can it be otherwise in multicultural political entities such as the USA, or Australia, where the public domain is public to a multicultural polis. Certainly, it cannot be otherwise in international affairs (and in most interrelated economics today, national affairs are international affairs). And then there are global problems — pollution, population, resources, peace. These are clearly problems which cannot be defined, let alone addressed, without intercultural communication. Critique, which involves problem-solving, although it goes beyond it, is then, necessarily intercultural.

The Critical-Pragmatic Specific Intellectual

The only alternative to a set of values completely confined to an area of professional knowledge is a set of values which are general enough to underpin all knowledge. Only when some common ground or touchstone can be found can we begin to have a methodological discussion about the differences which remain between us. If critical intellectuals must be intercultural intellectuals it is partly because the present condition of humankind is to be faced by global problems. For a pragmatist, these problems are themselves the guarantee of common ground. We are speaking of critical intercultural professionals — a new, critical-pragmatic cosmopolitan professionalism.

But there is a more important reason for an intercultural role for specific intellectuals and that is because we can *anticipate* the eventual solution of our most pressing global problems. It is not beyond our present imaginations to outline a global way of life that is ecologically sustainable. And despite its failures, the very existence of the United Nations is evidence that we have already imagined a global way of life that is politically sustainable and just. When these problems are solved what remains? Only the problem we present to ourselves — the problem of our own humanity and identity. And we already know that the solution to that problem cannot be obtained if we discard the information necessary to it — the cultural and individual variety of our human condition. The riddle of our human identity is an intercultural conundrum.

What some postmodern thinkers failed to recognise is that all inquiry is underpinned by common values and that these values concern the relationships among inquirers as members of an inquiring species. As Habermas has argued, the mysterious thing about the success of science is the open relationships among scientists, and their commitment, not the relationship between scientists and their objects of study. Government's view of action is confined to means–ends action and fails to encompass critical communicative action, despite tacitly relying on this in every way. Democratic dialogue among culturally diverse people relying on the role of communicative hope is the antidote to authoritarian poisons. It is this hope which expresses the motivation which is also part of the common ground upon which we all touch when we set out to understand each other and our world.

This book began with a wager. The wager still stands. At the level of specific professionals, that wager can be expressed in this way: if it is to be possible to find a way to solve our global problems, then that way will be possible for each and every professional in his or her specific cultural circumstances. Specific professionals are not at the margin of society, they are at the centre. They are the people who make postmodern society work. Foucault's analysis is contradictory. He argues both that the pastoral power of the new class is a crucial part of the system of power/knowledge and that possibilities for resistance are necessarily marginal and local — but the local is everywhere, even at the centre. The task of critical professionals is to make that centre a multicultural, democratic centre.

The critical-pragmatism of this book is a synthesis. Its purpose is to guide the critical process by reflecting on our general capacity for intercultural understanding and on our capacity to engage in critical institutional communicative and cultural analysis. That capacity may be acquired by all professionals and may be applied in every locality. We may conclude by asking a similar question to Emawayish: Don't they have critique and hope everywhere?

Index

213